INDUSTRIAL STRENGTH DESIGN

Y0-CAY-984

Brooks Stevens
INDUSTRIAL DESIGN

INDUSTRIAL STRENGTH DESIGN
HOW BROOKS STEVENS SHAPED YOUR WORLD

GLENN ADAMSON

Milwaukee Art Museum
Milwaukee, Wisconsin

The MIT Press
Cambridge, Massachusetts
London, England

Industrial Strength Design: How Brooks Stevens Shaped Your World

Glenn Adamson

The MIT Press
Cambridge, Massachusetts
London, England

© 2003 Milwaukee Art Museum and The Massachusetts Institute of Technology

All rights reserved. No part of this book may be reproduced in any form by any electronic or mechanical means (including photocopying, recording, or information storage and retrieval) without permission in writing from the publisher.

Library of Congress Control Number: 2003104427

ISBN 0-262-01207-3 (cloth)
ISBN 0-944110-81-9 (paperback; for sale at the Milwaukee Art Museum only)

Front Cover Image: Brooks Stevens, 1941
Back Cover Image: "Industrial Design by Brooks Stevens Associates" at the Milwaukee Art Institute, 1950

Designed by Steve Biel
Edited by Karen Jacobsen
Printed in Canada by Friesens Corporation

Table of Contents

Evinrude Lark 1956

Die Valkyrie Coupe 1954

INDUSTRIAL STRENGTH DESIGN

Foreword

DAVID GORDON, MILWAUKEE ART MUSEUM DIRECTOR

In 1950 the Milwaukee Art Institute—predecessor of today's Milwaukee Art Museum—hosted an exhibition about the works of Brooks Stevens. At the time Stevens had been in business for only fifteen years, but this institution had already recognized his importance to the city. "At this halfway mark in the century," declared Barton Cummings, the director at the time, "these industrial designs tie in with the very sinews of our community."

Cummings was evidently correct. Implicit in his remark was the fact that his museum customarily showed paintings, sculptures, and prints—not clothes irons and tractors. Yet more than fifty years later, Brooks Stevens still exerts a pull on the Milwaukee imagination. His name is inextricable from the city's history because his office shaped the products that have formed the backbone of its economy over the last century. Miller Brewing, Harley-Davidson, Briggs and Stratton, Evinrude (now a division of Bombardier Recreational Products), Allen-Bradley (now a subsidiary of Rockwell Automation), Cutler-Hammer (now a division of the Eaton Corporation): all were clients of Stevens.

These companies are all also supporters of this book and the exhibition that it accompanies. Generous financial support was also given by the Brooks Stevens family, the SC Johnson Fund, Inc., of Racine, the David and Julia Uihlein Charitable Foundation, the Stratton Foundation, the Globe Foundation, Kahler Slater Architects, the Kopmeier Family Fund and the Lynde and Harry Bradley Foundation. In this sense, Brooks Stevens's story continues to be a local one. But his achievements also have national significance, and it is therefore most satisfying to be able to bring his accomplishments to the attention of a wider readership.

The impetus for this undertaking came from a felicitous confluence of helpful people, who should be acknowledged here. Among them were the staff of the Milwaukee Institute of Art and Design; the members of Brooks Stevens's family; Jody Clowes, who was at the time the Milwaukee Art Museum's curator of decorative arts; and Russell Bowman, my predecessor as the Museum's director. All saw that a roomful of cardboard boxes could be transformed into a wonderful undertaking. In 1997, therefore, under Clowes's supervision, the wealth of photographs, renderings, models, products, and documents that now constitute the Brooks Stevens Archive came to the Museum as a part of the permanent collection. When Clowes left the Museum, Glenn Adamson, curator of the Chipstone Foundation, took a break from more traditional decorative arts and stepped in to curate this exhibition and assume a leadership role in producing this book. We are grateful to Chipstone for allowing Glenn to take on this additional role.

I am a transplanted Englishman and know well that England lost its lead in manufacturing in part because it ignored industrial design. Milwaukee is a typical American city whose industrial base is under threat from lower-cost producers. Good industrial design is a competitive advantage; this post-industrial economy could do with a few more "stylists" as well as engineers. It is important, therefore, not just to cherish the objects in this book and in the exhibition but also to be inspired by them to remain innovative in styling, function, form, and process. This book is about the way Brooks Stevens shaped the world, but it is also about the way that Stevens—one of the few big-league designers not to go to the coasts—shaped Milwaukee and other cities, and about how his example could yet reshape America's manufacturing.

Acknowledgments

GLENN ADAMSON

I hope that Brooks Stevens would have liked this book. My guess is that he would have, simply because it is filled with images that he dedicated his life to creating. It's also possible, however, that he would have been chagrined. He was always more interested in moving forward than in looking back, and he might not have liked the idea of being pressed between covers like a rare butterfly. As this project has progressed, in fact, I have become continually more impressed by the difficulty of accounting for him completely. So, on behalf of the Milwaukee Art Museum and myself, the first person I would like to acknowledge is Brooks Stevens himself. He was a curator's dream, that rare thing: a fascinating, underappreciated, yet thoroughly documented artist.

I use the word *underappreciated* advisedly. It is possible that a bias toward New York and the East Coast is partly responsible for Stevens's omission to date from the established canon of American industrial designers. It is also true, however, that until Stevens's papers were generously donated to the Milwaukee Art Museum by the designer's family and the Milwaukee Institute of Art and Design, it would have been virtually impossible to grasp the compass and depth of his career. A second thank-you, then, to these donors, and especially to Stevens's late wife, Alice, and to his children, David, Steve, Sandra, and Kipp. This project might have been initiated without their unflagging support, but it certainly would never have been finished.

The museum owes a similar debt to a small group of Stevens's confidants and supporters, all of whom played a role in bringing attention to the designer's papers and his firm's work. Alice Preston, a close friend of Stevens for many years and the curator of his automobile collection, had the prescience and dedication to preserve and organize the materials that now form the Brooks Stevens Archive before anyone else. Her knowledge, enthusiasm, and generosity have been of inestimable value to me. Gallerist Michael Lord and curators Gary Wolfe and Anne Woodhouse courageously staged early retrospectives of the work of Stevens's firm, establishing the basis on which the present effort was founded. All three have also given advice and assistance over the course of writing this book. Chip Duncan, an accomplished documentary filmmaker in Milwaukee, had the foresight to interview Stevens in 1990 and 1991. As the footnotes in this volume attest, his extensive footage constitutes the most complete primary source on Stevens's career. Last but hardly least, Michael Bersch devoted himself to Stevens personally and professionally during the last years of the designer's life. Acting variously as an archivist, personal assistant, and curator, he helped make Stevens's last days happy ones.

Although this book is in some ways monographic and biographical, it is also an exploration of the work of many hands and minds. Stevens claimed to be "a businessman first, an engineer second, and a stylist third," but he was primarily a salesman. Every image in this book bears the mark of one or more employees at his firm. Too often industrial design history ignores such contributions, and I hope not to have repeated the error. Even though Stevens was clearly the generative force at the heart of his company, his designs were always partially, and sometimes entirely, the work of others. Of Stevens's many design staffers, I would like to express particular gratitude to several who provided help and information: graphic designers Adrian Bonini and Gordon Robertson; product designers Joe Besasie, John Bradley, Bill Davidson, Tom Green, Stan Johnson, and Peter Stacy; and auto builder and designer Ray Besasie Jr. All of these men generously

Fig. 1
Brooks Stevens, 1947

members of the new society, a clear mark of recognition from his peers.

At the end of World War II the United States was economically preeminent to a degree rarely seen in history. Physically untouched by conflict, it had vast wealth and production facilities. In contrast, Europe and Japan were impoverished, their industrial base either destroyed or left with rundown equipment. An initial problem in satisfying pent-up demand in America, particularly in the automobile industry, was that only prewar molds and tooling were available. When Stevens was retained in 1947 to design new vehicles for Kaiser-Frazer Corporation, he emphasized the fact that radical innovations would be difficult due to limitations on tooling. Moreover, after years of concentrating on military products, there was inevitably some confusion initially about what to produce for the civilian market. The problems were solved, however, and an astonishing surge in automobile sales typified the boom that followed. According to historian James T.

Patterson, "new car sales in 1945 totaled 69,500. In 1946 they leapt to 2.1 million, in 1949 to 5.1 million, a figure that broke the record of 4.5 million set in 1929. Sales kept going up, to 6.7 million in 1950 and to 7.9 million in 1955."[10] American manufacturers had the market to themselves, the number of automobiles imported from overseas being insignificant.

All this was despite the mounting political tension stemming from what became known as the Cold War, highlighted by events such as the Berlin Airlift, which began in 1948, and the Korean War (1950–53). By the time the latter conflict ended, consumer spending exploded as waves of new products in every category for home and leisure use washed over the market. Fueling the boom was the phenomenon of the annual model change, intended to provide constant inducement to buy. For Stevens and every other leading designer, these were the glory days: work was plentiful, fees were substantial, and public recognition was at an all-time high. As ever, Stevens aligned himself with the interests of industry, claiming, "The industrial designer in today's business world should be basically a business man, an engineer, and a stylist—and in that direct order."[11] More significantly, by 1954 he began to articulate a concept of "planned obsolescence," a term he claimed to have invented.

Stevens may have coined the term, but the concept was already well established, stemming from the 1920s, with obsolescence identified as the main means of ensuring economic prosperity. Christine Frederick, an early advocate of applying Frederick W. Taylor's scientific management techniques in the home, became a convert, arguing the case for obsolescence in *Selling Mrs. Consumer*, a book published in 1929. "The machine and power era," she wrote, "makes it not only possible but vital to apply in the home the doctrine of *creative waste*. By this term I mean the relaxation, by those of us who can afford it, of the old desperate grip most of us had upon values and utility in goods." Instead of holding on to possessions, change was now the essence of the new order:

> *We are only beginning to see that there is tremendous significance in all this; and that America's triumphs and rapidity of progress are based on* progressive obsolescence. *… These are its characteristics:*
>
> *(1) A state of mind which is highly suggestible and open; eager and willing to take hold of anything new either in the shape of a new invention or new designs or styles or ways of living.*
>
> *(2) A readiness to "scrap" or lay aside an article before its natural life of usefulness is completed, in order to make way for the newer and better thing.*
>
> *(3) A willingness to apply a very large share of one's income, even if it pinches savings, to the acquisition of the new goods or services or way of living.*[12]

Depression and war hampered the full realization of these ideas, but in the 1950s they came to full fruition, with but one modification: savings did not need to be pinched. They were unnecessary, since if income was inadequate, credit to fuel purchasing was easily available on a previously unknown scale.

Stevens first published his version of the concept in 1953, in a brochure that proclaimed, "The great strides of industrial design are yet to come through Planned Obsolescence." He defined the term, in a phrase he was to repeat widely, as inciting the consumer's "desire to own something a little newer, a little better, a littler sooner than is necessary."[13] In September of the same year in a French publication, he stated: "Our task is to induce the public to buy or to possess something always new, and to thus promote the industries to go on with production." He added a further point, also widespread in business justifications of rapid model change: the population as a whole derived benefit, since "the used goods pass on to the second hand in a much better state of conservation than it would have been had it been used for a long time."[14] Stevens elaborated the argument in subsequent versions and repeated it on numerous occasions, earning him substantial publicity, some of which was not so welcome.

What some saw as the excesses of planned obsolescence, in all variants of the term, aroused fierce criticism, most notably in 1957 from Vance Packard, beginning with his book *The Hidden Persuaders*, a heavy indictment of the manipulative role of advertising. It struck a nerve, appearing at a point when a reaction was emerging against the cycles of constant change. Packard asserted that by the mid-1950s, "more and more ad men began talking of the desirability of creating 'psychological obsolescence.'… merchandisers of many different products were being urged by psychological counselors to become 'merchants of discontent.' One ad executive exclaimed with fervor: 'What makes this country great is the creation of wants and desires, the creation of dissatisfaction with the old and outmoded.'"[15] Stevens dismissed this view out of hand. In a 1958 interview he stated bluntly: "Our whole economy is based on planned obsolescence, and everybody who can read without moving his lips should know it by now. We make good products, we induce people to buy them, and then next year we deliberately introduce something that will make those products old fashioned, out of date, *obsolete*. We do that for the soundest reason: to make money."[16]

Fig. 2 (above)
Vance Packard, ca. 1960. Packard's book *The Waste Makers* criticized Brooks Stevens's theory of planned obsolescence.

Fig. 3 (right)
Walter Dorwin Teague and Brooks Stevens, 1950. The designers are shown at the Milwaukee Art Institute's 1950 exhibition of Stevens's work.

Nevertheless, Packard's reference to Stevens as "the crown prince of obsolescence" clearly rankled. Stevens reacted sharply in a 1959 draft for an article, attacking "the ivory-tower intellectuals and the newspaper commentators and TV commentators [who] come forth to condemn everything in business, including, of course, 'planned obsolescence.'" A version of the 1959 paper was published in the *Rotarian Magazine* in early 1960. Stevens added a citation from "an editorial in *Weekly People* (an official organ of the Socialist Labor Party)," which criticized the "form of waste [called] *planned obsolescence* or *forced obsolescence*. This consists of a deliberate scheme, carried out by means of advertising and product design, to persuade people to become dissatisfied with what they purchased a year or two ago, and to throw it away before it is worn out." Steven's response was to repeat his basic points: the large secondhand market meant planned obsolescence was not wasteful, and people were not duped into buying but did so freely, desiring the new. He cited the example of the failure of small cars to sell as support for consumer choice, saying that buyers preferred the larger vehicles produced by Detroit. Products were continually improving, and the practice of regularly upgrading to a new model ensured employment, economic prosperity, and a high standard of living for all. He also tried to suggest that it was really a problem of terminology: "This industrial designer feels that perhaps it is only the phraseology that may lead to debate but not the philosophy." He suggested "Planned Product Improvement" as a less contentious usage.[17]

In this instance, however, the effort to equate criticism with socialism fell flat, since Stevens's article was published together with one by Walter Dorwin Teague, whose Olympian gravity as the elder statesman of industrial design could not be tarnished with Red insinuations. Teague was forthright: "This practice of making previous models look outmoded when the new models have no better service to offer is known as 'planned obsolescence,' or 'artificial obsolescence'—the latter being the more accurate

Evolution

Revolution

The world-famous army 'Jeep' vehicle started it all. Then came the evolutionary changes. Sensible changes. Like more ground clearance. Stronger suspension. Weather proof tops. Fun changes. Like pink and white striped upholstery. Fringed surrey tops. Lively colors. A sports roadster. A station wagon — rugged, durable, designed for work and play.

Then came the 'Jeep' Wagoneer. A revolution! The Wagoneer is so revolutionary, it's hard to recognize your old 'Jeep' friend. It's a station wagon. *And* a looker! You'll be stunned. Slide into that luxurious interior. Beautiful. Comfortable. Visibility unlimited!

Turn the ignition key. You've got an overhead cam engine purring for you. The only one in any American

*Optional items at slight extra cost.

production car. Try that steering. Power.* The brakes. Power again.* The transmission. It's automatic.* Feel that ride. Pure luxury.

And the 'Jeep' heart and spirit are still there. Pull one simple lever and you're in 'Jeep' 4-wheel "Drivepower."† Then there's hardly a hill that can keep you down . . . hardly a mud hole that can bog you down. In fact, there's scarcely any driving situation that can get you down. You're free to go anywhere with the traction to pull you through.

Drop in on your 'Jeep' dealer. He's so enthusiastic about the 'Jeep' Wagoneer he'll be *glad* to give you a test drive. Actually, he gets a kick out of it himself!

KAISER Jeep CORPORATION Toledo 1, Ohio

†"DRIVEPOWER" is Wagoneer station wagon's new, improved and exclusive 4-wheel drive system.

ALL NEW 'JEEP' WAGONEER

See the Wagoneer demonstrated on "THE GREATEST SHOW ON EARTH." Tuesday nights, ABC-TV Network.

Fig. 4
Advertisement for the Jeep Wagoneer, 1963. Several of Brooks Stevens's automotive designs based on the military Jeep are featured in this ad, which might be considered a visual demonstration of the principle of planned obsolescence.

term but still not as accurate as just plain 'gypping.'" Instead, he asserted: "The function of design, simply put, is to realize the true character of the thing designed, and to reveal the values that have been built into it. If it is used for camouflage, it is being prostituted." Most firms, he wrote, were intent upon delivering products that were based on "honest, legitimate obsolescence," defined as making products "more serviceable, less costly."[18]

Stevens and Teague also differed sharply in their views of consumers. Stevens was unequivocal about his responsibilities: "The industrial designer's first obligation is to his client primarily because he is retained by his client and derives his income for his services from that manufacturer."[19] He viewed users pragmatically, even skeptically, in terms of what would sell: "You're asking me if designers are charlatans? I'd say yes, to a certain degree. I could not go on a full crusade for good design, I mean, really good, aesthetically good, artistically good design in a manufactured product because it wouldn't pay off. The public would not understand it or accept it. It would be beyond them. It just wouldn't sell." Teague, in contrast, while acknowledging the importance of clients, placed primary emphasis on the role of designers as representing users in the development processes. Industrial designers, for him, approach "the object as an outsider representing the user, the public; and he knows the thing should work better, not worse, for the attention he gives it." In summary, "it is his responsibility to see that the object is humanized."[20]

Yet rather than portraying the division between Stevens and Teague in terms of a personal polarization, it would be best to see their disagreements as representing the diversity of approach characteristic of American design, and indeed of American society, at that time. Henry Dreyfuss emphasized ergonomic methodology; Peter Muller-Munk cultivated European urbanity; Donald Deskey molded himself into the business executive incarnate. Stevens, in contrast, like Raymond Loewy, was described by Arthur Pulos in his history of American design as a showman, and he obviously enjoyed his reputation as the enfant terrible of industrial design.[21]

With the benefit of hindsight, planned obsolescence was indeed flawed in practice. The emphasis on superficial changes in form all too often meant that the quality of more fundamental aspects of the product was neglected, and the trajectory of stylistic change did not necessarily reflect the needs of people, but rather served the need of companies to sell more products. In his dogged insistence that the real measure of design was in the sales charts, however, Stevens was a man of his time, and he was not alone. Raymond Loewy's New York office at one time had the slogan "It's good design if it sells" set on its postal franking machine, so that every letter sent out carried the imprint. If some people thought that emphasizing sales was crass commercialism that tainted design, Stevens argued that it was a fact of business life, like it or not.

Ultimately designers must be judged in terms of their practice, not their pronouncements. Stevens's success as a designer demonstrated that he did deliver improved products on the terms he claimed for them, and they deserve examination on those terms. The best of them—such as the Petipoint iron, his Harley-Davidson Hydra-Glide motorcycle, or the generations of vehicles derived from his original concept of the Jeep station wagon—were striking aspects of the everyday visual language of their age. Their tangible legacy still strikes a chord long after the echoes of philosophical debates have faded.

In the 1960s Stevens seemed to retreat from public discourse. Times were changing, and the American market was being penetrated by new product concepts from overseas that did not necessarily hinge on the principle that bigger is better. The success of the Volkswagen proved Stevens, and the overwhelming majority of Detroit executives, to be wrong—there was a market for a small car if it was of the right kind and quality, a point underpinned by the flood of Japanese cars and other products that followed. While overseas competitors sought advantage through quality in technology and design, U.S. companies were being taken over by the new financial management and marketing techniques taught in business schools. Improving stock prices became more important than product quality. The consequences for design were noted in "The Decline of Industrial Designers," a *Fortune* article from 1968. "Radical innovation in design is now the exception rather than the rule," the writer asserted, and design "is likely to apply timid if tasteful talents." It concluded that design focused only on marketing targets could become outmoded. This caused some fluttering in the dovecotes of the design profession, a few letters of protest, and little more.[22]

The following decades were not easy ones for the design profession. Many design companies were reduced in size, and many closed. Yet Stevens's firm continued to prosper on the same basis as it had always done—a close relationship with clients that focused on improvements in form and utility to bring advantage in the competitive battles of the marketplace. He never really changed his fundamental approach, and neither was it necessary for him to do so, as long as clients were satisfied with the work he and his associates turned out and people bought the products.

In 1991, when the *Chicago Tribune* published a long article and interview to celebrate Stevens's eightieth birthday, it opened with the words: "Brooks Stevens is hardly a household [name]."[23] Yet he had been. In the interview he expressed regret at the loss of the innovative spirit characteristic of the American businessmen of his early career, who built the foundations of the nation's wealth. It is as an integral and exuberant part of that generation that he should be remembered.

1. Alfred P. Sloan Jr., *My Years with General Motors* (New York: Doubleday, 1963), 266.

2. "Modern Art in Business," *Business Week*, 28 September 1929, 30.

3. "The Eyes Have It," *Business Week*, 25 January 1930, 30.

4. Ron Grossman, "The Idea Man," *Chicago Tribune*, 3 June 1991.

5. Ibid.

6. Brooks Stevens Associates, "Design: Industrial, Packaging, Advertising," ca. 1940, Brooks Stevens Archive, Milwaukee Art Museum.

7. Brooks Stevens, introduction to 1943 reprint of "Your Victory Car," Brooks Stevens Archive.

8. Brooks Stevens, "Planned Obsolescence," *Finish Magazine*, September 1956, HL-12.

9. Brooks Stevens Associates, "Industrial Design…and How It Creates Business," 1949, Brooks Stevens Archive.

10. James T. Patterson, *Grand Expectations: The United States, 1945–1974* (Oxford: Oxford University Press, 1996), 70–71.

11. "Planned Obsolescence: Is It Fair? Yes! Says Brooks Stevens; No! Says Walter Dorwin Teague," *Rotarian*, February 1960, 2–5.

12. Christine Frederick, *Selling Mrs. Consumer* (New York: Business Bourse, 1929), 81, 246. For more on Frederick's early statements on obsolescence, and their relationships to concurrent developments in the automobile industry, see Roland Marchand, *Advertising the American Dream* (Berkeley: University of California Press, 1985), 156–60. For an early consideration of "conspicuous waste," see Thorstein Veblen, *Theory of the Leisure Class* (New York: Macmillan, 1899).

13. Brooks Stevens Associates, untitled brochure, 1953, Brooks Stevens Archive.

14. "To Sell Is Not to Waste," typescript translation of article from *L'Automobile*, September 1953, Brooks Stevens Archive.

15. Vance Packard, *The Hidden Persuaders*, rev. ed. (Harmondsworth: Pelican, 1981), 24.

16. Karl Prentiss, "Brooks Stevens: He Has Designs on Your Dough," *True: The Man's Magazine*, April 1958.

17. "The Crime of Planned Obsolescence," *Weekly People*, 18 October 1958, quoted in "Planned Obsolescence: Is It Fair?" 2.

18. "Planned Obsolescence: Is It Fair?" 4.

19. Stevens, "The Clarification of 'Planned Obsolescence,'" 1959, Brooks Stevens Archive.

20. Prentiss, "Brooks Stevens."

21. Arthur J. Pulos, *The American Design Adventure, 1940–1975* (Cambridge: MIT Press, 1988), 270; Prentiss, "Brooks Stevens."

22. "The Decline of Industrial Designers," *Fortune*, February 1968, 149.

23. Grossman, "The Idea Man."

Brooks Stevens, the Man in Your Life: Shaping the Domestic Sphere, 1935–50

KRISTINA WILSON

The editors of *House and Garden* penned these inspiring words in 1947 about the leaders in the field of industrial design, whom they dubbed "ten men in your life":

> You will see that the trend is towards appliances that are increasingly simple to operate, increasingly automatic. Once set in motion, they are expected to carry through an intricate succession of processes, to turn themselves off at an appointed instant. You will learn that an astonishing amount of thinking, a long trial-and-error process are behind your new, gleaming, silent servant. …Common to these ten men is the belief that nothing is quite good enough for the American homemaker. As a result, they are in a sense social revolutionists, helping to free the housewife from the drudgery of manual chores. They are not only making housework more inviting, they are giving millions of women new leisure and the unspent energy to make the most of it.[1]

Included in this group of "revolutionists" were Brooks Stevens and other well-known designers such as Henry Dreyfuss, Raymond Loewy, and Harold Van Doren. Stevens, like many of these designers whose careers began before World War II, found some of his earliest commercial successes in the field of domestic appliances: the Steam-O-Matic and Petipoint irons (1940 and 1941), the Hamilton dryer (1944), and the Coolerator refrigerator (1945), all of which were manufactured in larger quantities after the war, when industries had converted to peacetime production. Furthermore, two of his large-scale environmental designs from the years around World War II can be interpreted as multidimensional, mobile domestic appliances: a motor home, or "land yacht,"

for millionaire playboy William Woods Plankinton Jr. (1936) and the Olympian Hiawatha train for the Milwaukee Road (1947).

Echoing *House and Garden's* claim that such "gleaming, silent servants" would "free the housewife," Stevens, like many of his cohort, believed that clever gadgets could alleviate the drudgery of domestic work and that clever styling would attract the female consumers they sought. His frequently flamboyant designs did in fact garner much attention in the marketplace, but as historians of domestic labor have demonstrated, such gizmos did little to lessen the total amount of work required to maintain a mid-century household.[2] Indeed, new appliances often simply raised expectations for what tasks a housewife could accomplish on her own; in the years after World War II, as Betty Friedan powerfully argued, these expectations were often used to convince women to leave the commercial workforce (where they had labored during the war) and return to the solitary work of homemaking.[3] Although Stevens's appliances were no more or less guilty than any others of enslaving the housewife, his appealing, quirky designs—as well as his emphasis, in his design manifestos, on romancing the housewife—make a potent case study.

If, as a result of developments in domestic technologies, housewives throughout the first half of the twentieth century were increasingly isolated, surrounded at home by inanimate machines, then those who bought appliances styled by Stevens were surrounded by unusual, dynamic designs that prompted identification and emotional attachment. In short, his designs compensated for the loneliness they enabled through a sophisticated strategy of flattering the housewife. In their stunning appearance the objects flattered her taste, telling her that she was stylish enough to choose them. As commodities in a higher, but not prohibitive, price bracket, the objects became symbols of her (newly returned) husband, who, with his peacetime salary, was doting enough to buy them. And, with the imprimatur of the phrase "Styled by Brooks Stevens" emblazoned on them, the objects demonstrated that she was important enough to deserve the attentions of this other "man in her life," the famous designer who made appliances into luxury gifts. Stevens's designs didn't just flatter women, however. They also became tools for enforcing strict gender identities and for encouraging the large-scale differentiation of gendered spheres within the home in the years around World War II.

Brooks Stevens and the Profession of Industrial Design

In his later years Stevens was proud to claim that he had coined the phrase "planned obsolescence," which he used to describe a strategy for stimulating sales based on making products *appear*, through design, to be better than previous (equally functional) models. His attitude indicates a wholehearted embrace of the commercial use to which aesthetics can be put, and it is instructive to consider his biases within the context of his peers. From their earliest days as recognized professionals, industrial designers had struggled to explain the role of aesthetics in their work. The industrial design profession emerged in the late 1920s as manufacturers sought new ways to promote their products and diversify their potential audiences.[4] Over the course of that decade, the advertising industry had developed an arsenal of psychological and aesthetic tactics to lure customers to purchase an endless variety of goods. The redesigning of products appeared, to some manufacturers, to be a logical extension of advertising. A different design made the product seem "new" and might even improve functionality and, if it were eye-catching enough, could serve as an advertisement in and of itself. New designs carried more financial risks than advertising campaigns, however, because they entailed the retooling of factories, had the potential to affect (positively or negatively) the functioning of the product, and could alter the very character (again, positively or negatively) of the item. With so much at stake, manufacturers were thus wary of using only aesthetics—notoriously unpredictable and subjective—

as a base on which to expand, or resuscitate, their businesses. When they turned to the growing cadre of professional industrial designers for help in reconceiving a standard product, they demanded practical, concrete reasons for aesthetic changes.

Designers balanced the demands of function and appearance in a variety of ways. Walter Dorwin Teague, considered by many to be the founding figure of the profession, argued that for each functional product there existed an ideal efficient, aesthetically pleasing form. Although appearance thus took precedence in Teague's philosophy—all design was motivated by the pursuit of a Platonic form—the commitment to an eternal and constant form imbued his aestheticism with certitude and conviction. (It also, ironically, contradicted the popular practice of annual restyling.) He developed these beliefs in his 1940 manifesto *Design This Day*, in which he asserted that "only one set of aesthetic laws and one standard of judgement" informed great design, reminding his readers that "implicit in any man-made thing is the ultimate form that will most perfectly satisfy its maker and serve its user."[5] Henry Dreyfuss, another major figure in Stevens's professional world, rationalized his aesthetic decisions by developing forms that responded to intuitive use by the human body. As a critic in 1931 explained, "Dreyfuss brings to his work no special aptitude for mechanics and only a moderate gift in the handling of materials. He has to a high degree a sense of the ultimate use to which commodities will be put, a feeling for the comfort of the man who is going to use the fountain pen for writing more than as a decorative adjunct to his desk."[6] Norman Bel Geddes, undoubtedly the best showman among the early generation of industrial designers, prided himself on forward-looking, often fantastical and extravagant designs. Although he, like his peers, believed that a redesigned form must enable enhanced functional capacity, he did not allow function to take complete priority over aesthetics. Rather, as Jeffrey Meikle has written, Geddes believed that form should *express* function, that aesthetics should be used to make an object *look* functional.[7] This variation on the "form follows function" doctrine allowed Geddes to explore aesthetic devices that were not a direct result of the object's use—in short, it allowed him to experiment aesthetically, not infrequently to the detriment of the object's performance. Needless to say, many of his peers blamed Geddes for the flamboyant, impractical reputation that some companies ascribed to this young group of businessmen-artists.

Stevens set up business for himself as an industrial designer in Milwaukee shortly after his departure from Cornell University in 1933. He entered the trade several years after his New York colleagues had established themselves, and he inherited from them the vexing relationship between improved product functioning and eye-catching aesthetics. Although he navigated his own course through these philosophical waters, his solution owed a particular debt to Geddes, whose popular futuristic 1932 publication *Horizons* would have been known to Stevens.[8] From his first years as a professional designer, Stevens seems to have understood, as did Geddes, the consumer's attraction to eye-catching designs. Unlike Geddes, Stevens was able to develop new designs that were not costly to implement and that did not impede functioning. His concern for functionality took a decided backseat, however, to his inspired enthusiasm for design as an attention-getting strategy. Indeed, his mature design philosophy could best be described as the pragmatic use of aesthetics. As early as 1940 he reminded manufacturers that "in this fast moving day and age the purchaser … often buys on first appearance."[9] And in the years after the popular term "planned obsolescence" became commonplace in design circles, he further expressed his commitment to the manufacturer's bottom line by proclaiming: "The industrial designer, of course, creates his special niche in the economic and business life of his country by adding the stylist's touch to make manufactured products desirable to the consuming public and to give the products that last degree of 'buy-appeal' necessary to make the sale."[10]

As Stevens was all too aware, the primary audience for his "buy-appeal" designs was the housewife of the late 1930s and 1940s. While men tended to be the breadwinners of the family (except during the war years), women almost uniformly decided which products to buy for the home. They were not only the arbiters of taste in household furnishings, but they were also the experts on maintaining hygiene and order in that household

and were thus the logical audience for manufacturers of home appliances, as an ad from 1950 makes clear (fig. 1). Stevens himself invoked the housewife's buying authority repeatedly through the figure of "Mrs. Consumer": How to make a given product "appeal more to Mrs. Consumer?" How to modify a design "lest Mrs. Consumer shy away from a good product because [of how] it looks"?[11] More importantly, his rhetoric reveals a pervasive concern with establishing an intimate emotional connection with the housewife, with romancing her into buying his work. Stevens understood, for example, how an appealing design could acquire greater than average significance for his

Fig. 1
Advertisement for the Modern Hygiene vacuum cleaner, 1950

audience: it not only had to look pleasant but also had to inspire "pride" and "joy" in its owner.[12] Less unusual designs were "a step toward regimentation and … blandness" and would not establish a meaningful "identification" between the owner and the product.[13] His designs, by contrast, established themselves in the household pantheon of prized possessions and imbued their owner with a sense of her own good taste and, quite simply, importance. He confirmed this design strategy when he commented to a reporter in 1955: "Designers regard women as the yardstick for measuring the appeal of products. Men will never again be considered the country's most important buyers. …It was [during the Depression] that industrial design really got under way. We had to use a little romance, a little divining, and a little plunging to find out what women wanted to buy."[14] Ultimately, while his peers emphasized the enlightening and clarifying power of good design, Stevens—as evidenced by his propensity for the dramatic and unusual, and his embrace of commercialism—demonstrated a commitment to the seductive power of good design.

Early Domestic Appliance Designs

An in-depth examination of several of Stevens's domestic appliance designs—including irons, a clothes dryer, and refrigerators—reveals that the devices, while claiming to make housework easier, in fact only charmed the housewife and did little to lessen the amount of work in her day. Stevens's earliest commercially successful designs for the housewife were two irons: the Steam-O-Matic, the first domestic steam iron, and the Petipoint (for the Edmilton Corporation), an air-cooled electric iron with a smaller point at its rear for detailed ironing. The Steam-O-Matic was, of necessity, a bulky item: contained within its walls was a chamber for water, which, when heated, produced steam (fig. 2). Stevens's brief was to "minimize the apparent size" of the iron, so that "Mrs. Consumer" would not think it too heavy.[15] He achieved this with a series of swooping lines—highly polished, in contrast to the mottled surface of the remainder of the body—that originated from the iron's prow, traced its rounded contours, and terminated at the back, giving the iron a sense of forward-surging motion. The plastic handle complemented the dynamism of the body:

toward the front its molded form fit the housewife's grip, and at the rear it kicked upward with a featherlike flair. This iron had a sense of panache that belied its weight and transformed the bulky metal object into an efficient, aerodynamic instrument. As one ad asserted, "It seems like magic, but it's very simple… just fill the iron with water, plug in, and in a moment it is steaming lustily."[16]

The Petipoint, developed in the following year, had a similarly streamlined, forward-rushing aesthetic (fig. 3). Its prow seemed to burrow busily into the task at hand, achieving such speeds that its expansive wings appeared to lift the back of the iron from the horizontal surface. The handle again accentuated the body's motion: its front end leaned forward, pulling the heavier back end of the handle almost out of its seat. The elaborate wings did more visually, however, than simply enhance the aerodynamic sensibility. Their distinctive presence—which, according to Stevens, facilitated the iron's air-cooling function—transformed the iron from a workaday accessory into a unique, somewhat extravagant possession. The wings were an aggressive expression of technological innovation, confirming the iron's cutting-edge status. They were also an uncanny echo of the ruffles (or petticoats) that the iron itself was designed to negotiate; this reference, however subliminal, imbued the object with a preciousness and femininity more frequently associated with jewelry, ensuring the housewife's intimate attachment to the tool.[17]

Of course, Stevens also claimed that his designs enhanced each iron's functional capabilities; even if aesthetics and psychological responses were his primary interests, he was always careful to include practical considerations when justifying his designs. The Steam-O-Matic required a large body to house the water that became steam, and Stevens made that body as light and sturdy as possible by casting it in aluminum. The Petipoint's cooling fins allowed the heat of the iron to dissipate to either side, leaving the top surface, with its thermostat, and the plastic handle cooler than those of other irons of comparable size. And its smaller point at the back—the "petit point," designed "to accommodate small pleats and sleeve tucks in ladies' shirtwaists and blouses"— made the iron into a virtual two-in-one.[18] (The "petit point" also

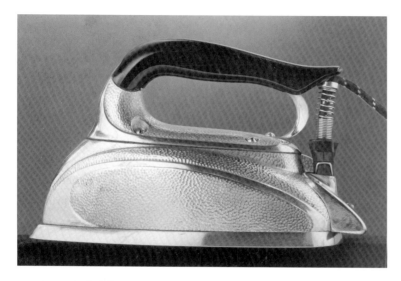

Figs. 2 and 3
The Steam-O-Matic clothes iron of 1940 (left) and its immediate successor, the Petipoint of 1941, both designed for the Edmilton Company of Milwaukee

eliminated the flat edge that had traditionally formed the base for an iron when it rested upright, not in use; the user of the Petipoint had to rest the iron on its side, balanced against the fins and handle, a decidedly awkward and impractical consequence of this "functional" design.)

Thus both of Stevens's irons apparently transformed a hitherto complicated or specialized process into an easily performed chore. The Steam-O-Matic enabled women to care for cotton shirts and heavy linens, which they had previously sent out of the house for cleaning and pressing.[19] The Petipoint offered a fine point for detail work within a larger iron, so that a housewife would not have to make do with the larger point for delicate ruffles or, worse, skip the ruffles altogether. In effecting these changes, the irons can be classified as what Reyner Banham called the "great American gizmo." In his formulation, a gizmo is "a small self-contained unit of high performance in relation to its size and cost. …The minimum of skill is required in its installation and use."[20] While there is no doubt that ironing requires skill, these two products allowed the housewife to iron heavy fabrics and details with less skill and fewer complicated maneuvers than previous irons had demanded.

Another central characteristic of the gizmo is that it operates "independent of any physical or social infrastructure"—that is, it requires no larger network of technology or people than its own body and that of its user.[21] With the exception of an infrastructure of electricity, both of Stevens's irons were independent; they eliminated the need for assistance from a household servant or a contracted, out-of-house service. In short, they enabled the housewife to be completely self-sufficient and completely isolated. Whereas before she might have used the in-house and out-of-house help of numerous people, these new irons enabled her to perform, and thus made her solely responsible for, all of the complicated tasks of clothing and linen care. As Ruth Schwartz Cowan has convincingly argued, technological innovation in the twentieth-century household eliminated many of the supporting tasks done by human servants but ultimately did little to lessen the total amount of work needed to maintain the home.[22] The housewife therefore had as much, if not more, work to do than when

she had human help; furthermore, instead of spending her day with other people doing housework, she now spent her day alone with her "gleaming, silent servants."

On an unconscious level, it was perhaps to compensate for this increasingly isolated life that Stevens and other designers imbued their appliance designs with such flair and panache. The goal of an eye-catching design was not merely to prompt the housewife to purchase a given product. It was, more importantly, to foster identification and attachment to the object over a period of time: the design reminded her that someone (that "man in her life") had thoughtfully considered her daily routine, thus transforming the object of work into a surrogate object of affection. In the years immediately following World War II, a flashy appliance, demonstrating a couple's participation in peacetime prosperity, was a particularly potent lure to the housewife returning to homemaking.

Stevens's design for the Hamilton clothes dryer enhanced another product that actually only reorganized chores even as it proudly came "to the relief of the little housewife" (fig. 4).[23] The mechanism for a self-contained drying unit had been developed by an independent inventor in the mid-1930s, at which time no automatic dryer was available to consumers; housewives instead had their laundry dried at commercial establishments or they hung it on a line (either outdoors or, in wealthier homes, in basement "drying rooms"), often with the help of family or a laundress.[24] Thus, when the Hamilton Manufacturing Company approached Stevens to provide a design for its new dryer, he had the opportunity to establish a form for a completely new appliance.

Stevens undoubtedly took inspiration for the dryer's basic white cube from Geddes's radically simplified white stove for Standard Gas (1933; fig. 5), which had codified the predominant aesthetic for case-piece appliances throughout the 1930s. Hamilton had placed the opening to the dryer in the front of the cube so that the top surface could be used by the housewife for folding or other "work" (which she was now able to do alone, without help). Stevens quickly realized, however, that such a basic design "would have no appeal and could never command the price required."[25] His solution was to place the service and adjustment controls behind two fluted panels on either side of the door and to put a window in the door. The fluted panels were an entirely extraneous element—a bit of ornament that dressed up the dryer, demonstrating that both it and the woman who used it deserved an extra dose of luxury and beauty in their daily routine. Indeed, in an advertisement from *Electrical Merchandising*, the dryer's flutes echo the housewife's apron, reinforcing an identification between her pristine, well-cared-for femininity and the machine (see fig. 4).

Although the window was conceived as a device to show off the dryer's capabilities—as Stevens later recalled, the Hamilton company asked, "Well how are we going to make [the public] know what it does? I said, put a window in the door"[26]—when coupled with the fluted panels, it offered multiple layers of associations. It was, in one interpretation, a window onto a stage set flanked by tall, rich curtains—imbuing the life inside the dryer, and the life using the dryer, with some of the drama of the daily radio soap operas. In another interpretation, it was simply a window—a house window, with white curtains—offering a mesmerizing view of the transformed fabrics of household life. In fact, when it was first introduced in stores, Stevens recommended that it be displayed tossing around a colorful pair of "the husband's shorts"; the shorts not only demonstrated the machine's function but also acted synecdochically, reminding the housewife that her work was not lonely, but rather was in the service of her husband and family.

Electric refrigerators, introduced in the 1920s, received some of the most celebrated makeovers in the 1930s and 1940s by designers such as Dreyfuss, Loewy, and Stevens. Dreyfuss's 1934 design for General Electric set a precedent that later models would imitate (fig. 6). He removed the condenser from its highly visible place in a monitor above the refrigerator and buried it at the bottom of the object; he then extended the sides of the case to the floor, creating a unified, simplified mass. Loewy's designs for the Sears Coldspot—updated annually between 1935 and 1938— offered a more stylish variation on Dreyfuss's rectangular box: its 1938 incarnation featured chrome-striped feet, a subtle vertical ridge running down the length of the front (intended to evoke an automobile's V-shaped radiator), and two ball handles (fig. 7).[27]

Fig. 4 (upper)
Advertisement for the Hamilton clothes dryer, 1944

Fig. 5 (lower)
Norman Bel Geddes, Oriole stove, ca. 1933.
Designed for the Standard Gas Equipment Company, Baltimore.

Fig. 6 (upper left)
Henry Dreyfuss, refrigerator, 1934.
Designed for the General Electric Company, Schenectady, New York.

Fig. 7 (lower left)
Raymond Loewy, Coldspot refrigerator, 1938.
Designed for Sears, Roebuck, and Co., Chicago.

Fig. 8 (upper right)
Brooks Stevens, rendering for a Luxury refrigerator, 1942.
Designed for the Hamilton Manufacturing Co., Two Rivers, Wisconsin.

Fig. 9 (lower right)
Brooks Stevens, refrigerator, 1948.
Designed for the Coolerator Co., Duluth, Minnesota.

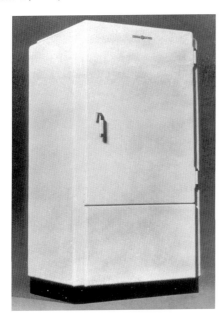

Stevens developed several refrigerator designs during and after World War II, each indebted to Dreyfuss's and Loewy's work in varying ways. Among the more fanciful of his designs was a proposed refrigerator for Hamilton with a translucent corner through which the user could see the contents (fig. 8). In the 1942 renderings the refrigerator is a seamless box with rounded corners and edges, sitting on a diminutive striped base. The translucent panel is engraved with a large, attenuated flower, and the word *luxury* is emblazoned in glistening chrome across the door. In this dreamlike view, arising in the midst of the war effort, the jewel-box aspect of a refrigerator is fully realized: from this machine's stylish exterior one can eagerly contemplate the delight of opening its doors and finding the treasures (bountiful, unrationed food) inside.[28]

For the Coolerator Company, Stevens designed a refrigerator that further simplified Loewy's stylish box (fig. 9). The body of the Coolerator has the same contours as the Hamilton design, with its seamlessly rounded rectangular form. The facade is interrupted only by the line separating the lower compartment from the refrigerator proper, its two handles—one horizontal and one vertical—and a dramatic chrome thread that rushes from over the top edge of the box, plunges down the length of the door, then whips off to the right, trailing the word *electric*. The chrome thread, like the fluted panels on the dryer, is an unnecessary, if restrained, ornament. Its simplicity is both understated and pronounced—the single curve shown off on a field of white—and it marks the refrigerator with a subtle sophistication, appealing to the housewife's sense of her own stylishness and uniqueness. Indeed, the early advertisements for the Coolerator proudly extolled the manufacturer's commitment to serving the needs and fantasies of the postwar wife: "Brook [*sic*] Stevens, famous industrial designer, and his staff worked for months to perfect a Coolerator to fit in the streamlined postwar kitchen. 60 designs were submitted. Of these 60, 8 were chosen for consumer and homemaker testing. In this way, the design of the New Coolerator was chosen the favorite of women everywhere! Yes, the New Coolerator is styled right—with all 17 things women want most in a postwar refrigerator!"[29] Although the advertisement did not enumerate those "17 things," it is clear that enlarged refrigerators with more efficient cooling systems allowed women to shop less frequently, so that they no longer had daily interaction with shopkeepers, but rather made weekly shopping trips to stock their own stylish refrigerated shelves.

Stevens's early appliance designs dressed up the gizmos of the domestic sphere, the silent, mechanical servants that had replaced the housewife's daily interactions with human help. Moreover, these servants flattered her: through their unusual designs they forged a sense of identification, so that their uniqueness, and the care with which they were designed, was transferred to their owner. The housewife herself became unique, the object of special care, even as she was stranded at home alone, left to ruminate on the world to which the flying Petipoint iron might take her, the world beyond the window of the Hamilton dryer.

Early Environmental Designs

Stevens's domestic appliance designs ultimately had ramifications far beyond the individual chores of isolated housewives. Because his designs were so explicitly intended for the women of America's homes, they ensured that certain tasks and spheres were made specifically feminine. If taking care of clothing and preparing food were incontrovertibly women's work, then the laundry and kitchen, outfitted with luxury gizmo "gifts" from Stevens to accomplish these tasks, became spaces within the house solely for women. Stevens used gizmos to similar (unconscious) effect in two large-scale environmental designs from these years, the Zephyr land yacht and the Olympian Hiawatha train. In both of these mobile domestic environments, gadget technology defined and differentiated gendered spheres, as it had done within the stationary home.

In the Zephyr land yacht, designed and constructed for William Woods Plankinton Jr. in 1936, Stevens built an entire home around the clever layering of gizmos (Plankinton even later gave the vehicle the nickname "Gadget").[30] With its electric icebox, electric stove, full bathroom with shower, living room, hunting and fishing equipment, and sleeping quarters for eight (including driver and manservant), the land yacht was, in essence, a large-scale gizmo. It operated as a completely self-sufficient domicile,

UNMARRIED MILLIONAIRES *Bill*

By Jack Stone

William Woods Plankinton Breakfasts in Gadget, His Mansion Trailer—
There Is Scarcely a Part of the United States the Millionaire Bachelor
Hasn't Visited in Gadget.

Fig. 10
William Woods Plankinton Jr. taking breakfast in his Zephyr Land Yacht.
From an article published in the *American Weekly*, 1947.

which could roam where it pleased without needing to put roots
into a larger permanent social or economic infrastructure
(fig. 10). Although the land yacht included space for Plankinton's
(male) visitors and servants—whereas appliances such as the
Steam-O-Matic or Hamilton dryer allowed for the presence of
only one person—their role in his mobile home can be seen as
that of a gizmo too. By joining Plankinton on one of his peregri-
nations, his friends and servants gave up their larger social
network and entered into the sole service of entertaining him;

conversely, their presence insulated—or isolated—Plankinton
from the larger world, providing him with a portable fraternity,
everything he needed within the easy reach of the Zephyr's
forty-five feet. As the housewife's gizmos made her kitchen and
laundry a specifically feminine sphere, so Plankinton's large-scale
roving gizmo defined the perimeter around an indubitably
masculine world.

In Stevens's designs for the Olympian Hiawatha train,
he created another mobile home, a large, self-sufficient gizmo
outfitted with gadgets, in which both men and women were given
gender-appropriate spaces. Stevens's firm oversaw all aspects of the
train design, from its interior compartments and accessories to
its exterior shape; in the totality of its design vision, the project
matches Dreyfuss's better-known work on the Twentieth Century
Limited (1938). The newly renovated Olympian Hiawatha train
was clearly marketed as a domestic sphere on wheels. Various
advertisements from the summer of 1947 depicted it as a family
home, with a mother, father, and son gathered before a window
in a mock living room in one image and a family of four around
a table in another (figs. 11, 12). Significantly, the press releases
for the new train frequently stressed its modern, homelike
environment and touted its highly gendered "lounge rooms."
An article from the *Milwaukee Journal* informed readers that
"the women's lounge quarters will emphasize a feminine note
while the men's lounge and smoking rooms will be definitely
masculine."[31] The "feminine note" was apparently achieved through
"soft grey green and ivory formica paneling" in the lounge, the
inclusion of a large divan, and "carefully selected French costume
prints," which were hung on the walls. The men's lounge, in contrast, had "red leather chairs, carpeting, and … sporting prints
covering the popular sport of trout and game fishing."[32]

And, indeed, the train's separate gendered spheres were
even writ large in its exterior design. Its major innovation was
its rear observation lounge, in which multiple panes of glare- and
heat-resistant glass created an egg-shaped, streamlined room for
viewing the landscape and sky above (fig. 13). This flashy tail
stood in pointed contrast to the engine of the train, which Stevens
fashioned into a charging bullet: two headlights, one above the

other, framed by horizontal lines, appeared to pierce the night air, streaking at top speeds along the narrow tracks (fig. 14). Stevens's engine was a machine for (the masculine occupation of) work, while his observation lounge was a machine for (the feminine occupation of) socializing. Furthermore, while the engine was a machine for *seeing*, the observation lounge, glowing as it snaked through the western landscape, was a machine for *being seen* (both from outside the train and from the social scene within). Ultimately the entire body of the train, a home on wheels, was anchored by the polar opposites of gender, the masculine engine and its feminine tail.

Throughout the domestic sphere—whether stationary or traveling—Stevens's gadget designs always worked on two levels: first, to perform a task (ironing, powering a train) and, second, to assign and confirm gender identities. His domestic appliances romanced the housewife, encouraging her to ignore the loneliness of housework and reconfirming the feminine character associated with such chores and the sphere of the house in which they are performed. Stevens's designs for the larger-scale gadgets of the Zephyr land yacht and the Olympian Hiawatha similarly affirmed traditional social gender codes such as the hunting male, the preening female, and the intact nuclear family. One may well ask why the women (and men, for that matter) of America made themselves such willing accomplices to this conservative social order. Undoubtedly the economic and social upheavals of the 1930s and 1940s fostered respect for the familiar, safe gender roles of previous generations. It may well have been comforting to a mid-century housewife, stripped of her mother's cadre of servants, to be given the tools to perform the tasks that in previous years she would have overseen—for a time, at least. It was not until the publication of Betty Friedan's book *The Feminine Mystique* in 1963 that women began to challenge the assumptions attached to their housework and encoded, unconsciously, in Stevens's designs. The legacy of Friedan allows us to envision a society—as yet unattained—where Bill Plankinton might find a niche in his land yacht to store his Petipoint iron.

Figs. 11 and 12
Advertisements for the Milwaukee Road's Olympian Hiawatha train. From *Better Homes and Gardens*, 1947 (above) and *National Geographic*, 1950 (left).

Figs. 13 and 14
The streamlined engine and the Sky Top Lounge observation car
of the Olympian Hiawatha

I am grateful to Glenn Adamson for his comments on an earlier draft of the manuscript.

1. "Ten Men in Your Life," *House and Garden*, September 1947, 125.

2. See, for example, Ruth Schwartz Cowan, *More Work for Mother: The Ironies of Household Technology from the Open Hearth to the Microwave* (New York: Basic Books, 1983); Christine Hardyment, *From Mangle to Microwave: The Mechanization of Household Work* (Cambridge: Polity Press, 1988); and Susan Strasser, *Never Done: A History of American Housework* (New York: Pantheon, 1982).

3. Betty Friedan, *The Feminine Mystique* (1963; reprint, New York: Norton, 2001).

4. One of the first book-length discussions of industrial design was published in 1932: Roy Sheldon and Egmont Arens, *Consumer Engineering: A New Technique for Prosperity* (New York: Harper and Brothers, 1932). The classic history of the industrial design profession is Jeffrey L. Meikle, *Twentieth Century Limited: Industrial Design in America, 1925–1939* (Philadelphia: Temple University Press, 1979).

5. Walter Dorwin Teague, *Design This Day: The Technique of Order in the Machine Age* (New York: Harcourt, Brace and Company, 1940), 49, 47.

6. Gilbert Seldes, "Profiles: Artist in a Factory," *New Yorker*, 29 August 1931, 22.

7. Jeffrey L. Meikle, "Coldspots and Heaters: The Formation of Industrial Design," *Industrial Design* 28 (July–August 1981): 25.

8. Norman Bel Geddes, *Horizons* (Boston: Little, Brown, 1932).

9. Brooks Stevens, "When Engineering Influences Design," *Durez Molder* 10 (April 1940): 10–11.

10. Brooks Stevens, "The Clarification of 'Planned Obsolescence,'" ca. 1959, Brooks Stevens Archive, Milwaukee Art Museum.

11. Stevens, "When Engineering Influences Design," 10–11. The phrase "Mrs. Consumer" originated with Christine Frederick's 1929 book on home economics, *Selling Mrs. Consumer* (New York: Business Bourse, 1929). See John Heskett's essay in this volume.

12. Ibid.; Brooks Stevens, "Industrial Design and Its Practical Application to Industry," lecture given on November 17, 1937, quoted in "November Meeting," *Milwaukee Engineering* 18 (November 1937): 9–10.

13. Stevens, "Clarification of 'Planned Obsolescence,'" 4.

14. "Most Products Designed for Female Buyer," *Milwaukee Journal*, 16 October 1955.

15. Stevens, "When Engineering Influences Design," 10–11.

16. Advertisement for Steam-O-Matic iron at Marshall Field and Company, ca. 1940, Brooks Stevens Archive.

17. A brochure promoting the Petipoint Iron, published by the Edmilton Corporation, 1941, explained its functions: "Now dainty ruffles, tucks, and hard-to-get-at surfaces may be ironed perfectly and easily as well as large flat surfaces … all with one iron" (Brooks Stevens Archive).

18. "Designer's Notes: Design Commissions Prewar and Immediate Postwar," Brooks Stevens to Richard Guy Wilson, 8 July 1985, collection of the author.

19. Cowan, *More Work for Mother*, 106.

20. Reyner Banham, "The Great American Gizmo," in *A Critic Writes: Essays by Reyner Banham* (Berkeley: University of California Press, 1996), 113; originally published in *Industrial Design* 12 (September 1965): 48–59.

21. Ibid. For a related discussion of the gizmo (or device) paradigm, see Albert Borgmann, *Technology and the Character of Contemporary Life: A Philosophical Inquiry* (Chicago: University of Chicago Press, 1984), chap. 9.

22. The "servant problem"—the shortage of women to hire for household help—started in the first decades of the twentieth century. However, as Cowan demonstrates, throughout the pre-World War II years, the area of housework for which wives consistently sought specific help was the laundry, either through a hired laundress or commercial laundries. Cowan, *More Work for Mother*, 106–107, 156–157, 174.

23. Brooks Stevens Associates, "Industrial Design … and How It Creates Business," 1949, Brooks Stevens Archive.

24. "Designer's Notes."

25. Ibid.

26. Brooks Stevens, interview with Chip Duncan, 1990, transcript, Brooks Stevens Archive.

27. Meikle, *Twentieth Century Limited*, 106.

28. In a 1990 interview, Stevens recalled the Hamilton refrigerator: "And you see this corner here? That is a transparent molded part of the cover, metal and plastic. Now you know when you walk up to the refrigerator when you come down at ten at night and you wanna look and see if there's anything there to nibble on. You would sneak the door open and look in real quick and close it because you're supposed to be wasting the cooling or whatever if you left the door open. So … this gave you the view point, I could see 90% of the content through the transparent door and then say, oh there is some cream cheese in there. I'll open the door now and take it out. And that was part of the romance that was in the showroom. This thing would light up inside and you'd see all the goodies in there" (Stevens, interview with Chip Duncan).

29. Advertisement for Coolerator refrigerator, published in *What's New in Home Economics*, April 1945, Brooks Stevens Archive.

30. Jack Stone, "Unmarried Millionaires: Bill Plankinton, Bachelor in a Trailer," *American Weekly*, 21 December 1947, 6–7.

31. "New Trains to Set Pace for Railroad," *Milwaukee Journal*, 10 November 1946.

32. "Designer's Notes: Olympian Hiawatha Railroad Train for Chicago, Milwaukee, St. Paul and Pacific Railroad," 12 May 1948, 5, Brooks Stevens Archive.

Stevens and his family, featured in an advertisement for Lawn Boy mowers, ca. 1962

Brooks Stevens: "Ego-Inspiring Styling" and the American Dream

JODY CLOWES

It is ironic that the Milwaukee Art Museum has devoted so much attention to Brooks Stevens, who repeatedly asserted that he was not interested in winning awards from New York's Museum of Modern Art (he never did) and that the "good thing … about what we did was that there was no signature. …There was no Brooks Stevens look."[1] A stylish man with a healthy ego, Stevens submerged his personal aesthetic in favor of what he thought would sell and judged success in mundane terms: client lists and sales volume. Late in life, asked how he felt about his designs being displayed as art, Stevens demurred. Instead he praised his firm's 1950 exhibition at the Milwaukee Art Institute, comparing his work with designs by Norman Bel Geddes, whose "pictures of streamlined oceanliners… never got any more than printed. I mean, they were never made or anything. The aeroplanes with multi-engines… those were predictions. This was reality, real products in there." His most important design contribution, he declared, was "dollars in the bank for the client."[2]

Brooks Stevens believed in business, and this was fundamental to his salesmanship and his success. Throughout the 1950s and 1960s he promoted industry to itself in a dizzying round of speeches and articles for businessmen's clubs, engineers' conferences, and trade magazines. Proud to have coined the controversial term "planned obsolescence," he defended annual restyling as an engine of growth. Stevens clearly believed that improved products with what he called "buy appeal" were essential to the American way of life.[3] As a designer he presented himself as a hardheaded pragmatist who happened to have a visionary streak and a great sense of style. He wielded his conservative political stance to deflect businessmen's traditional mistrust of artists and used his unconventional dress, fancy cars,

and elegant bearing to convince them that he knew something they didn't. This is not to say that Stevens's work doesn't merit the status of art. Many of his firm's commissions stand with the best of twentieth-century industrial design. But for Stevens art was beside the point. In his mind, good design was design that sold.

Practical Postwar Design

At the close of World War II, Stevens had a well-established client list and a high level of local recognition, nurtured through tireless lecturing and favorable press coverage. The public image of American industry, tarnished by Depression-era suffering, had been profoundly transformed through war production. Businessmen and manufacturers were recast as true patriots, defenders and shapers of the American way of life. In the expansive rhetoric of the Cold War era, corporate interests were explicitly identified with the survival of democracy and the "Free World." The postwar business community had a mission, and Stevens positioned himself as a stalwart partisan ready to answer the call of duty (fig. 1).

Stevens recognized that his ideological commitment to the triumph of business was also a useful marketing tool. During the war he had begun to make a conscious effort to set himself apart from his competitors. In a 1942 promotional brochure for plastics featuring leading designers, he was the only one whose biography stressed the bottom line.[4] He used hard numbers and a straight-talking style to assure potential clients that he spoke their language. He also sought opportunities to oppose himself to prophetic design—as when he prepared "The Practical Postwar Car" to follow William Stout's prediction of a flying automobile at a 1944 conference. "The wilder the prediction and the more extreme the rendering, the more renowned the stylist seems to be," Stevens noted wryly.[5] In a 1943 story proposal for *Industrial Marketing* magazine, he made it clear he was no "long-haired artist":

> *I have felt for the last year that… the marvels of the postwar world have been terribly exaggerated, and in no way represent the practical manufacturing side of the picture. It is all very well for theorists and artist designers to project the fantastic all-plastic world which will be the fruits of victory after this horrible war, but, unfortunately, they do not consult those manufacturers and engineering departments who will somehow have to work these fantastic things out, or explain to the public why they have been misrepresented. … Please be advised that the story will be on the conservative side, but in so being it will be one that the average manufacturer will recognize as a possible link with the future instead of the theories of the long-haired artist who is satisfied to project his own whims on paper.[6]*

The True Magic of American Expansion and Prosperity

Stevens came by his affinity for business honestly. He grew up among Milwaukee's industrial elite and readily absorbed their free-market conservatism. Toward the end of the war he was invited to join "The Different Dozen," a group of right-wing civic and corporate leaders who gathered over cocktails to discuss business and politics.[7] Perhaps it was this involvement that convinced him that his political views would help establish a rapport with prospective clients. Whatever the cause, by the early 1950s Stevens's speeches became overtly political. His conservative rhetoric allied him with business, shamelessly flattered his clients, and garnered glowing coverage in trade magazines and local newspapers. The following is typical of his prose:

> *American competitive free enterprise is the true backbone of the stability of this country and this same powerful medium is fast becoming the crutch, economically speaking, to the entire world. This typically American trait and*

> *uncanny ability will, in my estimation, continue to be supreme and prosperous under… any management other than all out socialism or dictatorship. Extreme governmental control and taxation would deter progress through the dilution of ambition and its just rewards.*

> *[The Depression] brought the industrial designer forth… to lift American business by the bootstraps. …It took the individual American manufacturer, who can be compared to the earliest pioneer, to have the courage of believing in the principle of free enterprise, manufacture and competitive sale, as being the true magic of American expansion and prosperity.[8]*

Throughout the Cold War, however, business and political leaders understood that magic to be under threat, and economists fretted that the gross national product was not growing fast enough to secure the gap between the American and Soviet standards of living. Stevens consistently alluded to the urgent responsibility of business and consumers to help overcome communism. In a speech to appliance manufacturers, he invoked the Soviet menace and the perils of big government:

> *Man will continue to exploit space age materials, to satisfy needs, to create markets, produce profits… and improve his way of life, barring excessive taxation, union pressures, regimentation, or world conflict. Invention and education, if properly merchandised to the world, could be the key to peace on earth. Space exploration as a friendly competitive goal might accelerate this state in man's development, and divert the mind from earth-bound petty ideologies and aggressions. I believe the appliance industry, gentlemen, can be counted upon to do its part in this stimulating challenge to humanity.[9]*

Although this sounds comical today, at the time industry was seriously credited with protecting the American way of life. One of Stevens's favorite catchphrases—"I'd rather compete in the marketplace than the rocketplace"—was a virtual restatement of Richard Nixon's position in his 1959 "kitchen debate" with

Fig. 1 (upper)
For this image from his firm's 1943 brochure "Industrial Design: War — Postwar," Stevens carefully modeled his gaze and posture after those of the supposed military strategist seen in a photograph mounted behind his desk. That photo, however, was also staged; the man in uniform is actually his friend and client William Woods Plankinton Jr. Stevens's colleague Anthony (Tony) Reed is seated to Plankinton's right.

Fig. 2 (lower)
Stevens with the Jeep Harlequin, a 1960 prototype variation on the Willys Jeep Station Wagon

Nikita Khrushchev.[10] Shortly after the Cuban missile crisis, Stevens described the success of his Brazilian Willys Aero sedan as a "bulwark against communism and Castroism in South America,"[11] knowing that his words would find a receptive audience. For confirmation, he didn't need to look any farther than the editorial pages of *Fortune* and *Business Week* or the influential men he called his closest friends.

Suspicion of labor unions and government regulations went hand in hand with Stevens's brand of anticommunism. He blamed unions for creating workers' "unfortunate mental concept of leisure time," with mandatory breaks that discouraged pride and efficiency,[12] and he railed against Ralph Nader, whom he viewed as a short-sighted meddler with no appreciation for the challenges businessmen faced. Nader's role in forcing safety regulations and emissions controls on the auto industry made him a convenient stand-in for big government, and Stevens, forever hobnobbing at road races and auto shows, found the straight-laced reformer an irresistible target. Perhaps even more damning, Nader was boring. In Stevens's mind, socialists were boring; true Americans were dashing individuals (see fig. 2).[13] "I think this whole new hue and cry championing a boring plainness in cars, dress, furniture and other things is a step toward a dangerous socialistic regimentation," he said. "The average American . . . resent[s] regimentation in anything, and is looking for individuality and ego-inspiring styling."[14]

Giving Consumers What They Want

Ego-inspiring styling, for Stevens, didn't necessarily mean modernist "good design" or high-culture tastes. "We were out to sell boats to coal miners and lathe operators," he said, "not to connoisseurs in blue yachting coats. If this new customer wanted his boat to look like a swept wing car, we made it look like a swept wing car."[15] He chided *Industrial Design* magazine for its "lofty idealistic design approach and often forgetting that the design of mass-produced products relies not only heavily but entirely upon consumers. I have the feeling that in a very cultured and artistic way with overtones of great functionalism, it is often forgotten that the consumer many times wants things that the pure idealist

does not think he should have. . . . This country's business effort, despite any ivory-tower effects, will be strongly based on consumer palatability."[16] Without naming names, Stevens readily extended his professed scorn for artists to the design elite. Just as he used Nader as a symbol of big government, he used the Museum of Modern Art (MoMA) as shorthand for purist eggheads and modernist snobs. Stevens knew MoMA's seal of approval wouldn't impress the executives and engineers he wanted on his side. Dismissing MoMA may have also been a neat swipe at New York, a little bonus for Midwestern clients tired of being seen as provincials.[17]

Stevens did work in the modernist idiom when it served him, but he didn't shrink from splashy flourishes and popular references (fig. 3). Compare the clean lines and broad shoulders of the Square D plant to the color and undulating graphics of his administration building for Miller Brewing, which freely riffed on the company's beer packaging. Stevens's engines for Briggs and Stratton and machine tools for Kearney and Trecker are cool, smooth, and functionalist; his Milano Room for the Milwaukee Athletic Club applied rich materials with beautiful restraint; the celebrated 1962 Studebaker Gran Turismo Hawk is crisp and understated.[18] Yet he seemed equally proud of his umbrella-topped, UFO-inspired Fisherman powerboat, Lady of the Lake ("New Orleans romance" in the guise of a Mississippi River steamboat), and Rolls-Royce–style golf cart for Jackie Gleason (fig. 4).[19] And while Stevens's flashiest designs were generally publicity stunts, most of his mainstream postwar commissions—like snowmobiles and outboards for Outboard Marine, wood-grained "gourmet centers" for Hotpoint, and plastic radios for Gamble-Skogmo—have an air of easy glamour that hovers just above the taste for kitschy pink leatherette.

Stevens said he "could not go on a crusade for good design . . . because it wouldn't pay off. . . . [The] mass buyer could not absorb, say, fine Swedish modern design applied to a box of razor blades. The competition would come along with something not . . . as *good*, not as fine, but it would be striking. It would be baroque, perhaps, but it would grab the eye and it would sell razor blades."[20] He did, however, go on a crusade for planned

Fig. 3 (left)
Stevens's understated, functionalist Bolens Grounds Keeper of 1966 merited a notice from *Industrial Design* magazine. His flashier designs were typically ignored by the design elite.

Fig. 4 (right)
Stevens on a Cushman Motors Excalibur golf cart (1974). This custom golf cart for Jackie Gleason was modeled on a Rolls-Royce, featuring space for clubs and a full bar under the hood.

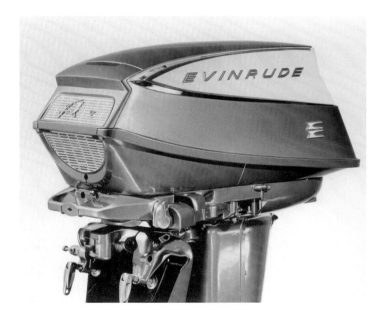

Fig. 5
Evinrude Lark outboard motors models III, IV, V, and VI, styled for 1959–62

obsolescence, for which he received a gratifying amount of publicity. Stevens's argument followed these lines: "At first, planned obsolescence sounds like organized waste. It isn't at all… You are not *forced* to buy the new products. You *like* to do it. …And when you do, you are making a contribution, and a fundamentally sound one, to the American economy."[21] By creating a market for used goods and maintaining high employment and wages, he argued, planned obsolescence "raises all of America by its bootstraps"(fig. 5).[22]

As usual, Stevens was in good company. While his critics painted planned obsolescence as vulgar, immoral, and wasteful, Stevens's view was widely accepted in the business community,[23] and he continued to lecture on the topic well into the 1960s. His eagerness to buck the critics ingratiated him with conservative businessmen, who felt that their vision of success and the "American way" should be self-evident.

Selling "Elegant Arrogance"

Despite Stevens's celebration of business, he disdained the look of an organization man. He knew the value of a good entrance and courted attention with distinctive clothing and an array of unusual cars. In Milwaukee's conservative social climate, he certainly stood out, and in Europe, he claimed, he was often taken for an Englishman, not a Midwesterner.[24] Stevens's workaday dress, although striking, was subdued. He strutted like a peacock, however, at the elaborate parties he and his wife, Alice, hosted for friends and associates. In 1958 he wore lemon yellow pants, a pink jacket, and a ruffled shirt to their annual supper dance, "the top event of the summer social season."[25] Stevens loved orchestrating these themed affairs, re-creating Monaco one year and a night in Venice the next, with scene paintings and gondolas in the swimming pool.[26]

In this setting, bolstered by his secure social position and easy, cordial manner, Stevens offered his glamorous eccentricity for the vicarious enjoyment of clients and Milwaukee society. The copy for a 1966 Excalibur advertisement—"Elegant arrogance for about $8,000"—seems tailor-made for the designer, who ranked appearance and demeanor among his most important sales

tools (fig. 6).[27] Careful to associate only with top management, he cultivated his relationships with executives through entertaining, gentlemanly road racing, and strategic involvement in clubs and charities. His confident style and precisely worked image, far from undermining his alignment with business, reinforced the impression of Stevens as a worldly man of substance.

This publication attempts to assess Stevens's design legacy, but the chameleon-like quality of his work makes it difficult to present a grand summation of his aesthetic. Although his personal taste was finely honed, Stevens wasn't embarrassed or put off by anything that might have broad consumer appeal. Judging by his cars, his home, and his fashion sense, he himself was drawn to "ego-inspiring styling," fantasy, and the allure of something a little newer, a little better, a little sooner than necessary. This fundamental sympathy with the consumer made Stevens approach all of his firm's commissions with integrity and concern. In using design as a selling tool, he truly believed that he made a difference for his clients and the national economy.

Implicitly, he also believed in his contribution to another American ideal: the pursuit of happiness. "If I increased the sales from 800,000 to two and a half million…," Stevens said, "then I pleased that many more people. That's beyond the client. I'm making them happy."[28] Against the drab backdrop of Soviet-style communism, the twin joys of ownership and fashion were reconfigured as essential freedoms, and the pursuit of happiness increasingly suggested the pursuit of wealth and style. Stevens clearly felt that the pleasure he took in antique Duesenbergs and custom-tailored suits, and that others might find in the Lawn Boys and powerboats he designed, was more than personal: it was crucial to the American Dream.

Fig. 6
Brooks and Alice Stevens with an Excalibur roadster

1. Brooks Stevens, interview with Chip Duncan, 1990–91, transcript, Brooks Stevens Archive, Milwaukee Art Museum.

2. "Revolutionary Display Pulls Crowd to Gallery," *Milwaukee Journal*, 11 January 1950. The exhibition, *Industrial Design by Brooks Stevens Associates*, included 125 objects by one hundred manufacturers (see page 84 in this volume).

3. Quoted in John Wickland, "Desire for the 'New' Called Economy Key," *Minneapolis Tribune*, 9 December 1953.

4. Durez Plastics and Chemicals, Inc., "In War We Must Prepare for Peace," 1942, Brooks Stevens Archive. Among the other designers included were Raymond Loewy, Henry Dreyfuss, Harold Van Doren, Peter Muller-Munk, and Egmont Arens.

5. "The Practical Postwar Car," presented at the Society of Automotive Engineers conference and reprinted in *The Iron Age* (15 June 1944).

6. Letter to the editor, *Industrial Marketing* 28 (August 1943): 123–24. Stevens used virtually the same language in "The Industrial Designer Is No Miracle Man," *Industrial Marketing* 28 (October 1943): 19–21, 148, and in his firm's promotional brochure "Industrial Design: War–Postwar," ca. 1943.

7. "The Different Dozen" was an informal group, apparently undocumented although remembered by many Milwaukeeans (William C. "Steve" Stevens, interview with Glenn Adamson, 30 July 2002).

8. "Industrial Design: An Insurance Policy against Depression," manuscript prepared for *Better Designs*, 1 August 1952, and excerpted in *The Bison* (North American Life and Casualty Co.), February 1955, Brooks Stevens Archive.

9. "Designing Down-to-Earth Appliances," undated presentation transcript, ca. 1965, Brooks Stevens Archive.

10. Brooks Stevens to William S. Pickett, 7 May 1968, Brooks Stevens Archive. On July 24, 1959, standing before a model home at the American National Exhibit in Moscow, Vice President Richard Nixon and Soviet Premier Nikita Khrushchev publicly compared their countries' technological achievements and quality of life. A transcript of what came to be called the "kitchen debate" was published in the *New York Times* the following day.

11. Partial clipping, *Milwaukee Journal*, January 1963, Brooks Stevens Archive.

12. "Industrial Design: Economic Visual Aid," presentation script for the Société des Ingénieurs de l'Automobile conference, Paris, 2 March 1959, Brooks Stevens Archive.

13. Brooks Stevens to Joel W. Eastman, 9 February 1970, Brooks Stevens Archive; Ronald Anzia, "Safe Car Need Not Be Ugly," *Milwaukee Sentinel*, 12 April 1969; John Bradley, interview with Glenn Adamson, 16 July 2002.

14. Quoted in "Prophet with a Purpose," *Let's See Milwaukee*, 23 January–5 February 1959, 11; "Sports Car Influence on American Automobile Body Design," presentation script, 1953, Brooks Stevens Archive.

15. Stevens was referring to the flashy "prophetics" designed for Evinrude's boat show displays; quoted in "He Put Tail Fins on Boats," *Milwaukee Journal*, 27 November 1960.

16. "Stevens on Car of Future" (letter to the editor), *Industrial Design* 10 (May 1963): 8.

17. Beat generation artists and writers were another favorite target. In particular, Stevens chastised them for rejecting planned obsolescence; see "No Room for 'Beat Generation' in Today's Economy, says Industrial Designer Brooks Stevens," press release, 1958, Brooks Stevens Archive.

18. Not surprisingly, Stevens's more purist efforts were the ones that won awards and professional attention. *Industrial Design* lauded an Evinrude fiberglass Gull Wing powerboat that his office designed in 1963: "The absence of chrome strips, flashing crests or outlandishly shaped fittings puts this design in a rare class" ("Eleventh Annual Design Review," *Industrial Design* 11 [December 1964]: 97). The Square D plant, cited as a "top plant of the year" in *Factory* magazine (May 1959), was also praised by William Henry in "Where Two Professions Meet, They Overlap," *Industrial Design* 6 (June 1959): 40–41. Kearney and Trecker's Milwaukee-Matic, a 1966 Master Design award winner in *Product Engineering* magazine's annual competition, was noted in "Machining Center Brings Small Shops Automation," *New York Times*, 14 August 1966, sec. F. The Milano Room (1957) was redecorated in 1994.

19. The Lady of the Lake, which was built to cruise Lake Geneva, Wisconsin, was modeled on Evinrude's "showboat" for the 1961 New York Boat Show; see Dorothy Kinkaid, "New Boat on the Lake," *Milwaukee Sentinel*, 28 May 1963.

20. Karl Prentiss, "Brooks Stevens: He Has Designs on Your Dough," *True: The Man's Magazine*, April 1958.

21. Ibid.

22. "Frank-Talking Designer Argues His Philosophy," *Milwaukee Engineering* 40 (April 1961): 12.

23. "Planned Obsolescence: Is It Fair? Yes! Says Brooks Stevens; No! Says Walter Dorwin Teague," *Rotarian*, February 1960, 2–5; Vance Packard, *The Waste Makers* (New York: D. McKay, 1960); "'Planned Waste'—or a Better Mousetrap," *Fortune*, October 1960, 131; John Chamberlain, "Unhidden Persuader Packard's Unplanned Obsolescence," *Wall Street Journal*, 7 October 1960; Vic Petchul, "Dear Vance Packard," *Appliance Manufacturer* 7 (November 1960).

24. Stevens, interview with Chip Duncan.

25. Prentiss, "Brooks Stevens."

26. Stevens, interview with Chip Duncan.

27. Advertisement for Excalibur Motors, *Wall Street Journal*, 9 August 1965.

28. Stevens, interview with Chip Duncan.

Fig. 1 Brooks Stevens, age seven

Less Than Perfect
Early Influences and First Designs, 1911–34

Kippy was always making things. Even when he was a little boy, a really little boy, he loved to make things, to "put them together," as he said. He'd spend hours on plans for something, and then he'd make it. And when it was finished, he'd give it to me, of course. Don't boys always make things for their mothers?

Sally Stevens (1955)[1]

Clifford Brooks Stevens, known to his family and friends as "Kip," was born on June 7, 1911, in Milwaukee (fig. 1). From the first, he was a person who liked to design and build. Fortunately for the history of industrial design, he never lost his taste for this activity, and his circumstances could not have been more favorable for it. In the nineteenth century Milwaukee had lost a contest with Chicago for control of trade routes from the East Coast to points west. Denied the role of entrepôt, the city became an industrial center.[2] Beer, machine tools, construction and agricultural equipment, leather, and other manufactured goods formed the basis of its economy.

Brooks's father, William Clifford (Steve) Stevens (b. 1884), thrived in this environment (fig. 2).[3] He was vice president of engineering for Cutler-Hammer, one of Milwaukee's largest machine tool firms, and moved steadily up the ranks of the company's leadership. In 1918 he invented the electric preselective gearshift, a pushbutton-operated device that enabled the driver to move into a new gear without needing to double-clutch the engine. His invention was reportedly inspired by his experience of seeing women operating military vehicles and ambulances during World War I, and he hoped that it would

make it less physically demanding to drive a car.

The young Brooks Stevens learned two traits from his father that would form the bedrock of his career as an industrial designer: salesmanship and a deep love of automobiles. He traveled with his father to Detroit and watched him try to sell his gearshift to the executives at various car companies. Though Cutler-Hammer had invested heavily in developing the technology, the effort to get it manufactured was ultimately unsuccessful. Nonetheless the sales pitch that Stevens heard many times as a child had a lasting influence on him, as did his father's mechanical ingenuity. W. C. Stevens would later invent a new version of his gearshift operated by a lever above the steering wheel, as well as a hand-pull dashboard emergency brake; as his accomplishments suggest, he was a steadfast auto enthusiast who owned "a different car every week."[4] He would often allow his underage son to test-drive the exotic Pierce-Arrows, Marmons, and other cars that he owned. Young Brooks was also brought along for the ride to the national auto shows in New York, Chicago, and Detroit.

As Brooks Stevens explained it, all this fatherly attention was "part of the reward for being less than perfect."[5] At the age of eight, the future designer had been struck down by a particularly

Fig. 2 (right)
William Clifford Stevens,
Brooks Father

Fig. 3 (below)
Brooks Stevens as coxswain
for the Cornell University
crew team, ca. 1930

severe case of polio. All of his limbs stiffened, and his right arm was rendered virtually useless. Doctors predicted that he would not be able to walk again. Stevens's father, however, was not a believer in bed rest. He piled sketchpads and model kits next to the boy's bed and encouraged him to build one miniature airplane and boat after another. Brooks took to this activity with great enthusiasm, and by the time he was in the eighth grade, his thoroughly researched hand-constructed model ships were displayed at the Milwaukee Public Library. Stevens's father also decided that the then-accepted practice of binding a polio patient's legs in braces would result in permanent weakening of the limbs. (This reasoning proved to be correct; in later years all polio patients were prescribed exercise instead of inactivity.) He challenged Brooks first to ride a bicycle and then to swim a mile in the pool at the Milwaukee Athletic Club, promising to buy him a Model T Ford when he succeeded. "They must have hauled me out hundreds of times short of that mark," Stevens later said. "But I finally got that car. My father knew how to motivate me."[6] By the time he was in high school, he was able to walk with the aid of ankle braces.

Another legacy of Stevens's youth was the social environment that surrounded him. While growing up he attended the private Milwaukee Country Day School, graduating in 1929. During these years he befriended several of the people who were to play an important role in his adult life, both personally and professionally. Ralph Evinrude, future head of the Outboard Marine Company, was a high school pal and eventually one of the first clients of Stevens's design business. Other childhood friends included Anthony (Tony) Reed, who would become an engineer and partner in Stevens's office, and Alice Kopmeier, who would become Stevens's wife. In addition to these personal relationships, Stevens had the good fortune to grow up in a world of well-to-do families—the leaders of Milwaukee's industrial and civic infrastructure. For the rest of his life, he would stay in this comfortable world and take advantage of all it had to offer.

From 1929 to 1933 Stevens studied architecture at Cornell University in upstate New York (fig. 3). It was the only time he lived outside Milwaukee, and by his own account, the experience made only a limited impression on him. "If I spent as much time on the bank building as I did on the cars that I drew on the rendering in front of the building," he remembers his professors telling him, "I could have been a good architect."[7] He nonetheless made a good-faith effort to learn the trade during his college years. His father arranged an annual summertime position for him at Milwaukee's leading architectural firm, Eschweiler and Eschweiler— an arrangement that was expected to evolve into a postgraduation job. By the end of Stevens's college career, however, it was clear to both father and son that the prospect was not a good one. It was the height of the Depression, and even Milwaukee's top architects were starving for business. Stevens left Cornell in 1933 without a diploma and returned to Milwaukee to work as an inventory manager, first for a pair of soap companies, and then for the grocery supply firm Jewett and Sherman. Bored and restless, he persuaded Lewis Sherman, the head of the company, to let him redesign some of the product labels.

This opportunity proved to be the first step toward Stevens's career as an industrial designer. Both he and his father were aware of the early stirrings of this new profession. By this time, all of the significant first-generation figures in the field were in business, among them the "big four" in New York City: former theater set designers Norman Bel Geddes and Henry Dreyfuss; advertising illustrator Walter Dorwin Teague; and Raymond Loewy, a French émigré who would later become Stevens's greatest rival.[8] In the Midwest the slightly lesser known Toledo partnership of Harold Van Doren and John Gordon Rideout had also gotten their start.[9] Though Stevens had no direct contact with any of these men during his formative years, he did have the opportunity to meet the debonair Russian émigré automobile designer Count Alexis de Sakhnoffsky in Chicago in about 1934 (fig. 4). A society page writer for a Milwaukee newspaper described the meeting: "Asked what his fees were, the count told Kippie between $350 and $400 a day. Whereupon Kippie fell off his chair."[10] Sakhnoffsky had helped to design many of the cars that Stevens revered, including a celebrated custom version of the L29 Cord that would eventually enter the young designer's own auto collection.

Given Stevens's background in architecture, his early hobbies of model building and sketching, and his love of cars— the ultimate design object, in that time and since—both he and his father thought that industrial design might be a perfect occupation. Their inclinations were confirmed when Stevens won a blind contest to redesign the corporate logo for Cutler-Hammer. Impressed, W. C. Stevens made his son the generous offer of five hundred dollars to start a design office. Brooks needed no help of this kind, however. Thanks in large part to his connections through family and friends, he made enough in billings his first month that he did not take a dollar of his father's proffered loan. After that, there was nowhere to go but forward.

Fig. 4 Count Alexis de Sakhnoffsky

1. Gertrude M. Puelicher, "Brookington Limited," *Exclusively Yours*, April 1955, 12, 14, 26.

2. See William Cronon, *Nature's Metropolis: Chicago and the Great West* (New York: W. W. Norton, 1992).

3. W. C. Stevens was born in Portland, Maine, and attended Cornell University. He first joined Cutler-Hammer in 1906 as an engineer. Brooks Stevens's mother, Sally Holladay *née* Morgan (1886–1970), was from Lexington, Kentucky. The family name Brooks can be traced through the Morgan family all the way back to Thomas Brooks, who emigrated from England to Concord, Massachusetts, in the early seventeenth century. The author thanks David and Gretchen Stevens for sharing their genealogical research on the Stevens family.

4. Brooks Stevens, interview with Chip Duncan, 1990–91, transcript, Brook Stevens Archive, Milwaukee Art Museum.

5. Ibid.

6. Quoted in Ron Grossman, "The Idea Man," *Chicago Tribune*, 3 June 1991. Stevens would have a final round of treatment in 1947 at the Kaiser Clinic in Washington, D.C.; that did away with most of the limp, though the symptom would return in later life.

7. Stevens, interview with Chip Duncan, 1990–91.

8. For a good introduction to the "big four," see Jeffrey T. Meikle, *Twentieth-Century Limited: Industrial Design in America, 1925–1939* (Philadelphia: Temple University Press, 1975). On this first generation of designers, see also Arthur J. Pulos, *American Design Ethic: A History of Industrial Design* (Cambridge: MIT Press, 1983); Russell Flinchum, *Henry Dreyfuss, Industrial Designer: The Man in the Brown Suit* (New York: Cooper Hewitt, National Design Museum, Smithsonian Institution, and Rizzoli, 1997). For texts by these figures, see Walter Dorwin Teague, *Design This Day: The Technique of Order in the Machine Age* (New York: Harcourt, Brace, 1940); Raymond Loewy, *Industrial Design* (Woodstock, N.Y.: Overlook Press, 1979); Norman Bel Geddes, *Horizons* (Boston: Little, Brown, 1932); Norman Bel Geddes, *Magic Motorways* (New York: Random House, 1940).

9. See Dennis P. Doordan, ed., *The Alliance of Art and Industry: Toledo Designs for America* (Toledo: Toledo Museum of Art; New York: Hudson Hills, 2002).

10. Isabel Mann, "Whatever Mr. Stevens' Name Used to Be, It Now Is Brooks," *Milwaukee Journal*, 18 June 1936.

Holsum Products peanut butter jar 1934

Brooks Stevens's earliest extant design is this humble peanut butter jar, designed for the Holsum Products brand of Milwaukee wholesale grocer Jewett and Sherman. Lewis Sherman, the head of the company, hired Stevens fresh out of Cornell in 1933 at the recommendation of the young man's father. Though Sherman first assigned Stevens to inventory management, he soon allowed him to redesign the firm's labels and was so pleased with the result that he then assigned him the containers themselves. One of the first jobs Stevens took on was the peanut butter jar. He transformed its overall shape, turning the tall, narrow-necked vessel traditionally used for peanut butter into a squat form with a wide mouth that gave easy access to the contents. Cartoon peanuts were mold-blown into the glass itself; bees were used for the similar honey jars Stevens designed for the company. (Though it seems trivial enough, this self-declarative ornament foreshadowed similar treatments in later work.) According to the designer's later testimony, his repackaging efforts paid off in the form of increased sales for the grocery. Jewett and Sherman retained Stevens for its packaging needs until 1936 and continued to use his ideas as late as 1950.[1] The wide-mouthed peanut butter jar is of course still with us.

1. Margaret Fish, "Industry to Hail Brooks Stevens," *Milwaukee Sentinel*, 9 January 1950.

Holsum Products peanut butter jar 1934

Cutler-Hammer motor control switch cover after 1935

Milwaukee has been called "the nation's machine shop" because many of its largest and most successful companies manufacture motors, machine tools, and motor controls. At one time or another Stevens worked for seemingly every one of the city's firms of this type—Allen-Bradley, Allis-Chalmers, Briggs and Stratton, Cutler-Hammer, Harnischfeger, Kearney and Trecker, Snap On Tools, and Square D—as well as their Chicago competitor Durant. He tapped into this rich vein of clientele before he even had a design office, and it would be a sustaining source of commissions throughout his career.

Stevens's father was a vice president and chief engineer at Cutler-Hammer. At the end of 1934 he arranged for his enterprising son to enter a general competition for the redesign of the company's nameplate. Stevens dutifully set to work at a drafting table he had set up on the third floor of the family house. His design was entered and was judged blind against submissions from several established advertising agencies. Much to Stevens's surprise, his proposal was chosen by a vote of four to one. This was not only his first

Cutler-Hammer motor control switch after 1935 (left)
Cutler-Hammer display ca. 1938 (above)

"logotype," or company insignia, but also led to his first continuing source of work. When he opened his design office the following year, Cutler-Hammer became a steady client, again thanks to the good offices of Stevens's father. Stevens went on to design machine control covers, thermometers, machine tools, and trade show exhibits for the company. The switch cover shown here is typical of this work. Its boxy proportions and echoing bracket shapes are some-what conservative, departing little from the standard industrial design idiom established during the early 1930s. The insignia itself has a rigid geometry that both looks back to the heraldic shield-shaped emblems of earlier decades and anticipates the fully realized modernism of Stevens's postwar logos.

Custom L-29 Cord automobile 1929/1938

The collecting and rebuilding of old automobiles was a pursuit that fascinated Stevens from his youth to his final days. Eventually he would assemble more than eighty cars for his Brooks Stevens Auto Museum in Mequon, Wisconsin; some of these were his own designs, but many were old cars that he admired. One design that he and other antiquarians regarded with par-ticular awe was the L-29 Cord, a paragon of the elegant streamlined style of the 1920s. Built at the behest of E. L. Cord, the pioneering director of the Auburn Automobile Company in Indiana, the L-29 was long, low, and luxurious. Its novel front-wheel drive made it an unusually smooth-riding vehicle for the period and also gave it outstanding handling and performance. It was a car that, in E. L. Cord's words, "requires no selling to those who can afford it."[1]

Brooks Stevens had seen his first Cord at a wedding in late 1928 and acquired his example in 1937 on the advice of his friend James Melton, an opera singer and fellow auto buff. The car was a two-door cabriolet, one of several models in production (the others were a sedan, a brougham, and a phaeton). Stevens soon conceived a plan to customize its already impressive lines, a process that was not uncommon at the time. In an era when the craft of coach building was still alive and well, small shops often produced unique version of elite autos. E. L. Cord himself displayed a range of custom L-29s in his Los Angeles showroom, where they were eagerly

Custom L-29 Cord automobile 1929/1938
4 views including interior dash and headlight assembly.

snapped up by Hollywood stars. Among the most famous of the unique Cords was a blue coupe custom-built under the direction of Count Alexis de Sakhnoffsky, a Russian émigré whose body designs for such firms as Rolls-Royce, Minerva, Hispano-Suiza, and Bentley had become well known from their reproduction in the magazine Esquire. In 1938 Stevens managed to acquire the Sakhnoffsky- designed Cord from the Hayes Body Corporation in Grand Rapids. His ownership of the car led to a lasting friendship with the Russian designer, who later spent a short time working in Stevens's office in the early 1950s.[2]

The first dated reference to Stevens's own customization campaign is a 1939 clipping preserved in the Brooks Stevens Archive, which reports that the young designer had altered the car "to conform with modern style trends." In particular, the article explained, "slight changes were made in body and fender contours; a sloping windshield was added; chrome discs were fitted over wire wheels; and the whole thing [was] finished off with a streamlined paint job."[3] Absent from this list is the most distinctive and historically important addition to the automobile:

the rounded fin that protrudes from the center rear. This may be the earliest tail fin to appear on an American automobile. Though quite different from the angular side fins that would come into fashion in the 1950s, it served the same purpose as those later ornaments by finishing off the car's lines with a satisfyingly grand gesture. Originally the car would have had a rumble seat and a folding top, both of which Stevens removed in order to enclose the entire rear quarter in sheet metal, joining the body seamlessly to the rear fenders. He also dramatically transformed the front of the car, which retains its original grille but has custom-sculptured chrome bumpers and "wood lights," which give comparatively little illumination but have an attractive teardrop shape. Finally, in an early prefiguration of the extensive dashboard and instrumentation studies that he would conduct later in his career, Stevens sheathed the Cord's interior front panel with a textured stainless steel plate. He kept his customized Cord until the end of his life, occasionally making additional alterations to it. It is still owned privately today in Illinois, its already fine state of preservation enhanced by a careful restoration. The only obvious departure from Stevens's first customization of the car is the absence of the chrome wheel rims that originally covered the wire wheels.

Though the Cord was Stevens's most ambitious custom car, he later undertook many similar custom jobs, including some for his friends and clients. These automobiles were not by any means hobby projects; they served both to establish his credentials in a competitive design field and as a source of ideas for his mass-production vehicles.[4] It should be noted, however, that Stevens did none of the manual work on these cars himself. According to those who knew him, the designer avoided garage work all his life, despite the fact that it surrounded him. Instead he had a long string of trusted associates who performed custom coachwork to his specifications. Stevens's reluctance to learn the craft himself may have stemmed in part from his childhood bout with polio, which left him maladroit at many physical activities. Even if this had not been the case, however, it is unlikely that this self-styled aristocrat would have had much interest in manual labor. Stevens's relationship with automobiles, though passionate, was of a visual rather than a mechanical nature.

L-29 Cord cabriolet ca. 1930

Brooks Stevens in his 1955 redesign of a 1939 Lincoln Continental
executed for Henry Uihlein of Schlitz Brewing

1. E. L. Cord, "Why We Introduce a Front Drive Automobile" (1929); reprinted in Dan R. Post, *Cord: Without Tribute to Tradition: The L-29 Front Drive Legend* (Arcadia, Calif.: Post-Era Books, 1974). See also Dan R. Post, *The Classic Cord* (Arcadia, Calif.: Dan R. Post Books, 1952); Don Butler, *Auburn, Cord, Duesenberg* (Osceola, Wis.: Crestline/Motorbooks International, 1992); Randy Ema and Jonathan A. Stein, "The Cord That Cord Built," *Automobile Quarterly* 40 (October 2000): 88–99. For limited-production front-wheel-drive cars predating the Cord, see Harvey B. Janes, "Front Wheel Drive," *Automobile Quarterly* 1 (winter 1962): 372–81.

2. Stevens told the story of his acquisition of the two Cords in "The de Sakhnoffsky L-29," *Automobile Quarterly* 6 (spring 1968): 453–57. In the article Stevens admitted to altering the front of Sakhnoffsky's car, but he later thought better of the change and restored the vehicle to its original condition. Sakhnoffsky was the art director at Vanden Plas S.A. from 1925 to 1929 and then art director at Hayes Body Corporation of Grand Rapids, Michigan. See also Beverly Rae Kimes, "Alexis de Sakhnoffsky," *Automobile Quarterly* 3 (winter 1965): 458–69.

3. Unidentified scrapbook clipping, dated 1939, Brooks Stevens Archive, Milwaukee Art Museum. Stevens is quoted as saying that the car was the first to enter his collection in Gertrude M. Puelicher, "Brookington Limited," *Exclusively Yours*, April 1955, 12, 14, 26. In a 1990 interview Stevens asserted that he had customized the car in 1938.

4. On the importance of early custom cars as the basis for serial production, see Gregory Votolato, "Industrial Drama: The Custom Car Myth," in *American Design in the Twentieth Century: Personality and Performance* (Manchester: Manchester University Press, 1998), 202–21, and Matthew C. Sonfield, "Custom Automotive Coachbuilding in the United States," *Design Issues* 12 (summer 1996): 47–60.

Fig. 1 Brooks Stevens, ca. 1936

The Right Place at the Right Time
Becoming an Industrial Designer in the Midwest, 1935–40

It may sound incredible for an industrial designer to announce to manufacturers he can redesign anything from a can opener to a locomotive for increased sales. How can this man do a better job than the engineering staff that has been associated with a firm for a number of years doing nothing but designing the product it manufactures?

Brooks Stevens (1939)[1]

If you had been listening to the radio station WTMJ on the morning of October 10, 1944, you would have heard an announcer describe Brooks Stevens as "the success story of the thirties."[2] The designer's office opened on July 1, 1935, at 340 North Milwaukee Street, above a fish store (figs. 2, 3). Right away the young entrepreneur had to make a variety of important decisions, beginning with what he wanted to be called. His real first name was Clifford, and growing up he had gone by his nickname, Kip, but he rejected both of these in favor of his middle name, Brooks, because it was catchier and easier to remember. That settled, he set about staffing his new firm and finding clients, both of which he did through established personal connections. His first employee was childhood friend Tony Reed, who grew up in Racine and held degrees in aerodynamics from the University of Minnesota and the Massachusetts Institute of Technology. For many years Reed was the only trained engineer in the office and handled the innumerable technical details of the firm's design projects.

Stevens next recruited James Rohan, a graphic designer with experience in advertising who had been educated at the Art Institute of Chicago. In 1938 the office grew to five with the addition of Karl Brocken, an auto designer formerly with the

Duesenberg and Auburn auto companies, and Byron Voight, a model maker who had helped to construct the General Motors exhibit at the New York World's Fair. In 1940 Stevens added S. N. Gellman, a designer from the New York University School of Architecture and Allied Arts who had formerly worked with Norman Bel Geddes on stage sets and had also spent some time in the office of furniture designer Gilbert Rohde. Even in the early days of the office, these staff members sometimes had a great influence on the designs that were identified as being "by Brooks Stevens." This was particularly true of two-dimensional design and packaging, which were entrusted largely to Rohan. Despite Stevens's early success with the Cutler-Hammer logotype, graphics were never one of his primary interests.

Stevens's client list grew even more quickly than his staff. Unlike other designers of his generation—who cut their teeth on furniture, theatrical sets, or store displays—his early jobs were all industrial in nature. His largest contract was with his father's company, Cutler-Hammer, but he soon contracted with many of the other manufacturers in the region: Briggs and Stratton, for which he did a farm lighting system; the boiler maker Cleaver-Brooks; Young Radiator Company of Racine; a washing machine

Fig. 2, 3 (above)
Milwaukee Street Office, ca. 1935

Fig. 4 (top right)
Durant Productimeter, before and after re-design, 1939

Fig. 5 (right)
Ziegler candy packaging, 1948

company named Barton; and the Durant Manufacturing Company of Chicago, which commissioned a redesign for its "Productimeter" (fig. 4). James Rohan did packaging on the firm's behalf for Woodley's soap and Ziegler candy bars (fig. 5). By 1939 Brooks Stevens Industrial Design could boast of thirty-three accounts, and by the following year it had more than fifty.

Stevens's personal life was also marked by a notable addition when he began seeing Alice Kopmeier (b. 1915) in 1935 (fig. 6). The two had recently finished their schooling (he at Cornell, she at the Garland School in Boston) and were of an age and generation to date casually among a group of acquaintances. One night Alice came to a party with another beau but left with Brooks. In her words, "All the other guys I went out with were nice—but dull!"[3] The couple married in 1937—the announcement read "A New Design For Living"—and Stevens's status as one of Milwaukee's social elite was cemented.[4] His new mother-in-law, Meta Uihlein Kopmeier (1884–1966), was a daughter of Henry Uihlein, who was president of the Schlitz Brewery. His father-in-law, Waldemar S. J. Kopmeier (1882–1976), was one of the heads of the company Wisconsin Ice and Coal (which later became Hometown, Inc.), which would become one of the first clients of Stevens's design office. The young newlyweds moved into a duplex apartment on Capitol Drive in Milwaukee, only a few blocks from their friends Phyllis and Fred Stratton; the firm Briggs and Stratton would later be another important client.

These new social contacts, as well as those Stevens had inherited from his own family, explain the ease with which he entered the professional design field. They do not, however, account for his continuing success in it. Stevens proved himself a master at salesmanship from his earliest days in business. He contributed free decorating services to local charity balls and designed *gratis* a traveling toy-lending center for orphanages in Milwaukee.[5] As soon as the firm had its first designs under its belt, Stevens began delivering slide lectures entitled "Industrial Design and Its Practical Application to Industry."[6] These talks invariably stressed his main selling point: that design would pay for itself many times over. To really make his business succeed in Milwaukee, he had to persuade his client base not only of his

Fig. 6
Alice Stevens, ca. 1936

own skills but also of the efficacy of his services. It is often assumed that Stevens and his peers operated in a kind of design vacuum—that they offered advantages that had never before been contemplated by corporate executives. But in fact he faced a deeply entrenched design establishment of a kind, and it was one that existed at every manufacturing company in America: the engineering department. As Anne Woodhouse pointed out in her pioneering 1993 study of Stevens's work, a redesign always had to be sold to the very people who were responsible for the old design.[7] Engineers did see design as one of their duties, and even if they saw it as an ancillary role, it was not a responsibility that they were eager to yield.

Stevens fervently preached the separation of engineers from the design process. As late as 1960 he wrote that "the engineer's proper preoccupation with the problems of making a product work as well and as efficiently as the limitations imposed by management will allow, tends to becloud for him the basic purpose of the product. …The engineer should not be asked to investigate and evaluate such factors as the influence of physical human limitations on product design. Readability, color and the esthetic relation of shape to function are also the tasks primarily of the industrial designer." But even as he maintained that engineers lacked the objectivity and savvy to devise a marketable

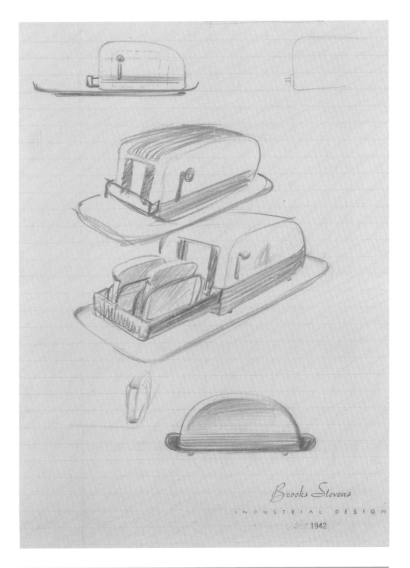

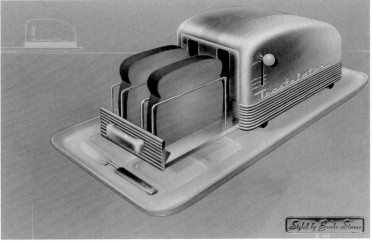

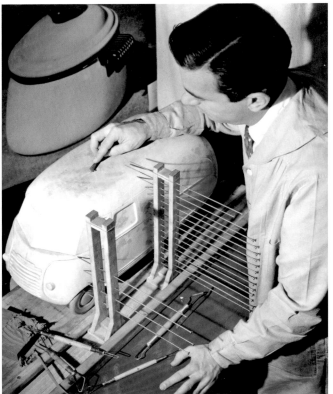

Fig. 7, 8 (left)
Brooks Stevens's sketch for a "Toastalator" drawer-front toaster, and the finished rendering, 1942

Fig. 9 (top right)
Staff drafting room, ca. 1943

Fig. 10 (lower right)
Staff model-maker Byron Voight at work, ca. 1938

product, he made it clear that the designer should try to understand, and occasionally even solve, engineering problems: "We know from experience that the industrial designer who honestly tries to understand and cope with engineering problems as such—despite his lack of formal training in engineering—is the one who wins the engineer's respect and cooperation fastest."[8] This co-optation was the first of various strategies to combat the jealousies of engineers, as well as the suspicions of money-conscious corporate executives who questioned the necessity of paying an outside design consultant's fees. One of his other tactics was simply to mock the instincts and actions of the untrained, thereby conveying the impression that design was a difficult and complex art. His favorite anecdote on the subject told how engineers at Briggs and Stratton would select the color for their new motors on the basis of how many cans of paint were left after repainting the factory walls and machinery.

Stevens's most effective strategies, however, were located in the subtle dynamic of his sales pitches. Like most designers of his generation, he cared deeply about the art of presentation and prized the rhetorical power of highly finished renderings. He carefully amassed data about the sales increase of products that he had redesigned, studiously ignoring other factors that might have contributed to these increases, such as innovative technology or aggressive advertising. On the strength of such numbers, he would present his ideas to a prospective client as surefire moneymakers—usually a wide variety of possible moneymakers, because he knew that it was important to demonstrate that he and his staff had thought long and hard about any given design problem. The plethora of options also helped Stevens create the impression that the patron was empowered. By giving a group of engineers and executives the chance to "play designer," he defused the territorial instincts that they might have harbored. Of course Stevens himself had definite opinions as to the relative quality of the various options he was presenting, but he would gently guide his clients toward the best solution. Occasionally the design favored by a company was not the one that he, or his staff, thought the most successful, but in these cases he would simply invoke the principle that the customer was always right and

move on to the next commission.

The way that Stevens's firm did business in these early years would change little over the next decades, despite changes in the technology and objectives of industrial design. He charged his clients in one of three ways: hourly or per diem "for creative and production work," a flat fee for a specific extended project, or a monthly retainer for ongoing management of identity and product design. The latter arrangement was limited to a few companies with which the firm had an especially strong relationship, such as the Outboard Marine Corporation and Miller Brewing. Because Stevens took a hand in directing the course of design for these companies, he had effective control over the amount and type of work that his firm would take on for the client during a given month.

Regardless of the type of contractual agreement, there were three stages in the execution of a particular design. First, Stevens or one of the senior designers on staff would execute quick preliminary sketches that outlined the general idea and vocabulary of the project (fig. 7). These were often done in direct consultation with the client's in-house designers and executives and, in the case of new accounts or product types, might be preceded by a presentation by the client's engineering staff.

The second stage, which Stevens called "formative," was devoted to the refinement of the initial scheme through hand renderings (fig. 8). In the early years these were always carefully finished drawings, executed in colored pencil or with an airbrush, which not only delineated the physical characteristics of the design but also tried to make it dramatic. Oftentimes, retrospective comparison between the renderings and the finished products they depicted can be a disappointing experience, but this only testifies to the artistry of the images, which were partly intended to persuade clients of the transformative powers of industrial design.

The final, "objective" phase provided whatever information would be needed to move the design into production. In the case of a three-dimensional product this often meant the hand construction of a full-size or scale model (fig. 10). In the 1930s this was done in plaster by the design firm's model maker, Byron

Voight; after World War II Dick Frank took over this position for the office, and the preferred material became modeling clay. In some cases, the model was then reproduced in plaster over a wood frame, painted to simulate the eventual production material and perhaps accented with details in plastic and sheet metal. (Because most products are symmetrical, these final touches were normally done on only half of the model.) Finished models were sufficiently accurate that they were often used to make direct castings, which in turn served as the basis for production molds.[9]

To the extent that Stevens's work exhibited a defined style at all during the late 1930s, it was one that he inherited from others. His most sophisticated designs at the time—like the Allis-Chalmers tractor or the Petipoint iron—were obviously rooted in the well-established modernist practice of "streamlining," in which disparate forms are integrated into a single sculptural mass. Ellen Lupton and J. Abbott Miller have written on the inherent aggressiveness of the streamlined style, whose clean, organic forms seem "incorruptible" and exert a sense of domineering perfection.[10] Stevens was certainly conscious of the fact that streamlining implied power, because he often used it in his vehicles despite his frequent acknowledgment that what he called "corner-rounding and hump-smoothing" did nothing to improve performance. He also seems to have been aware of the resonance between streamlining and functional integration, a principle that had been best articulated by Wisconsin architect Frank Lloyd Wright. The design goal of integration underpinned Stevens's early Zephyr land yacht and would play a large role in his design of the Olympian Hiawatha train of the late 1940s.

These attitudes did not set Stevens apart in any real way from his colleagues in New York, and indeed the commissions that his firm executed in the late 1930s can sometimes seem frankly derivative of other designers' work. It must be remembered, however, that Stevens operated in relative isolation prior to World War II. The slightly older and more established figures in New York were valuable role models for him, to be sure, but they were also distant ones. More important than originality was the response of the local audience, for whom industrial design itself was a novelty. It did not much matter if Stevens relied on tried-and-

true techniques if he could effect dramatic changes in a product's appearance. So much is clear from a "before and after" comparison of a Cleaver-Brooks tank heater (figs. 11, 12). The Stevens redesign communicates modernity in very clear terms, even though the function of the device—the warming of solidified industrial fluids held in large tanks—is not made any clearer to the nonspecialist viewer. Even if the rounded form and high-contrast graphics were relatively conventional within the overall spectrum of the day's industrial design, it is not hard to imagine that in Milwaukee the new look would have seemed more than sufficiently radical.

Recently the design historian Jeffrey Meikle has suggested that the typical look of Midwestern industrial design was in fact moderation of just this sort. Companies in the Rust Belt may have wanted a progressive image, but they certainly had no need, or wish, to seem avant-garde. Thus, according to Meikle, there was a regional preference among designers as diverse as Harold Van Doren, Viktor Schreckengost, and Dave Chapman for design that "tended toward restraint rather than flamboyance, towards an anonymous functional competence as opposed to a flashy stylistic individualism."[11] This general description certainly holds true for the initial stage of Stevens's professional life, when he was at pains to integrate himself with the local manufacturing base. It would become less applicable over time, however; indeed, "flashy stylistic individualism" became the very basis of his career. The roots of this transformation, like so many changes in American design, occurred during World War II. Within a decade, Stevens would leave the conformist streamlining of his early work far behind. What he would retain from his experiences of the 1930s, however, was arguably more important than any style. Over a span of five years he had already developed a working method and a comfortable relationship with corporate leaders that would enable him to become one of America's most prolific industrial designers.

Fig. 11 (left)
Cleaver-Brooks tank heater, before re-design

Fig. 12 (below)
Cleaver-Brooks tank heater, after re-design, 1941. The new design was described as "clean-lined and modern" with a "complete absence of projecting parts."

1. "Boost Sales by Redesigning Old Products," *Milwaukee News-Sentinel*, 16 September 1939.

2. Radio script, 1944, Brooks Stevens Archives.

3. Autobiography of Alice Stevens, Stevens family records. I am grateful to Steve Stevens for sharing this resource.

4. The wedding announcement is preserved in a scrapbook in the Brooks Stevens Archive.

5. *Milwaukee Journal*, 3 December 1939.

6. "November Meeting," *Milwaukee Engineering* 18 (November 1937): 9–10.

7. Anne Woodhouse, "Industrial Designer Brooks Stevens: Businessman, Engineer, and Stylist," *Wisconsin Academy Review* 39 (fall 1993): 10–14. On the early relationship between designers and engineers, see Meikle, *Twentieth-Century Limited*, 77–80.

8. Brooks Stevens Associates, "When the Industrial Designer Encounters an Engineering Problem," *Product Engineering*, 11 July 1960.

9. Brooks Stevens Associates, "Industrial Design … and How It Creates Business," promotional brochure, ca. 1950. Brooks Stevens Archive, Milwaukee Art Museum; Howard Andersen, "The Magic of Model-Making," *Milwaukee Engineering* 31 (October 1950).

10. Ellen Lupton and J. Abbott Miller, *The Bathroom, the Kitchen, and the Aesthetics of Waste: A Process of Elimination* (Cambridge: MIT List Visual Arts Center, 1992), 50–59. See also Kathleen Church Plummer, "The Streamlined Moderne," *Art in America* 62 (January–February 1974): 46–54.

11. Jeffrey L. Meikle, "The Midwestern City and the American Industrial Design Aesthetic," in Doordan, ed. *Alliance of Art and Industry*, 83–107. Dave Chapman has been little discussed by industrial design historians thus far, but he was an important competitor for Stevens over the years. Chapman left Montgomery Ward in 1936 after three years with the department store and opened his own office. In 1950 he became the youngest man to hold the position of president of the American Society of Industrial Designers (see "Chapman Talks Design," *Industrial Design* 8 [November 1961]: 38–39). For a time Chapman had responsibility for Johnson motors, which competed with Stevens's Evinrude designs in the marketplace despite the fact that both brands were manufactured by the Outboard Marine Corporation.

Zephyr land yacht 1936

Stevens's ability to succeed at excess is epitomized by this extraordinary two-part vehicle. It has gone by many names during its life. Stevens called it the Zephyr (after the engine that powered it), but most journalists called it the "Plankinton land yacht" after its owner, the eccentric Milwaukee millionaire playboy William Woods Plankinton Jr. The heir to a vast real estate and meatpacking fortune, Plankinton avoided work throughout his life and instead dedicated himself to creative self-indulgence. He commissioned the Zephyr from Stevens in 1935, when he was only twenty-nine. Conflicting reports put the original cost of the vehicle between ten and fifteen thousand dollars, but whatever Plankinton paid, he received the earliest professionally styled mobile home in history.[1]

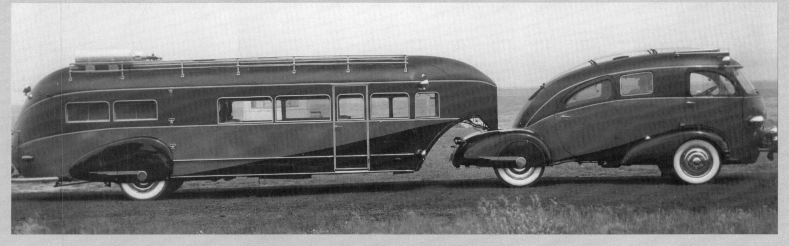

Zephyr land yacht 1936

Plankinton's own nickname for the vehicle was "Gadget," and it was an appropriate one. The Zephyr was crowded with innovative features. Its front, "tractor" portion was constructed by a local auto body shop on the chassis of an International Harvester truck cab. Stevens seems to have chosen this substructure because of its unusual design, which situated the driver directly above the engine. This facilitated the streamlining of the tractor's shape and reduced the overall length of the vehicle. The Zephyr's original engine was an International six-cylinder, but this was replaced after a year of operation with a Ford V-8 that afforded a seventy-five-mile-per-hour top road speed. In addition to two foldout beds (for Plankinton's chauffeur and his "valet-chef"), the tractor's seventeen-foot length held wardrobe closets, a refrigerator, a radio, a foldout wash basin, and an eighty-gallon water tank in the roof, which cooled the engine. Ten lights were mounted on the front: two standard car headlights, two long-distance lights, three fog lights, a searchlight that pivoted when the steering wheel was turned, and two spotlights. The long trailer to the rear, which was Plankinton's living quarters, was built on the frame of a Curtis Aerocar bus.[2] It slept up to seven people (including Plankinton) and had a living room with gun and fishing-rod racks, a full kitchen with "an electric stove large enough to roast a 24 pound turkey," and a bathroom with shower.[3] Taken together, the whole affair was two inches shy of forty-five feet long, the maximum legal length for highway travel, and—once loaded with is full complement of water, luggage, and passengers—weighed eleven tons.

Plankinton's mobile home has had a life nearly as interesting as its design. Its owner had already traveled 70,000 miles in it by the time of America's entry into World War II in 1941.[4] He was classified as 4H by the military, so he joined the Civil Air Patrol and became an army recruiter, traveling Wisconsin in the vehicle.[5] Eventually, after 185,000 miles and many decades of hard use, Plankinton sold the vehicle back to Stevens, who exhibited it outside his auto museum.

Unfortunately years of exposure resulted in the irreparable rotting of the wood frame of the rear trailer, which was broken up and discarded in the early 1980s. The front tractor cab survives, however, and is still owned privately in Milwaukee.

1. "Trailer Craze Has Two Firms in City Busy Making Equipment: New Tow Car for Plankinton," *Milwaukee Journal*, 18 October 1936. For the designer's account of the Zephyr, see Brooks Stevens, "Tomorrow's Luxury Land Cruiser," *Automobile Quarterly* 1 (spring 1962): 80–84, 98. For a general historical account of the automobile-pulled trailers that were the Zephyr's predecessors, see Roger B. White, "Planes, Trains, and Automobiles: The Land Yachts of Glenn Curtiss," *Automobile Quarterly* 32 (January 1994): 30–47; Stuart W. Wells, "Happy Campers: The Motor Camping Craze," *Automobile Quarterly* 36 (February 1997): 32–43.

2. "Truck Tractor Draws Deluxe Trailer," *Motor*, December 1937, 44.
3. "Unmarried Millionaires: Bill Plankinton," *American Weekly*, 21 December 1947, 6–7.

4. "Land Yacht Visitor Here," *Green Bay Press-Gazette*, 14 May 1941.

5. "Unmarried Millionaires."

Allis-Chalmers Model B tractor 1937

Curiously enough, Brooks Stevens cannot be credited with introducing the most important design element of the famous Allis-Chalmers tractors—their stunning Persian orange paint. That distinction goes to Harry Merritt, director of the tractor division of the Wisconsin-based company, who introduced the color in 1929 after being inspired by a field of poppies in California. Stevens did, however, fashion the silhouette that helped make the Model B one of the best-selling tractors of its day. With its teardrop-shaped gas tank, blue and white decal lettering, and bullet-nosed front end, the B was not the first streamlined tractor (the Oliver company's sleek Model 70 Row Crop predated it by two years), but it was the first tractor to be styled by a professional designer. In this respect Stevens anticipated a trend; Henry Dreyfuss began his well-known work for John Deere a year later, while Raymond Loewy designed his first tractor for longtime client International Harvester in 1942.

The Model B was the result of a concerted attempt to break into a market dominated by International Harvester. That company's Farmall tractors had accounted for as much as 70 percent of the total market in the 1920s. To compete more effectively, Allis-Chalmers developed fast, light tractors that were smaller and cheaper than the Farmalls. The company scored its first success in 1933 with the model WC, which rode on newfangled pneumatic rubber tires. The Model B carried the same sales strategy to an even smaller size and lower price point, almost half the cost of the WC, and was marketed directly to farmers who had previously been unable to afford any kind of tractor power. These small operators used the tractor to plant or cultivate one row of crops at a time, instead of two, as had been standard for tractor usage. The true competitors of the B were not other tractors, but draft horses.

Stevens reportedly faced stiff resistance from the engineers at Allis-Chalmers when he was initially hired, but he soon quelled their doubts. Reasoning that the rear fenders on a tractor

Allis-Chalmers Model B tractor 1937

Allis-Chalmers tractor advertisement 1938 (above)

Wartime version of model B ca.1942–45 (upper right)

Allis-Chalmers prototype model IB ca.1940 (lower right)

functioned only to protect the farmer from falling into the wheels, he made them smaller and moved them to the top of the tire. He also managed to design the new gas tank so that it could be made from two identical stampings fitted edge-to-edge—an economy of tooling that he would repeat many times later in his career when designing automobiles. The model B was so commercially successful that in 1938 the company restyled its previous hot seller, the WC, to match it.

For the next two decades all Allis-Chalmers tractor models featured the "tubular design," as one ad called it, that Stevens had created. Not until the introduction of the model D in 1957 was the signature teardrop shape abandoned for a blockier look. In the meantime, several variants of the B were developed using Stevens's basic design, including the Asparagus Special, the Potato Special, and the low-slung IB (meant for industrial use in factory settings). Rubber shortages forced the company to issue a steel-wheeled "wartime" model B. Stevens continued to work with Allis-Chalmers through 1955, developing front loader, switch gear, and motor control lines for the manufacturer; he also went on to design tractors and other equipment for Minneapolis Moline twenty-five years later.[1]

1. Norm Swinford, *Allis-Chalmers Farm Equipment, 1914–1985* (St. Joseph, Mich.: American Society of Agricultural Engineers, 1994); Norm Swinford, *A Guide to Allis-Chalmers Farm Tractors* (St. Joseph, Mich.: American Society of Agricultural Engineers, 1996); Norm Swinford, *The Proud Heritage of Agco Tractors* (Saint Joseph, Mich.: American Society of Agricultural Engineers, 1999); Andrew Morland and Peter Henshaw, *Allis-Chalmers Tractors* (Osceola, Wis.: MBI Publishing, 1997). The model B and its relatives were engineered by C. E. Fruden, the head engineer of Allis-Chalmers's tractor division.

Edmilton Petipoint clothes iron 1941

It is ironic that a designer who spent so much of his life creating larger-than-life vehicles should be known to design historians chiefly for a smaller-than-average clothes iron. Yet this is the case with Stevens, whose Petipoint iron has long been seen as an iconic example of the streamlined style. It is the only object from his career that has been regularly included in comprehensive studies and collections of American design. And although the Petipoint is not necessarily typical within Stevens's oeuvre, it is not difficult to see its appeal. The four cooling vents on each side of the iron are an outstanding example of the marriage of function and form prized by early designers. The upswept "tail" of the iron gives visual closure to the composition while adding an extra ironing tip for fine work such as small pleats and sleeve tucks (hence Stevens's name for the iron, from "petite point"). Because of this unusual feature, the iron rests on its side rather than its heel. The Petipoint was also one of the first irons to have a dual sole plate, fully automatic heat control, and a ceramic heating element.

The Petipoint was slightly preceded by another iconic clothes iron, the Steam-O-Matic. This design nearly matched the visual complexity of its successor, offering streamlined style in a larger, more conventional size. Prior to Stevens's involvement, the Steam-O-Matic had been released in 1936 as the first commercially available electric steam iron. (The innovation was partially necessitated by the introduction of synthetic fabrics such as rayon and acetates, which were melted by standard irons.) In redesigning the Steam-O-Matic, Stevens pared every ounce of unessential weight, altering the shape of both the body and the handle. He also changed the angle from which the cord protruded from the iron for ease of handling. Finally and most crucially, he added the single well-chosen detail of a curved, polished bead to create a sense of motion. The design was a great commercial success, supposedly boosting sales of the iron fifteen times over within thirty days.[1]

Edmilton Petipoint clothes iron 1941

In 1949 Stevens returned to the clothes iron one more time, in one of a series of commissions for the National Pressure Cooker Company. This time he eschewed the fine detailing of the Petipoint and Steam-O-Matic in favor of a unified curvilinear volume—an approach that may have owed something to Henry Dreyfuss's iron for Hoover, designed two years earlier.[2] The Presto iron was sleek and, at three and a quarter pounds, the lightest iron then on the market.[3]

1. Johnson Kanady, "One Man Industrial Design Show Opens," *Chicago Tribune*, 11 January 1950.

2. Russell Flinchum, *Henry Dreyfuss, Industrial Designer: The Man in the Brown Suit* (New York: Cooper Hewitt, National Design Museum, Smithsonian Institution, and Rizzoli, 1997), 83.

3. "Brooks Stevens Designer of New State Steam Iron," *Milwaukee Sentinel*, 8 July 1949.

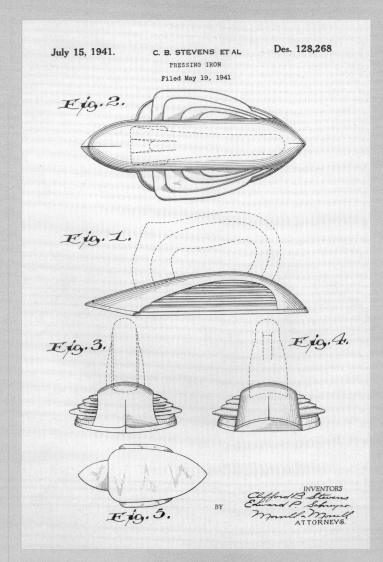

July 15, 1941.   C. B. STEVENS ET AL   Des. 128,268

PRESSING IRON

Filed May 19, 1941

Fig. 2.

Fig. 1.

Fig. 3.   Fig. 4.

Fig. 5.

INVENTORS
Clifford B. Stevens
Edward P. Schwyer
BY   Morsell & Morsell
ATTORNEYS.

Patent for Petipoint iron 1941 (upper left)

**Steam-O-Matic clothes iron, before and
after Stevens's redesign** 1936 and 1940 (upper right)

**Brooks Stevens and engineers designing
the Steam-O-Matic** 1940 (middle right)

Presto clothes iron 1949 (lower right)

When Engineering Influences Design (1940)

Today, everything is styled from an iron to a tractor. …In many cases manufacturers have been slow to recognize the value of appearance in their products. It is not enough to produce a functionally perfect device, for in this fast moving day and age the purchaser will not stop to have intrinsic worth demonstrated or proved but often buys on first appearance. …Progressive manufacturers are rapidly recognizing the extent of consumer resistance to equipment consisting of a shapeless mass of tubes, faucets, elbows, nuts, bolts, regardless of functional excellence. In addition to doing its work well, the object must look the price—must inspire the owner with sufficient pride for him to want to show it off. Parts must be correlated and housed to form a clean, well-proportioned whole.…

It is evident that the industrial designer must use the same fundamental approach to all design problems, whether it is an electric steam iron, or a tractor. In re-styling an electric steam iron we encountered a relatively new product, but one gaining in popularity. Its function requires a certain water capacity to create steam; therefore, it must be rather large and bulky. Aluminum castings are apt to be pitted, so some disguise or finish was required to overcome this fault. A hammered finish was chosen for it which closely resembles the pit mark we would hide. How to take those limitations, all dominated by the engineering of a successful steam iron, and through good proportion, line and form make the iron appeal more to Mrs. Consumer? Our first task in the re-design of the iron was to try to minimize the apparent size lest Mrs. Consumer shy away from a good product because it looks as though it might weigh 12 or 15 pounds!…

Here we begin by preparing preliminary sketches to experiment with a polished bead laid along the side of the high side wall, about $2/3$ up from the sole plate. This polished bead can be given a more graceful, stream-lined shape than the profile contours of the iron, and also tends to break down the appearance of height. At the same time the handle was worked with, so that its shape became graceful and congruous with the design as a whole. Here the methods employed by the outside handle manufacturer are most important, for in turning and shaping this handle in wood, there are many compound shapes he cannot readily produce. The hammered finish is a good example of some of the engineering limitations of this re-design task. The finish was not chosen for beauty, or to represent appearance in modern form, for it is more symbolic of old silver and copper jewelry and metal ware. The engineering logic of this case was: This steam iron must hold water; to hold water it must be large; because it is large the iron must be made from aluminum to make it light. In making it from cast aluminum we must disguise the pit marks in the casting and eliminate costly polishing and finishing. Therefore, the hammered finish is used because it most successfully takes care of all these factors.

Excerpted from Brooks Stevens, "When Engineering Influences Design,"
Durez Molder *(Durez Plastics and Chemicals, North Tonawanda, N.Y.) 10 (April 1940): 10–11.*

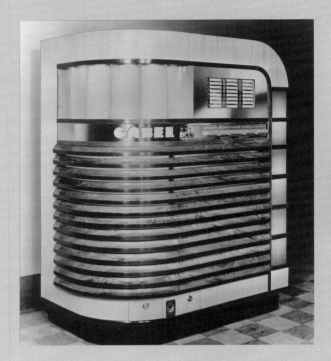

Gabel Kuro jukebox 1940 (left)
Louis Sullivan, Carson-Pirie-Scott building Chicago, 1899
Gabel "Twilight" Jukebox prototype ca. 1940

Gabel Kuro jukebox 1940

No Stevens design reflects his architectural training more than his 1940 Kuro jukebox. Its one-corner curvature and horizontal "speed lines" are reminiscent of Chicago architecture generally, and in particular the renowned Carson-Pirie-Scott Building by turn-of-the-century architect Louis Sullivan. The allusion may or may not have been a conscious one, but if intended, it was certainly appropriate. Gabel was Chicago's most venerable juke maker, having produced the first "automatic phonograph" in 1915.[1] Unfortunately the Kuro—named for two brothers in the Gabel family, Kurt and Robert—would be the company's last machine.

At around the same time, Stevens designed another twenty-four-record jukebox for Gabel called the Twilight. This jukebox may never have been produced, and no prototype is extant, but its design survives in photographs taken at Brooks Stevens Associates. The Twilight owed much to jukeboxes of the 1939–40 period designed by Paul Fuller for Wurlitzer, which broke radically with the Victorian styling of early 1930s jukeboxes. From Fuller's formula Stevens borrowed horizontal light fittings in the upper portion of the case and a dramatic contrast between colored illuminators and highly figured but simply formed wood. He then added a striking set of vertical elements that curved smartly at the case's top edge.

The Kuro is essentially the same design turned sideways. This time the principal compositional device is a sweeping curve that wraps around the front left corner. An echoing arc in the upper-right profile of the case and a row of illuminators on the right-hand edge balance the design. The Kuro is much more distinctive than the Twilight, chiefly because of asymmetry but also because the word *Gabel* is emblazoned across the rounded corner. Here Stevens added an additional note of modernity by using a blocked typeface fashionable in the 1930s. Unfortunately, due to Gabel's financial struggles, the Kuro almost suffered the same fate as the Twilight. Fewer than 250 machines were ultimately made, and only a handful are known to exist today.

1. Rick Crandall, "The First 'Modern' Juke Box," *Antique Phonograph Monthly* 7, no. 8 (1984): 3–14. The author thanks Grant Gabel for this reference.

Johnson Wax research vehicle 1940

A series of teardrop-shaped vehicles emerged from Stevens's design studio in the late 1930s, all inspired directly by the Zephyr land yacht. All had an ostensibly practical function but were intended primarily to attract attention. The first of Stevens's clients to order such a vehicle used it to sell products. The president of the Western Printing and Lithograph Company, a children's publisher, ordered a fleet of streamlined sales vans after seeing the Zephyr on the streets of Racine. Similar designs for other companies—including Miller Brewing, Oscar Mayer, and Wisconsin Ice and Coal—were employed as delivery trucks. Stevens's graphic designer James Rohan was given responsibility for the general layout and styling of the interiors of the vehicles, with the exception of delivery trucks that required refrigeration. These were lined with "Dry-Zero" insulation and a layer of waterproof cork veneer for more effective refrigeration—an idea that Stevens patented.[1] By 1949 twenty-six examples of this general design were on the roads in various roles; all were built on a cab-over-engine chassis built by International Harvester, the same as that used for the tractor cab of the Zephyr.

The style of the vehicles shows a great dependence upon other designers' ideas, perhaps evidence of Stevens's youth and impressionability. There is a particularly strong resemblance to the streamlined car designs of Norman Bel Geddes and the Dymaxion car of Buckminster Fuller,

The Johnson Wax research vehicle at the New York World's Fair 1939

Johnson Wax research vehicle 1940

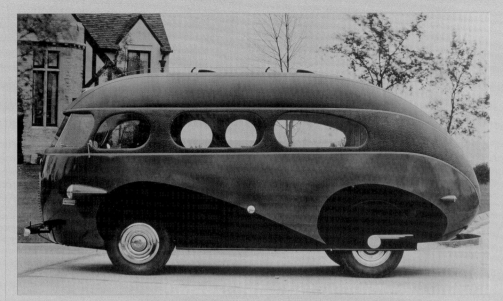

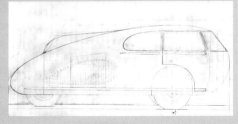

Western Printing van 1938

Interior of the Western Printing van 1938

Norman Bel Geddes, car model 1934

Playground equipment 1939;
*designed for J. E. Porter Company of Ottawa, Illinois,
for the 1939 New York World's Fair*

**R. Buckminster Fuller, rendering for
a Dymaxion Car** 1934

both of which had attained considerable notoriety by the mid-1930s.[2] In general, the exterior styling of Stevens's teardrop vehicles emphasized swooping horizontal lines that ran from nose to tail along the sides. Stevens noted that he did this to "[destroy] the illusion of height and bulk," because the need for interior headroom meant that the vehicles tended to be rather tall.[3]

The version of the design that won Stevens the most renown was a research vehicle created at the request of Herbert F. Johnson, president of the Johnson Wax Company in Racine. The vehicle was painted in Johnson's own Wax-O-Namel, tinted "Cherokee red" in tribute to the brightly colored office building that architect Frank Lloyd Wright had recently completed for the company. Unlike the Zephyr, which had been built on a wooden framework, the twenty-three-foot-long Johnson vehicle employed welded-metal construction. Like Plankinton's pleasure cruiser, however, it was fully stocked with amenities, including three bunks, running water, a bathroom, a gas-powered refrigerator and stove, a foldout desk, a wax-testing lab, and air conditioning.[4]

The somewhat farfetched premise for the vehicle's construction was that it would be driven to Brazil to conduct field research on raw carnauba waxes, drawn from tropical palm trees. This was, however, mainly a pretext for a brilliant publicity stunt. In July 1940 Stevens and Johnson together drove the research vehicle from Racine all the way to Queens for the New York World's Fair. According to H. F. Johnson's son, the vehicle was pulled over in Manhattan by a traffic policeman, who informed the pair that trucks were not allowed on Fifth Avenue. "This, officer, is not a truck," Stevens is said to have responded with some asperity. "It is a housecar."[5] Having survived this encounter, the vehicle made it to the fairgrounds, where it was publicly inspected by the commissioner of the Brazilian pavilion. This moment was quite significant for Stevens personally. The World's Fair was a triumph for American industrial design, as many companies turned to the likes of Norman Bel Geddes, Walter Dorwin Teague, and Henry Dreyfuss to design their pavilion displays, and thus it was important for Stevens to be represented there. He also completed a suite of streamlined playground equipment for Children's World at the fair, comprising a jungle gym, teeter-totters, a "Strato swing," and slides.[6] The Johnson vehicle, however, was undoubtedly his most high-profile contribution to the event. This was especially true after it was "televisioned" at the fair's RCA station and broadcast throughout the grounds, making Stevens's streamlined van the subject of one of the first live television broadcasts in history.[7]

After its star turn in New York, the Johnson Wax research vehicle returned to Wisconsin, where it toured extensively and was the centerpiece of further public relations events, including a viewing by the Green Bay Packers. The vehicle never made it to Brazil. With the onset of the war, it was instead donated to the Civilian Defense's Emergency Medical Service for use as a mobile blood bank. Its eventual fate is unknown.

1. "Traveling Salesmen Bring Their Office Right with Them," *Milwaukee Journal*, 24 October 1937; "Sales on Wheels," *National Lithographer*, April 1949, 35; "Last Word for Classy Icemen," *Milwaukee Journal*, 1 June 1938; "News Pictures," *Triple Diamond International* 11 (July–August 1938): 7; "Oscar Mayer's New Ice Truck Is Streamlined," *Madison Times*, 25 November 1939; "Insulated Ice Truck Streamlined for Extra Capacity and Eye Appeal," *Dry-Zero News*, October 1940. See also Brooks Stevens, "Tomorrow's Luxury Land Cruiser," *Automobile Quarterly* 1 (spring 1962): 80–84, 98.

2. Jeffrey L. Meikle, "Streamlining, 1930–1955," in *Industrial Design: Reflection of a Century*, ed. Jocelyn de Noblet (Paris: Flammarion, 1993), 183, 187; Norman Bel Geddes, *Horizons* (Boston: Little, Brown, 1932).

3. "Boost Sales by Redesigning Old Products," *Milwaukee News-Sentinel*, 16 September 1939.

4. "1940 Version of Covered Wagon Being Planned for Racine Man," *Racine Journal-Times*, 26 February 1940.

5. Samuel C. Johnson, conversation with the author, 17 June 2002.

6. "Stevens Designs New Playgrounds for World's Fair," *Milwaukee Journal*, 19 December 1938; "World's Fair Given Ottawa Firm," *Aurora (Ill.) Daily Beacon News*, 27 January 1939.

7. "Custom-Built Land Cruiser of Wax Firm Head Is Shown Here," *Green Bay Press-Gazette*, 19 September 1940; "S. C. Johnson's Land Yacht Complete Home and Laboratory," *Racine Journal-Times Sunday Bulletin*, 11 August 1940; untitled article, *New York Herald-Tribune*, 30 July 1940.

Brooks Stevens residence 1940

Historian Arthur J. Pulos has observed, "It was not unusual in the late 1940s for architects and designers to test their ideas by designing and furnishing their own homes and offices."[1] Stevens did both. Especially after moving to his second office in 1945, he received potential clients in surroundings that embodied sleek modernity. His greatest style showcase, however, was the house that he designed and built in Fox Point, a well-to-do northern suburb of Milwaukee. Designed in 1939 in conjunction with the local architect Fitzhugh Scott Jr., the building was clearly influenced by the model houses that had been featured at the 1933–34 Century of Progress exposition in Chicago. Stevens also cited the German Bauhaus as an inspiration for the design. But even if it was somewhat derivative, the new residence was by far the most significant architectural accomplishment of Stevens's career. With the possible exception of a handful of houses by Frank Lloyd Wright, it remains Milwaukee's finest example of modernist domestic architecture.

It is easy to imagine the bemusement that the new house created in a neighborhood made up of conventional colonial revival homes and bungalows. Locals jokingly referred to Stevens's cutting-edge home as the only Greyhound bus terminal in Fox Point, thanks to its austere concrete construction. And indeed the building was unlike anything previously seen in Milwaukee, both in overall concept and in the details of its execution. The facade followed the modernist precept of expressing the internal structure and was wrapped with aluminum bands that Stevens thought would prevent the walls from cracking. A tall window of glass bricks lit the main stairway, while the smaller windows were portholes with sliding metal shutters. Several details of the interior were quite innovative, including a radio built directly into the wall of the basement, a bedroom table that swiveled over the bed to serve as a breakfast or work surface, and a built-in Art Deco–style server in the dining room made of Lucite. The house also had an air raid shelter— Milwaukee's first. All in all, Stevens felt justified in claiming the home as "the embodiment of its owner's design for living as he sees it."[2]

Though the overall effect of the residence was quite severe, Stevens counted on a gradual softening through the growth of vegetation, and indeed once the exterior of the building was covered with ivy, its aspect was much altered. Alice Stevens, who had never shared her husband's taste for high modern, brought about similarly humanizing transformations on the interior appointments. When the house was new, the Milwaukee interior designer William McArthur had executed a decorating scheme using wood and metal furniture by the Dunbar Company. This was not much to Mrs. Stevens's liking, and in later years she gradually redecorated the house in the then-fashionable French Provincial taste. In 1951 a service area was added to the house. Eventually she replaced the glass block window in the facade with a stained-glass picture window. Apart from these alterations, the structure remains substantially unchanged today.

1. Arthur J. Pulos, *The American Design Adventure, 1940–1975* (Cambridge: MIT Press, 1988), 66.
2. "Milwaukee Designer's Home His Latest Creation," *Milwaukee Sentinel*, 3 November 1940; see also "A 'House of Tomorrow' Today," *Milwaukee Journal*, 17 November 1940.

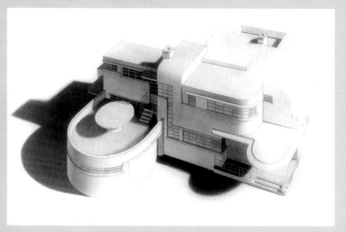

Clockwise from top:

Brooks Stevens residence 1940

Chicago Fair house of tomorrow 1933

Brooks Stevens residence, rear view 1940

Fig. 1 Brooks Stevens, 1941

The Prophet of Profit
Stevens in Wartime, 1941–45

As it was for most Americans, World War II was a major interruption in Brooks Stevens's life. He was classified 4F because of the lingering effects of his childhood polio and so did not serve in the armed forces. Several of his staff members left Milwaukee to fight, however, to be replaced (like factory workers in all parts of the country) by young women with no formal design education. Little is recorded about these new staff members, who must have been a marked change from the Chicago-educated, all-male staff of the past. This is a pity, because it was thanks to these women's efforts that Stevens managed to keep his office open throughout the lean years of the war. Some of his business came from ongoing accounts, including one with the meatpacking concern Cudahy of Cudahy, which commissioned a repackaging of its entire "Peacock" product line (fig. 2). For the most part, however, Stevens's traditional sources of income made for slim pickings during the war years. The majority of his 1930s clientele had been manufacturers who had now shifted over to military production.

Stevens gamely tried to act as a consultant for designs with a military or "home front" application. These presented an unusual challenge because aesthetics were rarely at issue—if ever engineers were to be preferred over designers, it was now. Stevens put a brave face on the matter, though, writing: "When American industry turns to an all-out program of material for war, there arises a new use for industrial design. Mechanized armies are the order of the day, this equipment must be studied and designed for maximum efficiency, simplification of form, and functional streamlining. This facilitates higher production and even ensures a definite measure of camouflage value when exposed to air attack."[1] He made good on this argument only once, through his work for the Clintonville, Wisconsin, truck

manufacturer Four Wheel Drive, which commissioned Stevens to design a snowmobile for use as a kind of "motorized cavalry" (fig. 3). A primitive affair, with a single caterpillar track to the rear and two skis in the front, the design predated America's boom in commercial snowmobile production by twenty years. The office also contributed to less exhilarating wartime designs for a paratrooper's field kit, an individual water filter, a mobile still, sterilizers, field stoves, and dehydration units.[2]

Stevens was much more at home when designing vehicles for the domestic theater of operations. In 1942 he came up with an ingenious plan for rebuilding existing Ford and Mercury passenger cars so that their maximum occupancy would rise from six to twelve. The rebuilt autos could then be used as personnel carriers for the Red Cross, defense plants, and army camps; with the seats folded down, they functioned equally well as ambulances or cargo transports. In the same vein, he collaborated in 1944 with local inventor Harry A. Kreuger on a device for legless veterans that replaced the foot pedals of a car with a mechanized steering column. To accelerate, one pulled back on the wheel, and to brake, one pushed in (fig. 4).[3]

A second and ultimately more profitable way that Stevens made ends meet during the hostilities was by helping companies plan their future products. This was a much-traveled path at the time. Many industrial designers saw themselves as having helped to lead America out of the Great Depression, and they expected to reprise the role in paving the way toward a healthy postwar economy. Naturally inclined to shake up the status quo even under normal circumstances, many in the design profession took the moment as an opportunity to prove their inventiveness. They began to flesh out the grandly impractical schemes that

Fig. 2 Peacock line of products for Cudahy of Cudahy, 1941

had been inaugurated at the 1939 New York World's Fair by Norman Bel Geddes, among others. "Rare indeed [is] the newspaper and magazine which has not shown at least one peek at the future," a writer for *Interiors* magazine noted. "This phenomenon, known as *pie in the sky* to Communists, fills the void created by lack of civilian production today, and soothes the average consumer by leading him to believe that postwar products will be worth waiting for. …Only the stodgiest reactionary will dare present a prewar model after all the publicity attending the present showings of postwar design. And the industrial designer will preside like an Indian Medicine Man…the arbiter of a product's appearance and its public appeal."[4]

For the most part Stevens chose to distance himself from this giddy optimism about the marvels of the postwar world. Whether this was because of his relationships to cautious captains of Midwestern industry, the fact that he was still relatively unproven, or an inborn conservatism is difficult to say. In any case he distinguished himself through writings and "prophetic" designs that bespoke a distinctively pragmatic stance. He made it his business to debunk his fellow designers' more outlandish predictions—cars with transparent roofs, all-plastic kitchens, and the like—as both improbable and foolhardy. Extensive retooling after the war would be time-consuming and expensive for manufacturers, he argued, and falsely raised hopes would result in poor reception for new products that looked like they had been made in 1941. "The truth," he wrote, "is that we must use the tools and dies in existence, and that means that for a time, at least, after the war we shall be having cars, homes, and trains that are not too far different from those we have been having."[5]

Stevens's most colorful exchange on this point came toward the war's end, when he and the renowned auto designer William B. Stout (author of the prewar Scarab, which was the last word in radical streamlining) delivered opposing papers to the Society of Automotive Engineers on the possibility of a postwar flying car. At the time, Stout was on the payroll at the Vultee Aircraft Corporation, and he made bold to predict the emergence of a "flyable automobile." Stevens, taking his customary cynical position, both dismissed Stout's ideas and took the opportunity

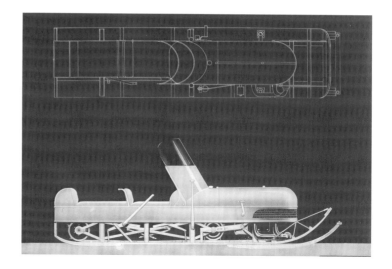

Fig. 3 (upper) Design for an FWD snowmobile, 1941

Fig. 4 (lower) Prototype steering wheel device for legless veterans, 1944

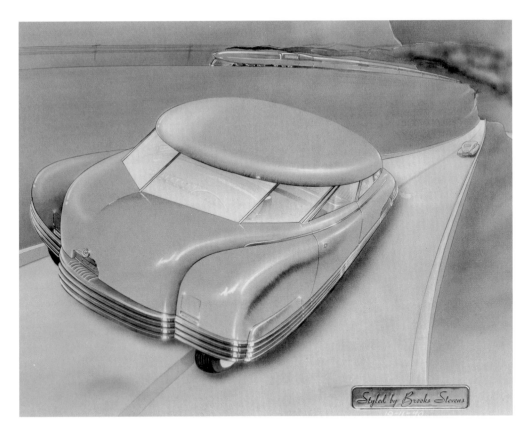

Fig. 5 (upper) Stevens' 1942 article "Your Victory Car" illustrated this rear-engine streamlined car as a possible postwar design.

Fig. 6 (lower) This bubble-topped vehicle was created by Stevens, but dismissed as "typical of many prophecies [with] a plastic body and transparent top presenting many problems."

THE VICTORY CAR
A DESIGN FOR
AN ALL-WHEEL
DRIVE CIVILIAN
"JEEP"
SCALE: 1⅛" = 1'   APRIL, 1942

Styled by Brooks Stevens

Fig. 7 Stevens had this drawing made to "show how a civilian jeep can be given grace and style." Willys-Overland would give him the chance to carry through on the idea after the war, first with the Jeep Station Wagon and then the sporty Jeepster.

to express misgivings about the practicality of aluminum and plastic car bodies and rear-engine automobiles.[6] Ironically, within fifteen years Stevens would propose his own cars in aluminum and fiberglass as well as a flying speedboat, but in the context of what he called "practical postwar design," he was having none of it.

This apparently no-nonsense position was more complex than it seemed, however. Stevens's wartime writings contained the germ of an equally vociferous, and contradictory, urge to follow the lead of his colleagues and outline a wonderful world to come. In a 1991 interview he laughingly admitted that in dealings with clients and the public, he "borrowed on realism, or fantasy, or whatever. Whatever I said that day. Maybe another story the next time."[7] This good-natured hypocrisy, which would play an increasingly central role in Stevens's public persona, began to emerge early 1942, shortly after America's entry into the war. In that year he began speaking about "the practical postwar car."[8] By December, under the title "Your Victory Car," his ideas on this topic made their way to the pages of *Popular Mechanics* and thence to the executive desks at Willys-Overland in Toledo, Ohio, where they paved the way for Stevens's first auto design commission.

On the whole the text was aggressively realistic, casting severe doubt on the likelihood that an all-plastic, rear-engine, or transparent-topped auto would emerge anytime soon. Yet Stevens cleverly found a way to flex his creative muscles, showing not only a "near possibility" but also a bubble-topped vehicle that he had ostensibly invented purely as a bad example of styling gone too far (figs. 5, 6). He also inserted, apropos of nothing in particular, images of his Zephyr land yacht and his streamlined research vehicle for the Johnson Wax company. In short, he showed his capacity to design for the present at various levels of practicality, while borrowing from the sensationalism of outlandish futurism where appropriate. The combination worked flawlessly. In the article Stevens had suggested that the military Jeep would be an ideal candidate for conversion to an inexpensive civilian passenger car, and Willys-Overland hired him to do just that (fig. 7). If Stevens needed any encouragement for his new blend of conservatism and creativity, he had gotten it. It would be a formula that would stand him in good stead for the next thirty years.

1. "Industrial Designers Exhibit Their Wares," *Milwaukee Sentinel*, 22 February 1942.

2. "Rotary Visitors Hear Address by Brooks Stevens," *Ripon (Wis.) Press*, 8 March 1945.

3. "It's Bare of Clutch or Brake, So Auto Runs on Push-Pull," *Milwaukee Journal*, 11 September 1944.

4. "What Is the Place of the Designer in Industry?" *Interiors* 103 (November 1943): 48–49.

5. "Predicts Few Changes in Postwar Automobiles," *Milwaukee Journal*, 1 February 1944. See also *Reflections*, pamphlet (Milwaukee: E. F. Schmidt Company, 1944), Brooks Stevens Archive.

6. "Postwar Auto to Don Wings, Inventor Says," *Christian Science Monitor*, 16 June 1944.

7. Interview with Gary Wolfe, 10 August 1991, Brooks Stevens Archive.

8. "Post-War Prophecies Made by Industrial Designer," *Racine Journal-Times*, 25 June 1942.

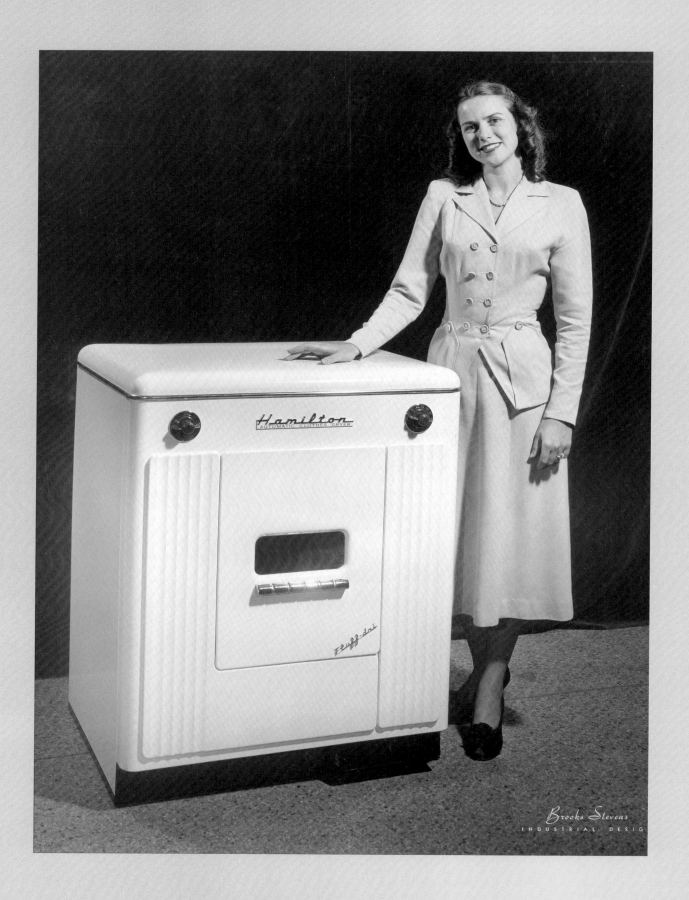

Hamilton clothes dryer 1941

Of Brooks Stevens's wartime designs, the one that he spoke about the most frequently and with the greatest fondness was his clothes dryer for the Hamilton Manufacturing Company of Two Rivers, Wisconsin. The dryer made for a great example of the designer's ingenuity, because it was made marketable (in Stevens's view) through a single alteration. Hamilton was one of the first companies to manufacture an automatic clothes dryer, but had an independent inventor not approached the company, it would never have entered the appliance industry. Previously it had been a manufacturer of institutional furniture, drafting tables, and the like. As Stevens later explained it, he was approached by the company with a featureless white cabinet and was asked for his input. "You can't sell this thing," he exclaimed. "This is a sheet metal box. People won't even know what it is. Who's going to pay $375 for what looks like a storage cabinet? Put a glass window in there, put it in the stores and it'll take off."[1] The dryer he ultimately designed resembled early television sets in its overall composition, and with a pair of shorts flying around inside (as Stevens often put it), it was in effect an advertisement for itself.

The dryer's front, in addition to having the window, was articulated with vertical fluting. Otherwise the finished design was not that different from the sheet metal box that Hamilton had planned to make in the first place. It was an example of what Stevens considered to be responsible design planning for the postwar period, and in fact the dryer turned out to be essentially a postwar product. Though it was ready for market by 1941, material shortages meant that it saw only limited manufacture until 1945. Stevens's firm, particularly his associate James Floria, continued working with Hamilton for decades thereafter, designing a washing machine for the company in 1953 and a new corporate logo in 1954. Though the dryer's innumerable annual model changes, Hamilton never strayed from the original concept of simple but salable design. As Stevens put it, "If it looks like you have to have a pilot's license to run the machine, you've lost."[2]

1. Quoted in "The Man Who Put a Whole New Spin on Design," *International Herald Tribune*, 19 July 1991, 8.

2. Unidentified press clipping, ca. 1967, Brooks Stevens Archive, Milwaukee Art Museum.

Hamilton clothes dryer 1941 (opposite page)

Hamilton clothes dryer prior to Brooks Stevens redesign ca. 1940 (above right)

Prophetic clothes dryer 1941

Let's Be Realistic about New Products (1945)

Let us look at an actual case history of the re-design of a pre-war product for the postwar period as offering a good example of the sound solution to postwar product acceptance. An automatic clothes dryer was put on the market several years before the war and had begun to gain real popularity. It commands the retail price of a major appliance because it actually involves an expensive mechanism and is a well-made unit.

In our first analysis of this product, when asked for recommendations by the management for the postwar version of this dryer, we pointed out that the prewar model, in its simplified square sheet metal cabinet, did not, upon the first impression, look like a major appliance. In fact, it was not evident what it was. It might have been considered anything from a storage cabinet to a small refrigerator. The clothes dryer field is not an old one. There are not many competitive makes and no precedents have been established or set in the appearance of clothes dryer devices in general.

It was our recommendation that we do everything to embellish the appearance of this product to convey its function and enhance its apparent value. Minimum overall cabinet dimensions were most desirable whether this unit was placed in the basement or in the kitchen with other counters. The top could be used as additional working space. With these facts in mind, plus the obvious problem of the increased cost of larger stampings, we were required to hold the rectangular box shape virtually as it was, housing the internal mechanism as closely and compactly as possible. The use of the window in the door immediately embellished the cabinet and made the product more intriguing when on display. The dealer could have a demonstration model using brightly colored fabrics to be tossed around in the drying drum, which would make an interesting display. . . .

The final design for this dryer cabinet was not arrived at by the execution of any single colored picture. The program constituted a complete analysis of the manufacturing program, the function of the dryer in the home, and a definite cost survey to determine how far the design could be carried without increasing the retail price.

The first actual step, as far as the drawing board was concerned, was the preparation of preliminary design sketches, all of which were made precisely to scale, showing a complete range of variation in cabinet styling from a very conservative plain treatment on through to a more completely styled appearance. Experiments were made with the accent on the vertical as well as the sketches featuring a horizontal emphasis. Symmetrical designs were made, and offset or unsymmetrical treatments were experimented with. Variations in trim, handle designs, nameplates, control knobs, and window shapes were exploited in a series of approximately twenty-five or thirty designs. These were carefully gone over in conferences with the management and the manufacturing department, as well as the sales and advertising departments.

As a result of these conferences, it was decided that there were no impossible treatments shown as far as manufacturing was concerned, and that the next move would be to expose these sketches to a cross section of the company, including the management, the women employees, and men closely related to the plant who would be the most production-minded. A questionnaire was mimeographed and distributed to fifty or sixty individuals who went over the sketches, which were on display and answered a series of questions. These questions covered their likes and dislikes with regard to simplicity or ornamentation, symmetry versus unsymmetrical design, the location of controls, even the size radii used on the corners and top of the cabinet.

These questionnaires were turned in and carefully cross-sectioned with very satisfactory and pleasing results. One design and one general treatment won out so overwhelmingly with all three groups that we felt assured of its acceptance with the general public.

After this survey was made, this design was refined and completed in detail and from finished working drawings handmade metal samples were built in which dryer mechanisms were installed, complete with controls, nameplates, and all details. From this makeup, the management could tell entirely what the new postwar dryer would look like and how it would operate.

The rendering accompanying this article showing the purely prophetic postwar dream-house clothes dryer [see page 73] is typical of the type of design that might have been proposed to the manufacturer if there had been no regard for cost, tooling, or any other practical phrase of the program. The transparent spherical dome provides an exciting display of the tumbling of the clothes, and aircraft-type controls seem to make the product much more important and intricate-looking, but when a careful analysis is made one realizes that this might have been executed by an artist indulging in wishful product design, rather than a designer seriously considering the limitations of the manufacturer's equipment as well as how the consumer would actually live with this unit. He has given no thought to cost, making this product completely out of range in retail price. It may seem incredible for an industrial designer to criticize too completely imaginative design work, when supposedly this is his stock in trade. My contention is, on the other hand, that the industrial designer has a serious part to play in reconversion and the industrial picture in general. He does not have to resort to fantastic interpretations of "things to come" to enlist a clientele. In fact, the wilder, more impractical suggestions, which are prophesied to excite the imagination, oftentimes become objects of scorn and disgust in the eyes of the engineer and manufacturer. There is a middle course. In fact, as a matter of experiment, we found that an airbrush rendering in full color of any product in even a purely practical design would intrigue the average consumer just as much. …

In summing up this discussion, I certainly do not wish to dampen the hopes of the consumer for marked and continuous improvement in the manufacture of consumer goods in general. I have only a strong desire not to see the average American propagandized into expecting miracles immediately, which may fail miserably if attempted, when we are going to need the soundest type of thinking, planning, and acting within the industrial picture to insure prosperity, continued employment, and the prevention of inflation or depression.

Excerpted from Brooks Stevens, "Let's Be Realistic about New Products,"
Contact *(Milwaukee Junior Chamber of Commerce) 25 (1 November 1945): 3–5.*

Supermix kitchen mixer 1942

The quintessential material of early industrial design was phenolic plastic—a heat-resistant substance popularly known by the trade name Bakelite. Invented in 1909 by Leo Baekeland, phenolic rapidly became, as its creator predicted, the "material of a thousand uses."[1] Few early designers failed to capitalize on the novelty and adaptability of the plastic, and Stevens's use of the material was typical in most respects.[2] Prior to the war, he had incorporated it in several designs, including a washing machine with a plastic agitator; in 1947 he would create the first radio entirely enclosed in plastic for the Trav-ler company. But Stevens's interest in plastic peaked during World War II as a result of his relationship with the Durez Company of North Tonawanda, New York, which enthusiastically embraced industrial design as a way of enhancing its public image during the war. Like most plastics companies, Durez could sell as much as it could produce to the military during wartime, but it was concerned that it would be difficult to sustain this high level of sales after the war. The company turned to Stevens and other well-known designers to make its case.[3]

In many ways the Durez campaign was a reprise of a similar effort launched by the Bakelite Corporation in 1933. For two years the pioneering plastics company had published advertisements in trade journals that exploited the natural marriage of industrial design and publicity. Plastic products by fifteen designers—including Egmont Arens, Norman Bel Geddes, Raymond

Supermix kitchen mixer 1942

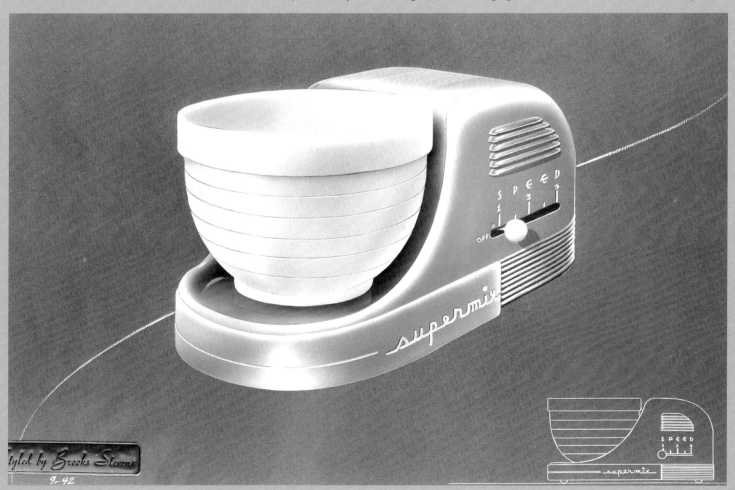

Loewy, and Walter Dorwin Teague—were promoted through the ads, and in turn, Bakelite became indelibly associated with sophisticated modernism.[4] Durez's approach followed this model closely, and the company's ads even included many of the same designers as the previous series. There was a key difference, however: all of the products in the Durez advertisements were prophetic. In 1942 the company published a booklet entitled "In War We Must Prepare for Peace," featuring military applications of the material, as well as Loewy's thoughts on civilian uses of a plastic-impregnated plywood developed for the navy.[5] Prominently featured was an image of Stevens's new Supermix kitchen mixer, trumpeted as "another design suggestion for modern living that's just waiting for America to win the right to enjoy it."

Stevens's inclusion in the booklet and in the company's associated ad campaign was ironic, given that much of his wartime rhetoric was given over to a tirade against plastic pipe dreams. Designers, he wrote, "have led the public to believe that on Armistice Day one will rise from a plastic bed, bathe in a plastic shower, drive to work in a plastic car, and so on. These exaggerations, if not tempered, may cause a serious condition in the consumer's mind regarding the first postwar merchandise."[6] After the war Stevens continued this line of argument. He was particularly critical of the impracticality of plastic auto bodies, which he thought would be difficult to repair after an accident and inordinately expensive because of the need for retooling and the cost of the raw material.[7] He therefore asserted that use of plastics should be restricted to smaller household appliances, luggage, and packaging.[8]

Stevens was apparently willing to overlook such misgivings in order to be included in the Durez ads. It is not difficult to see why, as his participation was a highlight of his wartime career. The series placed him among distinguished company, for the first time effectively pronouncing him the equal of designers who had attained notoriety in the 1930s. The Durez series featured not only the Supermixer but also a prophetic car by Stevens whose side panel extended to form the fenders in a unified volume. (Designs by others in the series included a refrigerator by Arens, a sewing machine by Peter Muller-Munk, and a Dave Chapman typewriter.) When asked to extol the virtues of plastic, Stevens was more than obliging, appearing in a Durez-sponsored television show and discussing how the material could be used advantageously. For one Supermix advertisement, he wrote: "Here's still another example of how Durez phenolic molding compounds help the designer translate ideas into reality. Obviously, an important specification for a food-mixer is light weight. And that's no problem when you design a housing with Durez plastics in mind. Furthermore, the lustrous, satin-smooth finish of these plastics gives the object excellent sales-appeal... beauty that's more than skin-deep, too. For plastic housings are durable, rugged, and resistant to mild acids and alkalis."

Will your <u>next</u> car look like this?

DUREZ... plastics that fit the job

DUREZ PLASTICS & CHEMICALS, INC.   DUREZ   1027 WALCK ROAD, N. TONAWANDA, N. Y.

Spartan vaporizer 1945
Durez ad with Stevens prophetic car 1942

Despite Stevens's confidence, the Supermixer's practicality was not tested in the factory or marketplace. It was never developed past the stage of an evocative sketch. The designer's other wartime ideas for the use of plastic also failed to reach the factory, including his ingenious

Trav-ler radio 1947

Boston Store Radio Display 1941

front-loading Toastalator. He did, however, see two of his commissions using Durez plastic marketed before war's end: a light-up compact called the Firefly for the Edmilton Company (for which Stevens had designed the Petipoint iron), and a vaporizer, or humidifier, designed for the Spartan Company in Minneapolis to remedy bronchial ailments.[9] Apparently neither was produced in large numbers—Edmilton complained of scarcity of raw materials due to the war— but both used plastic effectively. The Spartan vaporizer was particularly striking, with a stark juxtaposition of the matte plastic body and handle with a shining aluminum cover. As the original rendering for the vaporizer demonstrates, even casting seams were taken into account in the planning of the faceted form.[10]

1. Stephen Fenichell, *Plastic: The Making of a Synthetic Century* (New York: Harper Collins, 1996), chap. 4.

2. Jeffrey L. Meikle, "Streamlining, 1930–1955," in *Industrial Design: Reflection of a Century*, ed. Jocelyn de Noblet (Paris: Flammarion, 1993), 189.

3. On the wartime use and promotion of Durez and other plastics, see Robert Friedel, "Scarcity and Promise: Materials and American Domestic Culture During World War II," in *World War II and the American Dream*, ed. Donald Albrecht (Cambridge: MIT Press, 1995). On industrial design and plastic, see Jeffrey L. Meikle, *American Plastic: A Cultural History* (New Brunswick, N.J.: Rutgers University Press, 1995); Gregory Votolato, *American Design in the Twentieth Century: Personality and Performance* (Manchester: Manchester University Press, 1998), 131–39; and Deborah Allen, "What's So Special about Plastics?" *Industrial Design* 1 (February 1954): 57–67.

4. Meikle, *American Plastic*, 111–13.

5. See also John H. Love, "Values Studied for Use in Post-War Era," *New York World-Telegram*, 1 October 1943.

6. Brooks Stevens, letter to the editor, *Industrial Marketing* 28 (August 1943): 123–24.

7. "Autos of Plastic Just a Dream, Designer Says," *Milwaukee Journal*, 12 December 1946.

8. "Rotary Hears Talk Monday by Brooks Stevens," *Milwaukee Journal*, 11 December 1947. For a wartime text closely paralleling Stevens's outlook on plastics, see Joseph L. Nicholson and George R. Leighton, "Plastics Come of Age," *Harper's*, August 1942, reprinted in Richard Rhodes, ed., *Visions of Technology* (New York: Simon and Schuster, 1999), 147–49.

9. "Here's a Compact Men Will Favor," *Milwaukee Sentinel*, 23 November 1941, sec. B; *Durez Molder* 17 (March 1945): 10; "Plastics in the Post War World: Streamlining Our Future," *Canadian Plastics* 1 (August 1943): 89–92.

10. For more on the Durez industrial design campaign, see Arthur J. Pulos, *The American Design Adventure, 1940–1975* (Cambridge: MIT Press, 1988), 40, 45.

Firefly Compact Advertisement, 1942

Fig. 1 Brooks Stevens and Associates, 1945. Left to right: Anthony Reed, Jim Floria, Brooks Stevens, and John Hughes

The Organization Man
Steven's Best Years, 1946–55

An industrial designer in today's business world should be a business man,
an engineer and a stylist, and in that direct order.

Brooks Stevens (1959)[1]

Everything came together for Brooks Stevens in the decade after World War II. His personal life had never been better. Between 1939 and 1951 he and Alice became the proud parents of four children—David Brooks, William Clifford ("Steve"), Sandra Alice, and Kipp Kopmeier Stevens—each born four years apart. His social life also moved into full swing, as he became a member of several clubs, began throwing lavish summertime parties, and forged new connections in New York and Paris. Professionally, things were even rosier. Well in advance of the declaration of the armistice, he had expanded his staff in anticipation of post-war demand. On the occasion of the tenth anniversary of his firm, he had moved his office a short distance, from its original Milwaukee Street address to 622 North Water Street, thereby gaining enlarged quarters and a much more stylish space in which to meet clients.[2] The new office was lavishly appointed with ribbed glass windows and curved modernistic furniture custom-built to Stevens's design (figs. 2, 3).

Several of the staff members who joined the firm at this critical juncture proved to be invaluable additions. Karl Brocken, one of Stevens's earliest staffers, departed in July of 1944 to work for a Chicago architectural designer, but his place was more than filled by two new design associates, James Floria and John Hughes.[3] Floria was originally from Milwaukee and during the war had lived in Beverly Hills, California, working with the aircraft industry. Hughes, like many of Stevens designers' a product of the Layton School of Art in Milwaukee, had first worked as a designer at the Resettlement Administration in Washington, D.C., and from 1936 as a staff designer at Montgomery Ward in Chicago. He had gone into the engineering corps in the war and received a medical discharge in 1944. Floria was similar to Stevens in many respects. Both were natural salesmen with a flair for publicity—Floria had assisted in the design of a flying boat for Howard Hughes during the war—and shared an enthusiasm for automobiles and racing. Hughes was older and considerably more down-to-earth but was by all accounts a consummate professional and experienced stylist. Whatever authority the young and exuberant design staff may have lacked, Hughes provided.

Stevens formally recognized the importance of his two new colleagues by naming them, along with longtime friend and coworker Tony Reed, as partners of the firm. Though Stevens remained the sole capital investor in the firm, he now legally held only 50-plus percent of the company, with Floria, Hughes, and

Fig. 2, 3 Reception area and conference room for Brooks Stevens's Water Street office, 1947

Reed taking a little less than 20, 20, and 10 percent, respectively. The business was accordingly rechristened Brooks Stevens Associates, a name that lasted for the remainder of Stevens's career. This new business arrangement reflected a sharing of responsibility and a genuine chemistry among the four men (fig.1). A 1949 public relations brochure published by the firm describes the roles that each of the principals played:

> Stevens sparks ideas, keeps an attentive eye to new and old business and plays major domo of what for color and action compares with a three-ring circus. Designing engineer Reed is the genial, conservative paper-planner of the outfit who with his jack-of-all-trades abilities pieces together the technical inspirations of his partners. Designer Hughes is profound and methodic in his approach to every project and ably serves as a compensating factor in a business where stability and common sense are top requisites. Floria comes by design from the esthetic and academic side, with an effervescence of creative ideas, a showman personality and a love for the volatility of his profession.[4]

It is a measure of the rapid growth of industrial design during these years that Stevens's office, as large and successful as it had become, was not the only Milwaukee firm in the business during these years. The only real rival in the city was, ironically, Stevens's former employee Karl Brocken, who had returned from Chicago and opened his own firm with four staffers. In a pattern that repeated itself in later years, some of his clients were carried over from his work at Stevens's firm. In addition to Brocken there were a handful of other lesser-known local designers. Edward C. Klotz Jr. (b. 1915), a product of the Art Institute of Chicago, moved to the city in 1939 and somewhat pugnaciously called his company "Milwaukee Industrial Designers." Russel H. Bach, a graduate of the University of Wisconsin, had worked with Klotz during the war and went independent in 1945; he specialized in the emerging field of plastics design.[5] A few years later Jack Collins would form a design office in Milwaukee; he would become Stevens's main local competitor in the 1960s and 1970s.

Despite the presence of these other Milwaukee designers, Stevens was the only industrial designer from the city invited to be a founding member of the Society of Industrial Designers (SID) in 1944. This organization was itself designed to a high degree of precision. It arose as a defensive maneuver when the government refused to grant tax-deductible status to the business expenses of Walter Dorwin Teague's and Raymond Loewy's offices. Because SID was essentially an attempt to prove the legitimacy of Teague's and Loewy's freelance approach to design, initial membership was limited to independents rather than members of an in-house styling department. The line was drawn by requiring members to have an established record in designing at least three different types of products—which of course eliminated those who had worked only in the auto or appliance industry, even if they had decades of experience.[6]

The group was also very circumscribed geographically. Most of the fifteen founders of SID had their offices in New York (Harold Van Doren of Toledo, John Gordon Rideout of Cleveland and Joseph Sinel of San Francisco were the only other exceptions).[7] Stevens felt his difference from the rest of the group keenly before he arrived; he was not only geographically removed but also SID's youngest member. He described his first meeting with the organization as being like "going to meet the Gods on Mount Olympus."[8] Nor was his reception calculated to put him at ease. Stevens recalled, "George Sakier, one of the lesser lights, sidled over to me holding a double martini in one hand and an anchovy hors d'oeuvre, and asked, 'Where are you from?'" When Stevens replied that he hailed from Milwaukee, Sakier responded, "Oh, you mean from Sauerkraut Bay."[9]

Stevens had little to do with Sakier after that experience and indeed maintained relatively cool relations with all of his colleagues in New York. This did not prevent him from putting his new contacts to use, however. In 1947 he saw to it that the Milwaukee Art Institute (the forerunner of the present Milwaukee Art Museum) acted as a venue for a tour of SID members' work, shown in photographic form. By this time the organization had no fewer than seventy-four members, more than half of whom were included in the exhibition; only Stevens and his former staff designer Karl Brocken, however, were represented by actual objects.[10] The small show was notable mostly because it set the stage for the next significant milestone in Stevens's career: an exhibition entitled *Industrial Design by Brooks Stevens Associates*, which opened at the Milwaukee Art Institute in January 1950. This event was remarkable for several reasons. First, it was the first monographic museum exhibition devoted to an industrial designer. Perhaps it is unsurprising that a city like Milwaukee was the first to see the attraction of such an idea; as the institute's director, Barton Cummings, pointed out, "industrial designs tie in with the very sinews of our community."[11]

Stevens essentially acted as the curator of the show. He first hosted Cummings at his office and then conferred with him at every step as the exhibition was planned and mounted. Each stage in the process was fully documented and professionally photographed, attesting to Stevens's awareness of the significance of the project (fig. 4). The exhibition itself was an enormous logistical undertaking, comprising 125 objects and myriad photographs. "Never before in the history of the Institute has it welcomed an event of this magnitude," the *Milwaukee Sentinel* exclaimed. "Never before have such peculiar and violent assaults been made on the classical edifice on North Jefferson Street." One of Stevens's recent car designs, the Willys-Overland Jeepster, was inserted into the museum's small front door riding sideways on a flatbed truck; the car of the building's passenger elevator was removed to allow an Allis-Chalmers tractor to be hoisted up to the second floor using a winch (fig. 5). Stevens designed "modernistic scaffolding" for the display of photos (fig. 6) and painted the museum's walls in "deep modern shades," utterly transforming the space of the staid institution.[12] In spirit and in execution, the display technique was the antithesis of the white-walled "Good Design" shows being held concurrently at the Museum of Modern Art (MoMA) in New York.[13] Stevens's personal sense of disengagement from the MoMA design department, in fact, was such that if he saw one of his staff spending an inordinate amount of time on a model or rendering, he would admonish him, "This isn't for the Museum of Modern Art, you know." He nevertheless had no compunction about establishing the legitimacy

of his one-person show by putting together an accompanying design symposium. Entitled "The Designer as a Vital Link in American Industry between the Consumer and the Manufacturer," the one-day series of talks featured Stevens (who spoke on the subject of auto design), as well as SID president Egmont Arens, Walter Dorwin Teague, Dave Chapman, and James Plaut, director of Boston's Institute of Contemporary Art, who spoke on his efforts to connect designers to industry. Phillip McConnell, the executive secretary of SID, served as moderator (fig. 7).[14]

Even as he was hosting the national design community, Stevens's star was rising quickly locally. Among his most powerful new intimates was Miller Brewing president Frederick C. Miller, who spoke at the exhibition on the subject of design from the point of view of the industrialist. This was just the sort of contact that Stevens had cultivated over the past decade and a half, and by the late 1940s his efforts had begun to pay quite a dividend. Though Stevens considered people like Miller to be great friends as well as great clients, it is clear that by this time he had succeeded in entirely erasing the thin line between business and pleasure. Thus his closeness to Frederick Miller was inextricably bound with the many commissions he received from the brewing company in the late 1940s and early 1950s. Stevens kept up similarly lucrative relationships with Ralph Evinrude of the Outboard Marine Company, Francis Trecker of Kearney-Trecker, Fred Loock of Allen-Bradley, and many other local and national figures in business. Stevens did not have a predatory attitude toward men like these; they were, in fact, the best friends he had. Without such relationships, however, he would never have been able to introduce Milwaukee's biggest companies to the advantages of industrial design.

In the early 1950s Stevens consciously tried to expand his social and professional successes to new horizons. He began to take up residence in the Drake Hotel in New York, where he hosted cocktail parties in the hopes of mingling with potential clients. (This despite the fact that he considered such parties to be "a veritable font of useless information.") He redoubled his self-promotional efforts, hiring a French public relations manager named Guy Storr in 1954, and sought out international connec-

Fig. 4 (above) Brooks Stevens and Barton Cummings plan Stevens's 1950 exhibition at the Milwaukee Art Institute

Fig. 5 (left) Installing a Willys-Overland Jeepster

fig. 6 (above) "Industrial Design by Brooks Stevens Associates" at the Milwaukee Art Institute, 1950

fig. 7 (right) Stevens and colleagues at the opening of his retrospective. Left to right: Milwaukee Art Institute director Barton Cummings, Society of Industrial Designers president Philip McConnell, Walter Dorwin Teague, Egmont Arens, Stevens, Dave Chapman

tions by joining the Institut de l'Esthetique Industrielle and the Société des Ingénieurs de l'Automobile in 1950 (fig. 8). He managed to secure commissions for a series of spectacular custom cars, which invariably debuted at the Paris Auto Salon, and reveled in the ensuing multilingual press coverage. In an age of increasingly anonymous design, he did his very best to achieve a high profile while still playing the part of a company man.

The late 1940s and early 1950s must be considered Stevens's best years. It was a period in which he had as much business as he could wish for (he commented in 1951, "our business has gone up twenty-five percent in the last 18 months and we could add another thirty-five to forty percent to our volume, if we could handle it"), and yet he retained a high degree of personal control over his firm's designs.[15] This delicate equilibrium was not built to last. As the 1950s progressed, Stevens became more and more occupied with the hunt for new and larger commissions. He still had many good years of designing ahead of him, of course, but by 1955 the nature of his business had fundamentally changed. With the notable exception of car design, his primary role was now that of a "front man," with the execution of the actual product styling increasingly marked by the personal tastes of his staff designers. The corporate clients for whom he and his staff worked, furthermore, began to establish "captive" or in-house design departments, with which Stevens was forced to compete. Inevitably he and his fellow industrial designers were obliged to adopt a less unified (and even less "stylish") style, an approach that gave priority to the exigencies of corporate product development but sacrificed the subjective aesthetics of streamlining. It was Stevens's unique genius, in the face of this trend toward impersonality, to make himself a spokesman for this developing state of affairs. Though his most elegant designs were already past him, his career as a design theorist was only beginning.

Fig. 8 (above) Guy Storr and Brooks Stevens at the racetrack

1. "Prophet with a Purpose," *Let's See*, 23 January 1959, 8–11.

2. "Office Changed by Brooks Stevens," *Milwaukee Sentinel*, 1 April 1945.

3. "Brocken to Join Firm in Chicago," *Milwaukee Sentinel*, 10 July 1944.

4. "Business History of Brooks Stevens Associates," unpublished manuscript, ca. 1949, Brooks Stevens Archive.

5. "For the Abundant Life: Industrial Designers Provide 'Style' That Helps Keep Factories Running," *Milwaukee Journal*, 3 February 1946.

6. The exclusivity of the SID differentiated it from an older designers' organization called the American Designers' Institute (ADI), which listed among its members such luminaries as Alfons Bach, John Vassos, John Gruen, and Alexander Kostellow. The ADI argued that "the SID is blocking attempts to make id a full-fledged profession in order to keep the field to themselves," while the SID countered that "the ADI is loaded with fabric and furniture designers who don't qualify for the profession at all" (Bill Davidson, "You Buy Their Dreams," *Collier's*, 2 August 1947, 22–23, 68–69).

7. The organization's officers were Walter Dorwin Teague, president; Raymond Loewy, chairman of the executive committee; Henry Dreyfuss, vice president; Van Doren, treasurer; and Egmont Arens, secretary. Other members were Stevens, Donald Deskey, Norman Bel Geddes, Lurelle Guild, Ray Patten, Joseph B. Platt, Rideout, George Sakier, Joseph Sinel, and Russel Wright. See "Brooks Stevens among Industrial Design Group," *Milwaukee Sentinel*, 12 June 1945.

8. Stevens, interview with Chip Duncan, 1990–91.

9. Paul G. Hayes, "The Designer Who Roared," *Milwaukee Journal Magazine*, 6 December 1992, 5–17.

10. "Industrial Design Show July 2 to 27 at Art Institute," *Milwaukee Sentinel*, 29 June 1947; "Industrial Art Designs on Display," *Milwaukee Sentinel* 6 July 1947; "Art Is Giving Aid to Industry," *Milwaukee Journal* 3 July 1947.

11. "Revolutionary Display Pulls Crowd to Gallery," *Milwaukee Journal*, 11 January 1950.

12. Fred Haeuser, "Strange Things Happen to Art Institute Making Ready for Brooks Stevens Exhibit," *Milwaukee Sentinel*, 8 January 1950; ibid.

13. Kristina Wilson has pointed out the essential irony in this fact (conversation with the author, 2002). The traditional premise of the survey style of exhibition, she argues, is to promote consumerism, while the usual goal of a monographic exhibition is to demonstrate the accomplishments of the singular auteur. Yet the Museum of Modern Art maintained a high-minded rhetoric of quality during this period—even while tacitly acting as a sales mechanism through the proliferation of its Good Design labels—while Brooks Stevens, the ultimate salesman designer, was celebrated in Milwaukee for his genius. On the latent commercialism of the MoMA Good Design shows, see Terence Riley and Edward Eigen, "Between the Museum and the Marketplace: Selling Good Design," in *The Museum of Modern Art at Mid-century: At Home and Abroad* (New York: Museum of Modern Art, 1994).

14. "Six Week Display," *Torch Magazine*, January 1950, 21, 52; "Rubber on Concrete Is Railroad's Future," *Milwaukee Journal*, 29 January 1950.

15. Felicia Anthenelli, "Industrial Designers: Product Blueprinters Thrive on Manufacturer Effort to Save Materials," *Wall Street Journal*, 17 November 1951.

Johnson Wax Company desk lighter 1946

Nearly fifty years after the fact, Stevens remembered his first encounter with the architect Frank Lloyd Wright quite clearly. The year was probably 1938 or 1939. The young designer was at the

headquarters of the Johnson Wax Company in Racine, showing Herbert F. Johnson his firm's renderings for a new research vehicle. In the middle of the meeting, Wright, who was involved with the design of the company's headquarters at the time, walked into the office and promptly pronounced the proposed design to be a "shapeless mass."[1] Fortunately for Stevens, Johnson did not agree, and the vehicle went on to be a great triumph at the New York World's Fair.

The next encounter of the two men was no less intimidating for Stevens. This time the setting was the Layton School of Art during World War II, and the young designer was given the nerve-wracking task of introducing the architect. "So I introduced the man," Stevens recalled, "and did the best job I could with a few words regarding his prowess and so forth. And then I brought him to stage. He arrived in… a big flat rimmed and low porkpie hat, and the flowing cape with the red inner liner and this sort of thing. And he just burst upon this audience as though they were just peasants who had come to the theater to hear him. So when his final speech was over he bowed to the public and stopped and said, 'and now, if you have any questions.' And, of course, this was almost what he had been waiting for, I'm sure. And this poor little mayor was sitting there with his mouse-like wife, and said, 'Mr. Wright, I have a question. What would you do with the city of Milwaukee?' And he looked this poor man in the eye, and looked down at him, and said, 'Bomb it.' I thought that was rather typical of his personality."[2]

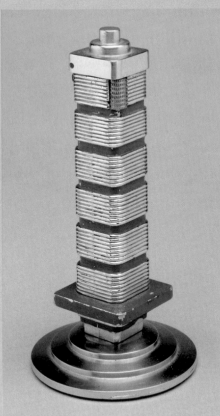

Despite misgivings about Wright's egotism, though, Stevens patterned himself after the older architect in many ways. At a time when there were few celebrity designers in the country, much less the Midwest, Stevens was highly aware of Wright's eccentric public persona, aggressive modernism, and expert showmanship. He emulated these qualities and sometimes even dressed the part; Ray Besasie Jr., who later became one of Stevens's mechanics, remembers seeing the designer wearing a black cape and fedora and carrying a cane.[3] This imitative impulse rarely expressed itself in Stevens's design work, which he considered to be salable and populist in a way that Wright's grandiose, idealistic architecture never was. A significant exception came about in 1946, however, when Stevens was asked to create a desk lighter to mark the fiftieth anniversary of the Johnson Wax Company. He responded with a miniaturization of the famous Research Tower that Wright had designed two years previously for the company's plant—a tall, horizontally banded structure that made for a surprisingly ergonomic design when shrunk down to hand size. The narrow waist at the lighter's bottom mimics the construction of the real building, whose entire 153-foot height is cantilevered from a base only thirteen feet wide at its narrowest point. It is tempting to see the lighter as a little tribute, evidence of an inferiority complex on Stevens's part. But it is much more likely that Stevens saw his desktop design, on the contrary, as literally knocking the great Wright down to size. In this respect, the lighter is a gesture of supreme self-confidence—the very characteristic that Stevens shared most completely with his fellow Wisconsinite.

1. Brooks Stevens, interview with Chip Duncan, 1990–91, transcript, Brook Stevens Archive, Milwaukee Art Museum.
2. Ibid.
3. Ray Besasie Jr., conversation with the author, August 2002.

Frank Lloyd Wright, Johnson Wax Research Tower
designed 1944, completed 1950

Johnson Wax Company desk lighter 1946

Globe Mastercraft runabout 1946

From the standpoint of design, boats are something like appliances, in that their essential functional elements are mostly hidden from view. Just as the complex inner workings of a radio or kitchen mixer are inside a case, most of the engineering on a boat lies below the waterline. Because of this opacity, the designer of the boat's upper half often tries to convey its functional qualities through aesthetic means. This was certainly the case with the Globe runabout. This small and highly maneuverable boat was a collaboration between Brooks Stevens and the naval architect Douglas Van Patten, with each man taking responsibility for one half of the hull. The sleek styling of the boat's upper, visible portion directly refers to the innovative and unusual convex underside. Its creators were justified in pronouncing their new craft to be "functional and esthetic but thoroughly nautical, yet ahead of its time."[1]

Van Patten had previously worked at Minette-Shields, a power yacht producer, and had helped to design landing craft during the war. He had also experimented with convex-section hulls on racing boats and knew that this approach could reduce water resistance to produce a more level, "non-pounding" ride. Van Patten brought this idea to the Globe project, as well as a wedge-shaped rudder that provided great stability at high speeds. Although Stevens had nothing to do with the planning of the experimental underbody, he did try to express it in stylistic terms. The windshield on the runabout departed from the usual V or flat shape used on small craft and instead curved across the boat's front in a "panoramic" shape. All the hardware, including a plastic two-spoke steering wheel, was custom-designed for the boat. Most strikingly, Stevens created a two-tone effect through the contrast of natural and bleached mahogany plywood and articulated the shape with a graceful raking sheer line that swept downward to the stern. Stevens later characterized these stylistic touches as "automotive" in character, but in actuality they were drawn from pre-war aerodynamic streamlining—a visual language that was conventional by the late 1940s but still novel when applied to a small passenger boat.

Unfortunately the Globe Corporation had not previously been involved with boat manufacture. Having originally been in the coal business, the company concentrated on the construction of airplanes during the war, but its experiment with peacetime conversion to nautical production proved to be short-lived. Versions of the boat were reportedly planned in eight different lengths, ranging from eleven to twenty-one feet, but only the standard fourteen-foot "Mastercraft" model was made in any significant numbers. About three hundred were made before 1951, when the project was abandoned due to material scarcity during the Korean War. Two nineteen-foot runabouts were also built, both of which survive in private hands in Wisconsin. At first the runabouts were powered by forty-five-horsepower outboard motors, with an inboard option being introduced in 1949. Stevens's connection to Evinrude was apparently outweighed by Globe's connection to Mercury through Getz's friend Carl Kiekhafer, and the boats were fitted with Gray and Mercury motors.[2]

Globe Mastercraft runabout 1946
Globester Scooter 1947

Like many of Stevens's early projects, the Globe boats were tied to other commissions for his design firm. Stevens became friendly with all the principals in the project, including Van Patten; Globe's chairman, George F. Getz Jr.; and the production manager at the Mastercraft construction plant, Russell Gage. With Van Patten, he later collaborated on his prophetic Evinrude Jetstream catamaran. Globe had previously hired Stevens to style a smart little scooter made of aluminum called the Globester, produced in conjunction with McCulloch Aviation. Russell Gage went on to employ Stevens as a consultant when he produced his own line of boats under the company name Gage-Hacker in the early 1960s, exclusively for sale and use at Lake Geneva in south-central Wisconsin.[3] Stevens himself went on to design enclosed-deck cruisers for Chris-Craft in 1954, fiberglass boats for the Owens Yacht Company in 1959, and Evinrude's first line of water-craft in 1963.[4]

1. "New Lines of Speedboats Incorporate Radical Ideas," *Milwaukee Journal*, 5 January 1947; "Brooks Stevens," *Rudder*, February 1961, 40, 60–62.

2. Bob Huber, "Reflections on the Globe," *Classic Boating*, March–April 1997, 26–31. The author thanks Larry Larkin for this reference. See also Dean Smith, *Tall Shadows: The Story of the Getz Family and Globe Corporation* (Scottsdale: Globe Corporation, 1993).

3. The author would like to thank Larry Larkin and Bert Getz Jr. for information on the Globe Mastercraft commission and subsequent designs.

4. Jeffrey L. Rodengen, *The Legend of Chris-Craft* (Fort Lauderdale: Write Stuff Syndicate, 1988).

Willys-Overland Jeep Station Wagon 1946
Willys-Overland Jeepster Phaeton 1948

By the close of World War II the military Jeep had become a symbol of America across the world and a symbol of vehicular reliability. There was little doubt that the postwar period would see some kind of civilian version of the rugged little car—the psychological impression made by countless images of Jeeps doing their duty at the front lines was too valuable a commodity to ignore. It was Brooks Stevens's good fortune to understand that fact sooner than anyone else. In 1942, with America only one year into the war, he delivered a talk on the subject of postwar automobiles at the Society of Automotive Engineers conference in Detroit. The presentation became the basis of an article entitled "Your Victory Car" for the magazine Popular Mechanics. In it, he dismissed prophecies of teardrop-shaped cars and spherical plastic domes, instead insisting that designers take a pragmatic look at the logistical difficulties of rapidly producing cars for peacetime. This might well mean that the "new" cars would be only slightly altered versions of 1942 models and, furthermore, that the American consumer might have to accept a smaller automobile than had been popular prior to the war. In particular, Stevens presciently argued that "today's Jeep could become tomorrow's popular car with a minimum of tooling and fabrication cost." He illustrated the point with a small, stylish car that compensated for the short frame of the Jeep through the blending of individual fenders into a continuous volume that ran down the flanks of the car [see page 69, fig. 7]. To decrease cost, he explained, the auto would have a minimum of ornamentation, using stylish lines as its main selling point.[1]

Stevens could not have known how important the article would be. Willys-Overland, the company that provided the army with the majority of its wartime Jeeps, was one of the few independent car manufacturers remaining in the country.[2] Before the war it had been on the brink of following innumerable other small producers into history's dustbin. Though it had managed to hold on to a tiny corner of the market with sedans of admittedly inferior quality, few at the company could have missed the opportunity that the Jeep represented. The young designer's article therefore caught the eye of the executives at Willys, who had already been thinking along the same lines but thought that Stevens could put the idea into action.

So it was that in January of 1943 the imperious vice president of engineering at Willys, Barney Roos, was instructed to summon Stevens for a consultation. Stevens was thrilled to have his first chance to design a car for mass production. He immediately drove to Chicago and took the

sleeping train to Toledo, Ohio, where he arrived for his 11 a.m. appointment, only to be left waiting nervously in the lobby. At lunchtime Roos strolled past him without a word. Finally, toward the end of the day, Stevens was called up to a fifty-foot-deep office on the fourth floor and was allowed to present his ideas. Roos heard him out and then gruffly informed him that he would be hired to style a line of postwar autos for Willys. Stevens returned to Milwaukee elated and immediately commenced work.[3]

Strangely the sedan that soon emerged looked very little like a Jeep. Probably with encouragement from the company's swashbuckling president, Joe Frazer, Stevens and his design staff took the prewar Willys sedan as their starting point. Though their creation was relatively plain and utilized a standard Jeep engine, the car called for an entirely new chassis and body tooling to create the rounded curves that Stevens and Frazer thought were needed to make the car sell. By 1944 they had designed and built three prototypes under the names 6/66, 6/70, and 6/71, all meant for the 1947 model year. Stevens turned to his onetime role model Count Alexis de Sakhnoffsky for assistance with the project. Though the extent of the collaboration is unknown, one might detect the Sakhnoffsky touch in the lines of the car, particularly its distinctive sloped rear quarter. The prototypes were outfitted with six-cylinder Willys engines and, unlike the military Jeeps, had sprung suspensions on all four wheels.[4]

Willys-Overland Jeep Station Wagon 1946 (upper)
6/70 Sedan 1946 (lower)

Despite the virtues of the prospective Willys sedans, they were abruptly canceled due to a change in leadership at the company. Frazer had a bitter falling out with the chairman, Ward Canaday, and was replaced by Charles Sorenson. Nicknamed "Cast Iron Charlie," Sorenson was a manufacturer rather than a salesman, as prosaic as his predecessor had been flashy. He thought that the sedans were a terrible idea—insufficiently connected with the wartime Jeep and unrealistic in their new tooling requirements. He favored a more conservative approach that would preserve the utilitarian character of the Jeep. He was also intent on performing the transformation on the cheap. His solution was to acquire an appliance manufactory and give Stevens the near-impossible assignment of restyling the Jeep using metal stamping equipment that had originally been intended for manufacturing washing machines. The presses had a maximum draw of six inches, which naturally made the expressively curved sedans, or any other streamlined automobile, out of the question.

When Sorenson broke the news to Stevens, the designer was in Toledo on a one-day consultation visit. Asked how long he could stay, Stevens answered, "Mr. Sorenson, I can stay until spring if necessary." As it turned out, he stayed only three days. For the first and only time in his career, he produced the color renderings for a vehicle by himself. The solution he presented to Roos, Sorensen, and Canaday was as simple as it was brilliant. Instead of a passenger car, he drew a station wagon. This was doubly unexpected, because the paneled wooden sides of older station wagons made them an expensive class of auto. They were suburban leisure vehicles, used by groups of well-to-do motorists for touring country estates or club grounds. Stevens's car, however, was unlike any station wagon ever seen. Though it had a two-tone pattern on its flanks that evoked the "woodies" of the prewar period, it was made entirely of steel. Its boxy lines made a virtue out of the limitations imposed by Sorenson's washing-machine presses, communicating the solidity of the military Jeep rather than the aristocratic luxury of a prewar station wagon. It also had only two doors instead of the conventional four, because Stevens felt that this was safer for a family car. (One of his nieces had once fallen out of the rear door of a station wagon, and though she was unhurt, Stevens took the lesson to heart.)

Willys-Overland's staff designers Art Kibiger and Robert Andrews eventually developed the Model 463 Jeep Station Wagon from Stevens's original concept.[5] The final result was pioneering in functional as well as visual terms. Despite the short 104-inch wheelbase inherited from the military Jeep chassis, there was a full hundred cubic feet of storage in the rear of the car, permitting its use as a load-bearing vehicle. In essence, Stevens had invented the sport utility vehicle— a car that performed equally well for family outings and moving furniture. The formula proved so successful that the station wagon was immediately recast as an all-purpose family car for the American middle class. By 1949 Plymouth had come out with its own all-steel wagon, to be followed by Ford and Chevrolet in the next few years; nonetheless, in 1950 Stevens was still able to claim that seven out of ten station wagons sold in America were Jeeps.[6] The 463 was manufactured for a total of sixteen years with minimal exterior design alteration, until it was finally displaced in 1962 by the Jeep Wagoneer, another Brooks Stevens design, which in turn stayed in production until 1991. The Jeep Station Wagon was also the basis for a "Station Sedan" (which came in more eye-catching colors, had a more powerful engine, and improved interior appointments), a commercial version called the Panel Delivery Wagon, and a series of pickup trucks.

Not content with his success with the Jeep Station Wagon, Stevens continued to push the executives at Willys to follow through on Joe Frazer's plan to manufacture a stylish postwar passenger car based on the Jeep. The company finally relented, once again putting strict limitations on new tooling for the vehicle. The name "Jeepster" (reportedly a coinage of Frazer's) was chosen, and Stevens once again set to work, using the chassis and front body of the Jeep Station Wagon as a base. He turned to classic prewar cars for inspiration.[7] This time he was on the more familiar turf of the stylish sports car, and the body type he chose was one only an enthusiast would have considered: the phaeton. There was no such car on the market in the 1940s, and for good reason. A phaeton is simply a roadster with four seats rather than two; in the prewar period the back seats had been for the car's owners, the front for a chauffeur. It has an open top, and like a roadster, is meant for driving at thrillingly high speeds. In other words, a phaeton is a thoroughly

impractical car. The Jeepster could function only as a second, "fair weather" vehicle; it had no hard top at all, and no side windows. In case of rain the driver's only recourse was a set of curtains. A further strike against the Jeepster came as a result of poor judgment on the part of Willys-Overland. At $1,886 (a figure that Stevens considered "steep") and powered by a comparatively weak four-cylinder L-head engine, it was both overpriced and underpowered. Sales were strong in 1948, its first year of release, when slightly more than ten thousand Jeepsters were built. Thereafter market reception dropped off precipitously, despite the introduction of an optional six-cylinder engine in 1949.

Yet for all its faults, the Jeepster was a wonderfully jaunty design. Fully intending it to "capture the fancy of the youth of this country, as well as the adult," Stevens called for it to be painted in bright primary colors and embellished the car with distinctive touches.[8] He and his codesigners at Willys, Delmar Roos and chief body engineer E.C. De Smet, superimposed a chrome T atop the iconic vertically slotted Jeep grille. (The grille was altered for the 1950 model year, and the new version was retained on the Jeep-based vehicles Stevens would later design for Willys do Brasil.) Boldly angled box-shaped fenders reused from Stevens's Jeep pickup truck framed the rear wheels. Relatively light at twenty-five hundred pounds and equipped with separate springing on the front wheels, the car was unusually agile and provided a firm ride meant to appeal to driving enthusiasts. The total package amounted to a quixotic anachronism. Though it was the last true "touring auto" built in America, it was also prescient in its appeal to a youth demographic. Willys's advertising for the car suggested that it was aimed at young buyers who might treat

Willys-Overland Jeepster phaeton 1948
Jeepster advertisement 1948

a car as an accessory rather than a necessity. Of course, this exact combination of affluence and indulgence would become a central feature of America's teen-oriented popular culture during the mid-1950s, but by that time it was too late. Production of the Jeepster had ceased in 1951. The car became immediately collectible, however, and in 1967 Kaiser Motors issued a new Jeepster that emulated the look of the original, proving that Stevens's phaeton was not only stubbornly behind the times but also ahead of them.[9]

1. Brooks Stevens, "Your Victory Car," *Popular Mechanics*, December 1942, 82–85, 162; see also "Postwar Panorama," *Goodwill Journal* 16 (September–October 1944): Joseph Geschelin, "Cars of the Future, Part One," *Automotive and Aviation Industries* 87 (1 September 1942): 26–27; "No Blackout of Thinking," *American Automobile* 19 (December 1942): 5–8, 19. The first version of the "Victory Car" talk may have been delivered at the Wustum Museum in Racine, where a selection of designs by Stevens's firm was on view. See "Post-War Prophecies Made by Industrial Designer," *Racine Journal-Times*, 25 June 1942.

2. The story of how Willys carried out this lucrative business is a complex one. Briefly, the Jeep was originally designed in 1940 by Karl Probst for another independent, American Bantam. Once the design was identified as the workhorse for the U.S. Army, however, it became clear that Bantam lacked the production capacity to supply the requisite number of vehicles. Willys managed to win the contract instead. During the war it in turn contracted Ford to build almost three hundred thousand of the vehicles but retained the exclusive licensing rights to the name and format of the Jeep.

3. This is the canonical version of events leading to Stevens's contract with Willys-Overland and the version that Stevens himself told and retold in later life. In some details, however, the narrative is in conflict with an unpublished early business history. According to this manuscript, Stevens had approached Willys in about 1940 or 1941 in the hopes of acting as a consultant; it was at this point that he had his frustrating experience with Roos, after which he returned to Milwaukee and received a commission to design of a postwar line of passenger cars. The sudden opportunity to build Jeeps for the army intruded, however, and Stevens's contract was canceled. Following the publication of "The Practical Postwar Car," however, Joseph Frazer contacted Stevens directly, asked that he come to Toledo for consultation, and then rehired him. In this account, Stevens's work for the firm did not begin in earnest until 1944 ("Business History of Brooks Stevens Associates," unpublished manuscript, ca. 1949, Brooks Stevens Archive, Milwaukee Art Museum).

4. "I.F.S. [Independent Front-Wheel Suspension] for the Jeep," *Motor*, 15 January 1947, 563.

5. Robert Andrews has challenged Stevens's authorship of the station wagon, but it is clear that Stevens was responsible for the overall concept if not the detailed execution of the vehicle. See William Porter, "Toledo Wheels: The Design Story of Willys-Overland, The Jeep, and the Rise of the SUV," in *The Alliance of Art and Industry: Toledo Designs for a Modern America* (Toledo: Toledo Museum of Art; New York: Hudson Hills Press, 2002), 109–27.

6. Brooks Stevens Associates, "Industrial Design . . . and How It Creates Business," promotional brochure, ca. 1949, Brooks Stevens Archive.

7. At this time Stevens wrote a paper entitled "Future Body Styling in Retrospect," which argued for mining the cars of the past for new ideas. See "Is This The Year of the American Revolution?" *Autocar*, 6 January 1950.

8. Gertrude M. Puelicher, "Brookington Limited," *Exclusively Yours*, April 1955, 12, 14, 26.

9. For more on the Jeepster, see Patrick R. Foster, "The Sport's Car," *Automobile Quarterly* 35 (March 1996): 6–17. The author would like to express gratitude to James Lee for his research on Willys-Overland. For other accounts of Stevens's work for the company, see Richard M. Langworth, *Kaiser-Frazer: The Last Onslaught on Detroit* (Kutztown, Pa.: Automobile Quarterly Publications, 1975); Robert Ackerson, *Jeep: The Fifty-Year History* (Newbury Park, Calif.: Haynes Publications, 1988); Patrick R. Foster, *The Story of Jeep* (Iola, Wis.: Krause Publications, 1998); and Peter Sessler, *Jeep Prototypes and Concept Vehicles* (Hudson, Wis.: Iconographix, 2000).

Evinrude Sportwin outboard motor 1947

In 1937 the Outboard Marine and Manufacturing Company (OMC), led by its Evinrude brand, joined forces with Johnson Motors to become the dominant force in outboard motor making. The timing could not have been better for Brooks Stevens, who had just opened his design office. Stevens was a boyhood friend of Ralph Evinrude, the son of the company's founder and the current head of the firm, and it was natural for OMC to become one of Stevens's earliest clients. Over the ensuing decades, the increasingly diversifying company would become the designer's most constant and profitable source of commissions. As OMC acquired and developed new divisions, including Lawn-Boy (outdoor equipment) and Cushman (light electric vehicles, such as golf carts and scooters), Stevens was employed again and again to formulate brand identity and product styling.

Ralph Evinrude's father, Ole (1877–1934), had patented the first outboard motor in 1910. As legend has it, Ole Evinrude was courting his future wife, Bess Cary, and attempted to row across Okauchee Lake with an ice cream cone for his young paramour. The ice cream melted en route, and Evinrude was rudely awakened to the need for a power motor. Prior to the late 1930s the outboards that he and a few competitors manufactured were definitely predesigned objects: contraptions of open mechanical parts and wires with a decidedly nonergonomic pull cord. The color of the motors was neutral silver, and the only graphic embellishment was the name of the manufacturer in block lettering. Eventually Brooks Stevens would change all that, but the work he performed for the company prior to World War II was limited. Although he was able to tailor the aluminum shroud with the aim of unifying its mass and to redesign the decal bearing the company name, he was not able to alter the basic look and color of the motors.

Evinrude Sportwin outboard motor 1947

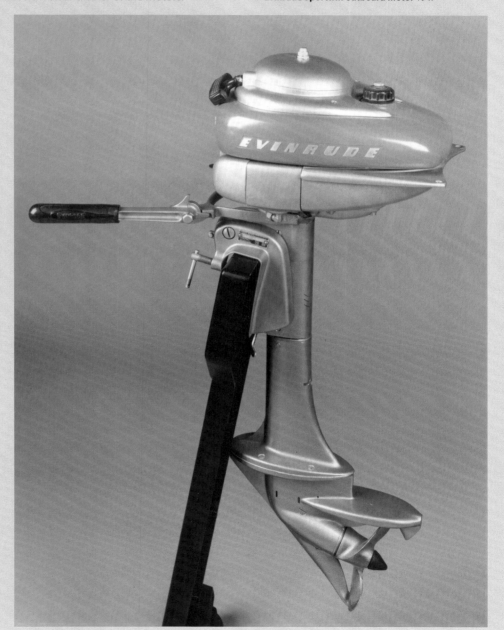

In the wake of the war, Stevens persuaded his client to finance a much more sweeping set of design changes. The design office developed separate identities for each of OMC's divisions (Gale, Johnson, and Evinrude), which had to be carried across a line of motors ranging in size from two to seventy-five horsepower. Soon Stevens's firm settled into a rhythm of annual styling changes, which were usually effected through the rearrangement of paint schemes and decals. These superficial alterations were punctuated by an occasional reshaping of the shroud itself to reflect an internal mechanical change. Each year care was taken to change enough that the new design would seem new, but not so much that the motor would lose its continuity with the previous version. Stevens and his staff were usually given responsibility only for the upper part of the motor, which would be visible above the water line. They did, however, accommodate a variety of technological innovations, including a pushbutton electric start, electric gearshifts, the "V" engine, and rubber linings that reduced noise.[1]

Beginning in the 1940s Stevens introduced a distinctive sea blue color to Evinrude's entire outboard line. Though this choice seems logical enough, it was in fact part of a ploy on the designer's part to appeal to a new sector of the marketplace: women. Prior to World War II outboards had been conceived as a man's accessory, for use when hunting and fishing; color coordination was not a consideration. This changed when the greater size and power, automatic starter and controls, and reduced noise of new motors made them appropriate for family boating and, as Stevens put it, "Mrs. America went into the driver's seat."[2] Like most design theorists and consumer analysts at the time, he operated under the principle that men were interested in mechanics and women were interested in looks. This assumption was, of course, much more widespread than the boating industry; it had an impact in automobiles, architecture, and myriad other areas of design. Penny Sparke has written of this "housewife aesthetic" as the first true domestication of modernism. Products like the Evinrude motor were a curious blend of avant-garde design and older Victorian concepts of elegance and grace—a combination that betrayed participation in age-old stereotypes of female superficiality but that also acknowledged the newfound power of women in the marketplace.[3]

A good example is the Javelin motor that Stevens and his head product designer, Gordon Kelly, designed in 1955, marketed under the Johnson trademark as "the 'Cadillac' of the outboard field."[4] Typically the Johnson outboards were given a conservative overall appearance in an attempt to capture a different market demographic from the stylishly streamlined Evinrudes. The Javelin was an exception to this rule. Though small in comparison to later power motors, it was, at thirty horsepower, the top of the Johnson line of its day. Its "holiday bronze" color was advertised as an ideal accessory to appeal to the female buyer; in Stevens's words, "there is no doubt that women's demands for color to harmonize with both sports clothes and boat interiors have influenced our selection of a reddish-brown metallic tint for 1956. Horsepower and operational advantages are taken for granted by women purchasers. Experience in many industries has shown that design and color are the two major influences on women buyers."[5] Yet the outboard also sported highly polished steel emblems and trim, which were a typical example of Stevens's habit of borrowing from automobile design. The combination, while intended as a blend of feminine and masculine attributes, was actually an object that anyone could find seductive—in the words of one advertisement, "the crest on the family silver, the jewel in your lady's hair. It's *fashion* in outboard boating—HIGH fashion and no mistake!"[6]

The Javelin was the swan song for Stevens's work with on Johnson line; shortly thereafter design of the brand was transferred to his Chicago-based competitor Dave Chapman in order to promote variety within OMC's products. Thanks in large part to Stevens's continuing friendship with Ralph Evinrude, however, his office continued to do all the styling and promotional work on the company's other outboard brands, Gale and Evinrude. Over the years leadership of the crucial account passed from Gordon Kelly to John Bradley, but almost everyone associated with the firm had some part of the work—including graphic designers such as Adrian Bonini, who prepared the decals for the motors, and product designers such as Bill Davidson, who was responsible for the new shapes of the 1958 Evinrude Lark and Starflite motors. The account eventually expanded to include snowmobiles, boats, and even a corporate jet. In the 1960s responsibility for the Johnson brand was returned to Stevens's firm, where it stayed until OMC's sale to the Montreal manufacturer Bombardier in 2001.

Johnson "Javelin" Outboard Motor 1955

1. For an overview of the company's technical developments in the postwar period, see Jeffrey L. Rodengen, *Evinrude, Johnson, and the Legend of OMC* (Fort Lauderdale: Write Stuff Syndicate, 1993).

2. "Runabout Aided by Two Pontoons," *New York Times*, 19 January 1960.

3. Penny Sparke, *As Long as It's Pink: The Sexual Politics of Taste* (London and San Francisco: Pandora, 1995).

4. Johnson Motors, advertising booklet, ca. 1955, Brooks Stevens Archive, Milwaukee Art Museum.

5. "Outboards Parade Color," *Milwaukee Sentinel*, 16 September 1955.

6. "1956 Johnson Outboard Debut," *Boston Evening Globe*, 7 September 1955; advertisement in *Field and Stream*, October 1955.

McCulloch Aviation plant 1947

One of the curiously underrated expressions of twentieth-century modernism is factory architecture. Early avant-garde architects such as Le Corbusier and Walter Gropius were entranced by vernacular industrial spaces, with their no-nonsense efficiency, repetitive forms, and broad, uninterrupted floor plans; the International Style in general was both influenced by and expressed in factory architecture.[1] Given Stevens's own architectural training, and his awareness of the nearby Johnson Wax plant by Frank Lloyd Wright, it was inevitable that he too would explore factory design. In this effort he was ably assisted by James Floria, an architect who had joined his design firm as a partner in 1944. An opportunity arose just after World War II when

the McCulloch Corporation, a Wisconsin manufacturer specializing in motors, announced its plans to move its aviation division to California following World War II. Stevens was friendly with Robert McCulloch and Sherwood Egbert, the corporation's president and vice president, respectively, and was hired to create a new facility in Inglewood, near the site of the Los Angeles airport.

Working in collaboration with a Los Angeles architectural firm, Stevens's staff designed an administration building, down to office layouts and custom furniture. They also consulted on the layout of the factory building on the site. The motif of an airplane wing was carried throughout the facility, notably in the canopy of the administration building's facade and in an enormous, irregularly shaped reception desk. As Wright had done in the Johnson Wax plant, Stevens and Floria departed from the International Style norm of factory design and instead created a vaulted interior space. Stevens later wrote that the building "[provided] shelter and ingenuity, which could never be matched by the simple transparency of glass walls revealing grinding machinery within."[2] Completed in 1947, the McCulloch plant accommodated one thousand workers and was capable of producing more than one aircraft engine per minute.[3] It was arguably the most striking example of an industrial building that Stevens's office produced, but it was only the first in a series. In the 1950s the

McCulloch Aviation plant 1947
Square D manufacturing plant 1959

firm went on to design factories for Miller Brewing, Square D, Power Products, and Kearney and Trecker, in each case working with a local architect on the project. Most of these later designs hewed more closely to the established International Style and were typically furnished with Knoll or Herman Miller furniture.[4] Stevens also continued to work with McCulloch, executing an engine supercharger for the company in 1946. This design led to an automobile prototype called the Paxton, which was intended to employ steam power (though this did not in fact transpire) and an experimental body made entirely of fiberglass.[5]

Interior view of the McCulloch Aviation plant 1947

Reception desk for the McCulloch Aviation plant 1947

1. See Spiro Kostof, *America by Design* (New York: Oxford University Press, 1987); Lindy Biggs, *The Rational Factory: Architecture, Technology, and Work in America's Age of Mass Production* (Baltimore: Johns Hopkins University Press, 1996); and Betsy H. Bradley, *The Works: The Industrial Architecture of the United States* (New York: Oxford University Press, 1999). The author thanks Anna Andrzejewski for these references.

2. Brooks Stevens, "Factories Also Have Faces," *Industrial Design* 8 (April 1961): 12.

3. "McCulloch Firm Begins Mass Engine Output at Los Angeles," *Milwaukee Sentinel*, 7 January 1947.

4. "Begin Construction on New Square D Addition," *Milwaukee Commerce*, 24 May 1956, 4; "Built for the Coming Boom," *Factory* 117 (May 1959): 108–11; "Cite Square D's Glendale Facility," *Milwaukee Sentinel*, 1 May 1959; James D. Floria, designer's notes on the Square D Good Hope Road Plant, 26 May 1959, Brooks Stevens Archive, Milwaukee Art Museum. The Square D plant was later used by the lock division of Briggs and Stratton.

5. McCulloch experimented with the Paxton between 1951 and 1954; working with Stevens were engineers James L. Dooley and Allan F. Bell. See Joseph Lowrey, "The Steam Revival," *Automobile Quarterly* 2 (summer 1963): 130–39. According to Stevens, the Paxton's bumpers were made of chrome-plated fiberglass, which was a first.

Olympian Hiawatha train for the Chicago, Milwaukee, St. Paul and Pacific Railroad 1947

The greatest single achievement of Brooks Stevens's career was the Olympian Hiawatha train for the Chicago, Milwaukee, St. Paul and Pacific Railroad—popularly known as the Milwaukee Road. It was one of the celebrated "streamliner" trains that streaked across America's railroad tracks in the mid-twentieth century—a few of which had been styled by two of the country's top designers, Henry Dreyfuss and Raymond Loewy.[1] Dreyfuss's Twentieth Century Limited, designed in 1938, was virtually unchallenged as the symbol of prewar industrial design. Not only did it culminate in an iconic, powerful locomotive, but the entire train was tailored to Dreyfuss's exacting specifications, from table linens and waiter's uniforms to ticket stubs. Outside of a World's Fair exhibit, it was the only chance most Americans had of experiencing a total industrial design environment.

Stevens's opportunity to match Dreyfuss's once-in-a-lifetime achievement came in 1945, when he was contacted by the Milwaukee Road's chief mechanical officer, Karl Fritjof Nystrom, to consult on the production of a new set of trains. The railroad had been operating equipment under the Hiawatha name since 1935 and had also introduced an Olympian train with streamlined coaches and dining cars before the war. The new Olympian Hiawatha train for 1947 was to be a complete Speedliner, with an integrated streamlined design; a year later a similar treatment was also applied to the Hiawathas that ran between Chicago and Minneapolis. Stevens and

Nystrom were both interested in using a novel approach to the construction of the train: curved plywood with an exterior laminate of aluminum. Once fabricated, these panels could be fitted together to form the sides and roof of the train cars, arcing all the way from the ridgeline to the bottom of the skirt. Unfortunately this approach was scrapped after a good deal of research because of concerns about cost, and the team resorted to conventional steel construction.

Though Stevens and Nystrom took the leading role in developing the concept of the train, the entire staff at Brooks Stevens Associates assisted in preparing the plans—from Anthony Reed, who provided engineering analysis, to Stevens's personal secretary, Betty Meyer, who contributed to the interior treatment of the women's lounge. The designs were finally completed by November of 1946, specifying every particular—from the exterior styling to such interior details as lighting fixtures, furnishings and wall treatments. Instead of emphasizing the surging locomotive, as Dreyfuss and Loewy had done in their earlier trains, Stevens saved his grand gesture for the rear of the streamliner. The Milwaukee Road's Hiawathas had always had enclosed solarium "Beaver Tail" observation cars, and he did this idea one better. The "Skytop" observation car that punctuated his Hiawatha was an open cage of glass—"as close to the prophetic plastic domed futuristic renderings of cars of the future as possible," Stevens said, while remaining "within practical boundaries of manufacture and service."[2] Because curved safety glass was not yet a reality, the open-air effect was achieved through a multitude of flat glass panels set between steel mullions; two thicker beams curved down toward the end of the train to provide structural integrity in case of a rear-end collision.

Olympian Hiawatha train 1947

Ten Sky Top cars were built in total: four Lounge cars for daytime Hiawatha routes, and six Skytop sleeping cars for the Olympian Hiawatha trains that made the long trip to the West Coast. The Skytop Lounge cars were divided into a seating area and a parlor, with custom swivel chairs and chrome tables—making for an interior swank enough that Frank Sinatra reportedly used the car as his entourage's accommodation suite when he traveled through the Midwest. The Skytop sleeping car was built by Pullman-Standard and had a larger glass-enclosed area, along with eight bedrooms.

The proposed exterior styling was marvelously synthetic, with a paint scheme (in the railway's traditional orange and maroon colors) that both reflected the use of space on the interior and tied the train cars together into a unified graphic design. Maroon frames embraced the rows of windows, with the rear of each car identified by a porthole or oval aperture and an angled panel in maroon that interlocked with the pattern on the next car in line.[3] Stevens went so far as to have his design painted on the side of an old Hiawatha car in an attempt to persuade his client to use it. In the end, however, the trains received a conservative solid band of maroon instead, with the 1947 Olympian Hiawathas sporting a "broken" stripe around the windows and

the 1948 trains a continuous stripe down the length of each car.[4] The Fairbanks-Morse six-thousand-horsepower diesel locomotive that pulled the Olympian Hiawatha lacked the grandeur of the faceted rear, but its ribbed stainless steel front panel and bright orange paint job still projected an image of speed and power. Behind it rolled between ten and sixteen cars, depending on the route, including a baggage car with conductor's offices; day coaches with reclining seats, adjustable foot rests, and smoking rooms; club cars, called "Tip Top Taps"; sleeping cars with unfolding bunks; dining cars with full kitchens; reserved-seat parlor cars with drawing rooms; and the Sky Top Lounge.[5]

The interiors of the cars were enlivened by a variety of amenities, including full carpeting, universal air conditioning, custom seating with two-tone upholstery, live plants, and walls decorated with patterned Formica. The latter choice, quite ahead of its time in the use of plastic laminate, was motivated by Nystrom's demand for durable materials. Stevens explained that "maintenance and long life in first class condition [were] the controlling factor in material choices, color schemes, and the like. There have been interesting trains produced in the past, which, on their maiden voyages looked most attractive and intriguing, but after very little use became shabby and shopworn, all of which became a continual detraction from the initial effect."[6] Formica was used to greatest effect in the men's and women's washrooms, which were planned according to strictly gendered sensibilities. While the men's room had overstuffed leather chairs and wood-grain decoration, the ladies' lounge had a divan and French prints reproduced in Formica set into green and ivory walls.

Most of the train's sleeping cars were standard-issue Pullmans, which precluded such niceties, but special "Touralux" sleeping cars were custom built at the Milwaukee Road's local shops with an upper berth that swung down from the bulkhead. The furnishing of the club car was similarly inventive, with angled tables that created "unregimented seating" for varying numbers of diners.[7] "I had been riding the Twentieth Century Limited and top trains in the country already for some years," Stevens later said, "and felt that the most ridiculous situation was to walk into the club car in the Century with one row of chairs on one side and one on the other side facing each other…wondering whether to speak or not. [It] made an uncomfortable sort of seat arrangement, and we felt that a lounge car should take on the look of a club room or a night club or a café."[8]

Sky Top Lounge interior 1947
Sky Top Lounge exterior 1947

The Olympian Hiawatha entered service on June 29, 1947. Six complete train sets were required to maintain everyday operation of the route between Chicago and Seattle—a forty-five-hour trip. In 1952 the equipment was updated with "Super Dome" cars, which had overhead skylights running the entire length of the train. Stevens had no direct hand in this change, though he foresaw a similar treatment in his original proposal, which called for continuing bands of windows from the Sky Top Lounge forward along the coves of the roof. This improvement marked the last hurrah for the midwestern luxury train. The Olympian Hiawathas officially ended service on May 22, 1961, and though some of the individual cars were in use until Amtrak took over the route in 1971, many were sold to the Canadian National Railway or were demolished. The long rail trip to Seattle was a thing of the past. In 1973 Stevens reflected grimly on the deterioration of train travel during his lifetime: "I almost fainted a couple of years ago when … I took the Hiawatha to Chicago and I went into the lounge and diner. In the lounge, I found that all the carpeting was gone and in its place there was corrugated tile on the floor or some such thing. I went into the dining car, which I had once thought of as one of the handsomest diners in the business, and now there was a cafeteria

Observation car interior 1947

lined up on one side, and you walked down and took old plastic-appearing lemon pie slices off some shelf . . . and you drank milk out of cartons. I went home by car."[9]

Even so, this was not the end of the story. Several Sky Top cars also survive, many painted yellow from a stint of usage in the Canadian National. Stevens's eldest son, David, surprised his father in January of 1972 by purchasing one of the Sky Top lounge cars—the "Cedar Rapids"—before it was destroyed. It survives in excellent condition today and is used as a mobile classroom to teach visitors about the history of the midwestern railroads.[10]

1. Angela Schonberger, *Raymond Loewy: Pioneer of Industrial Design* (Munich: Prestel, 1990), 76–80.

2. Brooks Stevens, "Design Commissions Prewar and Postwar" (designer's notes), 11 October 1991, Brooks Stevens Archive, Milwaukee Art Museum.

3. "New Trains to Set Pace for Railroad," *Milwaukee Journal* 10 November 1946.

4. Brooks Stevens, "Styling the Hiawatha," lecture, 18 May 1973; reprinted in *The Milwaukee Railroader*, third quarter 1997, 4–22. The author thanks Robert G. Donnelley and Anne Woodhouse for this reference.

5. "The Milwaukee 'Hiawathas' for 1948," *Railway Age*, 14 August 1948, 54–57.

6. Brooks Stevens, designer's notes on the Olympian Hiawatha, 1947, Brooks Stevens Archive, Milwaukee Art Museum.

7. Cedric Adams, "In This Corner," *Minneapolis Star*, 12 March 1948, 42.

8. Stevens, "Styling the Hiawatha," 11.

9. Stevens, "Styling the Hiawatha," 13. Milwaukee Road authority and former employee Jim Scribbins notes that Stevens may have been exaggerating for effect here: "We used carpeting only in dining, parlor, and sleeping cars; lounge (and other) cars always used tile flooring. The cafeteria cars enabled us to hold the line on food prices. Food quality remained high. Mr. Stevens should have received a glass into which he could pour his milk. A failure on the part of the waiter?"

10. For a general history of the Milwaukee Road, see Jim Scribbins's books on the subject: *The Hiawatha Story* (Milwaukee: Kalmbach Books, 1970); *The Milwaukee Road Remembered* (Waukesha, Wis.: Kalmbach Books, 1990); *The Milwaukee Road in Its Hometown* (Waukesha, Wis.: Kalmbach Books, 1998); and *The Milwaukee Road, 1928–1985* (Forest Park, Ill.: Heimburger House, 2001). The author thanks Mr. Scribbins for his many helpful suggestions and corrections to this account of Stevens's trains for the Milwaukee Road.

The Industrial Designer's Approach to Passenger Car Styling (1950)

It is indeed a pleasure to be invited here this evening to meet with you in your fine city to bring you a message on Industrial Design as it applies to your particular field, what the profession embraces generally, and to dispel the impression of the industrial designer as one who merely creates pictures. I will point out that this profession has really earned its way over a long period of time. Historically we have always had industrial designers, even though they were not known as such. Going back to the Civil War period, replicas of Gothic church windows in locomotive cabs, gold striping, brass trim, and even oil-painted murals of landscapes on the sides of locomotive cabs, were aesthetic touches added by the artist engineer of that time. Coaches were equally festooned, including stained glass windows and highly ornate interiors. "Plush," "pleated," and "brass-plated" were the words of the day for parlor car luxury….

The industrial designer does not like to be referred to singularly as an artist. That implies merely the superficial execution of an illusion of how some situation ought to be. His definite interest centers around the improvement of the product from the sales and eye-appeal standpoint. He does not presume upon engineering, but through his exposure of the problem he has been known to make definite contributions of function. His goals are good appearance, definite economy of production, if possible, and in many instances, through the proper simplification of the product in concept and styling, this reduction in cost can be the result. The industrial designer must live closely with the client's own staff and they must co-operate with him completely. The feeling of initial resentment must be cast aside and they must weld themselves into a team so that in the end there will be a satisfactory result desirable to the general public. It must be remembered at this point that we are always dealing with the same consumer—the individual who buys the automobile, who rides on the railroad train, purchases domestic appliances, or utilizes amusement facilities….

In the general architecture of the railroad train as a whole, and the railroad passenger car individually, the designer must deal with a rather inflexible set of dimensions and proportions. The railroad car is long and narrow, mounted relatively high on swivel trucks, and must contend with the necessary gap in coupling cars together in a train. The cross-sectional contours cannot be deviated from often, and must maintain definite and general similarity with older equipment so as not to obsolete cars ten or twenty years old which are still serviceable. It is naturally the designer's dream, in the creation of a new train, to give it a theme, design it as a unit, and have it remain intact during its service. I hardly need to mention the fact, however, that unavoidable situations occur in railroading today, demanding the occasional use of older equipment in emergencies, and suffice to say that this causes an aesthetic jolt in many of our up-to-date trains.

In discussing the limitations of the exterior design as it pertains to eye-appeal or passenger appeal, the designer can work with the surface styling of the outer skin with the use of corrugated sections, stainless steel, applied trim, skirt contours, window spacings and shapes, and colors. The more modern trains today have fallen roughly into two categories—namely, the bright, stainless steel treatment, fluted or otherwise, and the painted steel car. One manufacturer has practically established a trademark with the use of fluted stainless side walls. In the painted steel versions, we have fallen into a logical but rather stereotyped pattern of horizontal bands of color beginning with the traditional letterboard and varying in width and proportion over the rest of the surface. Most of the top trains in the country are now following the general pattern of horizontal stripes running through the windows and letterboard, leaving only a color scheme for individual identity.

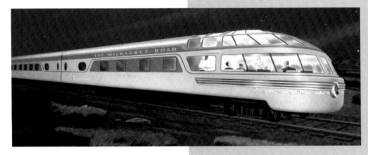

I feel that infinitely more individual identity and passenger appeal can be injected into the railroad car paint styling today. In the design of the new Olympian Hiawatha train for the C. M. St. P. & P. RR., we have injected a "new look" in paint styling. We have departed from the traditional horizontal bands, and in working with the colors of The Milwaukee Road—Harvest Orange and Royal Maroon—we have created individual identity that has become recognizable on the spot as the trademark of the Olympian Hiawathas. The principle of the paint scheme is based on the fact that it tells the story of the interior, architecturally, or the car. The average car is broken up into three areas: the large central areas, being the passenger area, with coach seats, sleeping sections in the Touralux car, and roomettes [and] bedrooms. The areas at each end are generally allocated to men's and women's lounges, and passageways from vestibules to the central passenger area. The window pattern area has been changed between the passenger area and what may be referred to as the "utility" area. Rectangular windows were used in the passenger area, contrasting with portholes and elongated portholes in the vestibules and lounge rooms. The maroon horizontal panel embracing the main central passenger area is thereby divorced from the two end areas, which remain in the overall orange field. A wide trim stripe, beginning under the portholes in the utility area, rises upward and over the central maroon panel, to return down again and carry under the portholes of the opposite end utility area. With two cars butting together at the vestibules, we find an obvious continuous pattern of portholes or utility type windows joining visually together, as well as the joining of the trim stripe. This combining of similar porthole patterns minimized the necessary joint between the cars, making the surface appear more continuous. The reoccurrence of this pattern from car to car in a long train relieves the monotony of the already exaggerated continuous length of a group of cars, and in turn, we have a strong individual pattern entirely original with this new train. At each vestibule door a large aluminum and maroon emblem is employed carrying out the symbolic figure of Hiawatha.

All the roofs of the equipment are painted in a dark sandy gray to offer the least possible change in appearance from dirt and weathering. The trucks and entire underbody are painted in a dull shadow black to minimize its irregularity, which would normally detract from the sleekness of the upper car body. Deep superfluous sheet metal skirting has been eliminated from these cars entirely in favor of maintenance, continuous good appearance, and to eliminate the unnecessary carrying of tons of ice and snow during the winter months. To carry on with the limitations necessarily placed upon the designer, it is almost needless to point out that car costs must be held within reason.

Many things, interesting and unique to the public, could be done with "carte blanche" or unlimited initial expense.

Safety must certainly come into the industrial designer's approach to the problem. His goal is to intrigue and please the passenger with the equipment, but it should not be at the expense of their safety and well-being. Many dangers lurk in the more aesthetic ways of styling lounge cars, diners, and even coaches. With the high speeds of today, we have sway despite our great improvements in riding qualities and suspension design. People may still be thrown against bulkheads, partitions, and furniture. One must be tremendously careful with the use of glass, sharp-cornered appendages, doorways, and the like. It is on important matters such as this that the designer depends heavily upon the experience and knowledge of the operating departments and the car builder's engineers….

Last but not least, in the limitation picture, we have tradition—something which I shall call "train-dition" (precedent adherence). There is a definite leaning toward approaching the new car design problem from the standpoint of materials, methods, and even shapes, with which there has been a long record of tried and proven experience and a definite desire to hold on to, to do it that way again—but just to change the color. This borders a little bit on Mr. Henry Ford's famous declaration in the days of the model T, "Gentlemen, you can have any color you want as long as it's black."

An interesting and stimulating battle is going on between tradition, convention, and the "new look." We find definite passenger acceptance to much of our good-looking equipment of today. In general, there is some flexibility in the plan of each car, based, of course, first on maximum payload with maximum comfort. The passenger today is not going to be satisfied with drab, monotonous, pure mechanical interiors that represent the zenith in fabric simplification and maintenance ease. The dark, glossy woods of the past, with a shiny layer of varnish, drab plush fabrics, and "busy" flowered rug patterns, have given way to a greater use of color, woven patterned fabrics, simplified pattern carpeting, rubber tiles, linoleums, and individuality in color schemes between cars. Lounge areas for women can take on an individualized, feminine appearance, or check the powder room atmosphere, and for the man, the den-like masculinity of the club with red leather chairs.

Railroad car equipment today can borrow, in a sense, from two other sources appealing to the passenger—the home, and some of the brilliant styling of the motor car. A cross between these can be cleverly woven into the scheme so that the warmth and cheerfulness of the home, coupled with a dash of our most popular means of transportation, can combine to be both practical and attractive. The occasional use of carefully selected pictorial subjects for lounge room areas, as well as passageways and bulkheads, can brighten any interior….

The tendency for regimentation of seating is functionally required in the coach of today, but there are possibilities for breaking the monotony of the long, narrow room with wall treatments, window spacings and shapes, and even color schemes of certain groups of seats. The latitude in wall coverings is expanding tremendously with the introduction of low-maintenance, synthetic materials of the decorative Formica types, as well as impregnated cloths, vinyl leather simulations, and many types of floor coverings. I personally do not believe in the use of high-gloss, hard-surfaced, enamel panels, or plastics, studded with stainless decorative moldings over every seam and joint. Despite the chances to use warm colors, these interiors are apt to become cold and kitchen-like in their appearance. Wood grains in the blond finishes can go a long way toward softening this effect and increasing their homelike character, but the use of genuine wood with lacquered or varnished surfaces is obviously subject to brutal wear and tear. Melamine laminates can be obtained in a tremendous variety of wood grains and patterns which have the surface toughness to withstand hob-nailed boots, metal cornered suitcases, and other damaging forces….

In lounge and club cars today there is tremendous opportunity for individual styling. Seating need not be regimented with chairs lined up on both sides of an aisle, but can be arranged in the smartest restaurant and nightclub groupings, with changes in fabric and color schemes, so planned as to offer privacy, different sized groupings, and even improved scenery appreciation. The use of living plants and hardy, green foliage can go a long way toward styling and softening the interiors of observation and club cars. Edge-lighted plastics, decorative lighting, colorful and cheerful patterns in fabric, and interesting architectural treatments can make the lounge car a great part of the answer to the threat of high-speed air transport….

Observation cars can be treated in very much the same manner as a club car, but with an even greater emphasis on vision. The new solar lounge for the Olympian Hiawathas and the Twin Cities Hiawathas features one solution to this problem with its aerodynamically contoured safety glass dome, all built into single-level contours of the conventional car, offering 180-degree panoramic vision in the horizontal plane to the rear, and 180-degree in the vertical plane, with sufficient structural strength to combat roll-over and rear-end collision. The use of heat and glare-resistant glass will minimize the conditions in bright weather and offer the maximum visibility for an appreciation of the countryside….

Railroad travel should be made as interesting and pleasant as possible at the lowest possible cost. If the surroundings are pleasant, the service and facilities good, there should be a proportionate share of allegiance and attendance on the part of the public who would choose this pleasant means of relaxation as compared to high-speed air transport. Railroad equipment is sizable, expensive, and must be used profitably over a long period. It should not be freakish in design, and should not involve momentary fads and trends in its execution because of the obsolescence problem.

Excerpted from Brooks Stevens, "The Industrial Designer's Approach to Passenger Car Styling," lecture to the Canadian Railway Club, 1950.

Wheary Streamguard luggage 1947

Most of Stevens's designs were literally industrial, in the sense that they were destined to be mass-produced. An exception to this rule was the luggage that he styled for the Wheary Company of Racine, which was constructed using traditional leatherworking techniques. Four lines (called, in ascending order of quality, Standard, Side Saddle, Grill-guard, and Streamguard) were designed, each with a slightly different composition of metal guards and leather patterning. Stevens also redesigned the interior fixtures and linings of each line and created a special oversize storage bag for holding bell-shaped "New Look" dresses in the fashionable Christian Dior idiom. In the set of deluxe Streamguard luggage shown here, the precision imparted by the designer makes for an interesting contrast with the varied color and texture of the calfskin. Handles of cast Lucite and metal—etched with the name of the company—stand out especially well against the luxurious old-world feel of the leather. Stevens was friendly with company president George Wheary, and eventually he became sufficiently integrated with the firm that he was placed on its board of directors.[1]

1. "Brooks Stevens on Wheary Board," *Milwaukee Sentinel*, 5 April 1950.

Wheary Streamguard luggage 1947

Workman sewing luggage

Wheary Advertisement Photograph

Harley Davidson Hydra-Glide motorcycle 1949

In retrospect the pairing of Brooks Stevens and Harley-Davidson seems inevitable: Milwaukee's great industrial designer and the city's greatest industrial design product. Yet only once in Stevens's long career was he consulted in the styling of a motorcycle for the company. His first contact with Harley had been in 1947, when he designed a new nameplate or tank badge for the entire line of motorcycles. Shaped to suggest a stylized streamer blowing back in the breeze, the accessory contributed in a small way to the sense of forward movement in the overall design. Through this experience Stevens came to know William Davidson, the head of styling at the motorcycle company. The relationship was close enough that in the late 1950s Davidson sent his son to cut his teeth as a product designer in Stevens's office. After a few years of working on outboard motors and the like, the younger Davidson returned to the family business and became known to the world as "Willie G"—one of the most prominent figures in the history of motorcycle design.[1]

More important to Stevens, however, was a commission to assist in the development of Harley-Davidson's 1949 Hydra-Glide motorcycle. As is often the case with auto design, the authorship of the bike's various elements is difficult to establish with absolute certainty. On the basis of Stevens's own later testimony, it seems that his contributions were clustered toward the front of the bike. The front fork is completely enclosed, with telescoping hydraulic cylinders that both provide and visually dramatize the suspension of the front wheel. The headlight is sunk into a solid mount in the top of the fork to create a unified mass on the front of the motorcycle—an effect that is enhanced from the rider's viewpoint by an oversize single-dial instrument panel that suggests the controls on an airplane. The bike also has an overall "low-slung" look, achieved by swelling the teardrop shape of the gas tank, fitting the wheels with wide chrome rims, and reshaping the handlebars so that they raked down slightly, though it is unlikely that Stevens had any direct hand in these styling touches. He was responsible, however, for the most distinctive element of the design: a new front fender with a deep, square skirt whose strong horizontal line implies an axis of motion running down the length of the bike. This accentuates the sense of power in what is already a very muscular composition. All in all, the Hydra-Glide is an elegant demonstration of Stevens's central precept of this highly charged area of design: "People want motorcycles to look like motorcycles."[2]

Jan. 13, 1948.   C. B. STEVENS   Des. 148,397

NAME PLATE FOR MOTORCYCLES

Filed Oct. 11, 1946

Patent for a motorcycle nameplate 1946

1. See Willie G. Davidson, *One Hundred Years of Harley-Davidson* (Boston: Bullfinch Press, 2002).

2. Brooks Stevens, interview with Chip Duncan, 1990–91, transcript, Brook Stevens Archive, Milwaukee Art Museum.

**Harley Davidson Hydra-Glide
motorcycle** 1949

**Hydra-Glide motorcycle seen
from rear**

Hydra-Glide motorcycle fender

Cleveland Welding Roadmaster bicycle 1949

"My introduction to the toy industry," Brooks Stevens recalled in 1959, "came when I followed a fast-moving bicycle parts conveyor through a slot in the wall of a then 'modern' toy factory. Out of sight, on the other side, where the conveyor slowed to a crawl, I found a dozen aged gentlemen. These men, the artisans of the factory, were perched on high, three-legged stools, painting, with quivering hands, the traditional gold stripes on bicycles. This was bike styling, as I found it twelve years ago. I will never forget those ancient craftsmen, but I hope the toy industry will."[1] Stevens was never one to be swept away by the romance of hand craftsmanship, and one can readily sense from this description of the Cleveland Welding bicycle factory that he was not going to leave well enough alone there.

Upon being hired in 1947 (thanks to a connection at a department store called Gamble-Skogmo, which carried Cleveland Welding's bicycles), Stevens focused first on the Roadmaster, the top-priced model in the line. He eliminated the delicate tonal shading that the company had often used on its bicycles, thus "reducing costs and increasing production efficiency."[2] In its place he created a stark two-tone color scheme that was both modern in appearance and inexpensive to produce; men's and women's versions had paint schemes in mirror image of each other. In an attempt to make the new design look like "more than a bicycle," Stevens used hollow construction to create an impression of increased size and bulk without adding much weight to the frame. The Roadmaster was also outfitted with a heavy tank, a spring fork, teardrop-shaped lights, and chromed details that recalled the styling of a motorcycle. At key areas on the bike he added a ribbed chrome grille that played nicely against the concentric circles of the main pedal gear. The redesigned bicycle sold well, leading to further work for Stevens's firm with Cleveland Welding and, in the late 1950s, the American Machine and Foundry Company (AMF).[3]

Cleveland Welding Roadmaster bicycle 1949

1. Brooks Stevens, "Why an Industrial Designer in the Toy Industry," *Toys and Novelties*, March 1959, 378–79, 471.

2. Untitled feature, *Interiors* 108 (December 1948): 118.

3. For more on bicycle design, see Jay Pridmore and Jim Hurd, *The American Bicycle* (Osceola, Wis.: Motorbooks International, 1995).

"Skylark" Formica pattern 1950

The "Skylark" pattern that Stevens executed for the Formica Company was a direct outgrowth of the designer's prior experience with the material. In the late 1940s Stevens had participated in the development of a Formica product called Realwood, which was composed of an actual wooden veneer sandwiched between two plastic laminates. As Stevens later said, "we decided it was just ridiculous to try to embed real wood from a forest into this thing," so he suggested replacing the wooden flitch with a photographically reproduced grain pattern printed on a third layer of plastic.[1] The company named this new product "Luxwood," and it remained the

"Skylark" Formica pattern 1950 (right)

Isamu Noguchi, Coffee Table designed 1947 (lower left)
*Milwaukee Art Museum. Gift of Gilbert and J. Dorothy Palay,
M1990.58a–c*

Proposal for a Formica pattern 1951 (lower right)

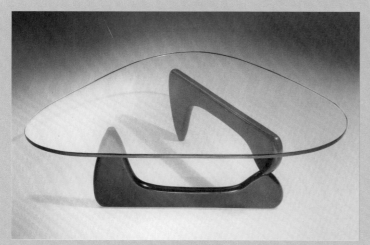

essential recipe for faux-grain Formica for several decades thereafter. This effort was coincident with Stevens's extensive use of Formica in the interior detailing of the Olympian Hiawatha train, for which he sheathed several of the car interiors with patterns of plants, wood grain, and parchments. The tables of the dining cars also had Formica tops.[2] Stevens was evidently impressed with the material, which had the advantages of being easily cleaned, durable, and aggressively modern. By 1948 he was predicting that Formica would soon be used in the interior of cars, to be followed shortly in bathroom and kitchen walls, den trimming, and even living-room paneling.[3] (Stevens actually did use Formica in an automotive context on at least one occasion. A pair of custom station wagons he designed for the Miller family in 1951 sported gray Formica panels on the inside of the doors.)

The Skylark pattern itself was a departure in that it was a much more "contemporary" pattern than had ever been used in Formica, by Stevens or anyone else. The design anticipates the biomorphism that Stevens would bring three years later to the "soft cross" logo for Miller Brewing. The amoebic forms of the pattern intersect chaotically, making it unclear which lies atop the other, creating free form not only laterally but also in implied depth. This was a common technique in Surrealist painting and collage and was used to great effect by other postwar designers. Isamu Noguchi's well-known glass-topped coffee table, for example, was made only a few years before the Skylark pattern and offers a similar set of overlapping biomorphic forms in three dimensions.

It seems likely that the innovation of the Skylark pattern was the work of one of Stevens's graphics specialists, rather than of the designer himself. Unfortunately it is not known who on the staff was responsible for this particular pattern, or for the Formica account more generally. The history is further muddled by the fact that Raymond Loewy's firm was subsequently hired by the Formica Company to alter the color scheme of Skylark. This seems to have occurred in about 1954, at which time the pattern was renamed "Boomerang." Formica revived Loewy's recolored version in 1988 and produced it until 1999.[4] Stevens's firm continued to generate patterns for the company through 1952.

1. Brooks Stevens, interview with Chip Duncan, 1990–91, transcript, Brook Stevens Archive, Milwaukee Art Museum.

2. Stevens's train was not the first to use Formica; the plastic was also employed in Canadian National Railways and Southern Railways System lines. See "How Good Can a Train Be . . . ?" *This Formica World*, fourth quarter 1949, 10–11, 14. On Formica use in the Hiawatha, see "Olympian Hiawatha," *Plastics Newsfront* 2 (October 1947): 4–7.

3. Cedric Adams, "In This Corner," *Minneapolis Star*, 12 March 1948, 42.

4. See Brooke Kamin Rapaport and Kevin L. Stayton, *Vital Forms: American Art and Design in the Atomic Age*, 1940–1960 (Brooklyn: Brooklyn Museum of Art; New York: Harry N. Abrams, 2001), 229, 241.

Kaiser-Frazer "Frazer" sedan 1951

Kaiser-Frazer, like Willys-Overland, was one of a handful of independent car manufacturers in the country and possibly the most adventurous. The firm had been founded in Willow Run, Michigan, at the close of World War II. The timing was not propitious; this was exactly the period in which most independent manufacturers began to struggle against the might of the "Big Three." The principals in the new firm, however, were not just any ordinary entrepreneurs. One was auto industry insider Joe Frazer, formerly the head of marketing for Willys-Overland and one of the great car salesmen of the century. His partner was the California aluminum and construction magnate Henry J. Kaiser. Frazer brought to the company years of experience and a great deal of personal flair, but it was Kaiser who provided the capital and much of the enthusiasm. In the late 1940s he was among the most powerful men in the country, having astounded the nation through his company's heroic shipbuilding efforts during the war.

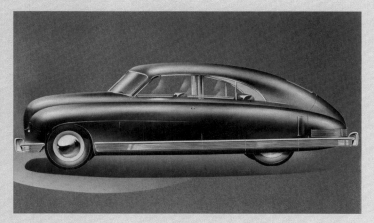

Rendering for an automobile 1944

Both Frazer and Kaiser had a deep personal interest in auto styling, and they first turned to veteran auto stylist Howard "Dutch" Darrin for ideas to supplement the work of the company's in-house staff. According to Stevens, however, Darrin's designs for the 1946 model year were poor ones, leading the company to dismiss him and bring in Stevens as a consultant in 1947. This was partly in recognition of his successful work for Willys-Overland, but it also continued a relationship between the designer and the Kaiser family that had been forged in the early 1940s. The McCulloch Corporation, for which Stevens designed a factory and office building, was closely tied to Henry Kaiser's businesses in California. The two firms had collaborated on an experimental front-wheel-drive car during the war, for which Stevens had acted as a design consultant. Through this experience Stevens met both Henry

Kaiser-Frazer "Frazer" sedan 1951
*Styling by Kaiser-Frazer's design staff, with consultants Duncan McRae,
Brooks Stevens, and Henry "Dutch" Darrin.*

Rendering for a Kaiser-Frazer automobile dashboard 1948

Willys Forward Control Commuter 1956

Kaiser and his son Edgar, who would go on to be the head of the Kaiser-Frazer auto company. In 1947 Stevens was the recipient of a successful round of polio therapy at the Kabat-Kaiser Clinic in Washington, D.C., which Henry Kaiser arranged personally.[1]

In his capacity as a design consultant, Stevens worked with Kaiser-Frazer's in-house design staff, led by Duncan McRae, and also with Dean Hammond, the company's chief engineer. At the time, Stevens's former idol Alexis de Sakhnoffsky was also on the design staff in Milwaukee and, according to Stevens, had some influence on the Kaiser-Frazer cars.[2] Immediately upon being hired, Stevens made some minor styling adjustments to the already-planned 1949 model year and began work on an overhaul of several models for 1950. His staff also prepared auto show exhibits and dealer showrooms for the company. Though Stevens's office was now the primary consultant for Kaiser-Frazer, "Dutch" Darrin was able to temporarily insinuate himself into the planning for the 1951 model year using his old contract as justification. This infuriated Stevens, who considered Darrin to be incompetent, and the two became bitter adversaries. In later years the truth of who did what for Kaiser-Frazer would be hotly contested by the two designers. Darrin eventually went as far as to sue for libel when Stevens was quoted in the press as saying that his rival was unable to draw a straight line with a ruler.[3]

The dispute between the two designers makes it impossible to reconstruct exactly what happened between 1948 and 1952. The difficulty is compounded by the fact that the existing history of Kaiser-Frazer, Richard Langworth's *The Last Onslaught on Detroit*, was highly influenced by Darrin's view of events.[4] Langworth corresponded with Stevens on certain details only after his book had gone to press, and though a series of letters between the two men survives, it is difficult to say how the book would have differed had its author had better information.[5] It should be noted that the Stevens-Darrin rivalry mirrored a longstanding personality clash between Edgar Kaiser and Joseph Frazer. Frazer had hired Darrin on the strength of a prior relationship at the automaker Graham-Paige, while Kaiser favored Stevens based on their previous experience together. After Frazer left the company in 1951, it is likely that Darrin's influence lessened dramatically. For example, Langworth attributed the 1951 Frazer convertible to Darrin. Stevens, however, asserted that he and Duncan McRae were primarily responsible for the car, with Darrin responsible only for the upper profile of the windshield and the shape of the rear window. There is considerable evidence to back up Stevens's claim to the car's authorship. The distinctive low-belted "pontoon side" and wraparound bumper look that first appeared on Kaiser-Frazer's cars in 1949 was clearly related to that on Stevens's wartime prophetic automobiles, which he had originally hoped to produce at Willys-Overland.

Stevens's other major achievement at Kaiser-Frazer was of a more prosaic but arguably more substantial nature. Like any good industrial designer, he gave a good deal of thought to "human factors" such as comfort, legibility, or improved utility—the class of design variables now referred to under the heading of "ergonomics." In car design these concerns led naturally to a consideration of safety issues. Accordingly, Stevens introduced a range of innovative features in Kaiser-Frazer's cars, including a thickly padded dashboard, narrow windshield corner posts that provided excellent driver visibility, and instrumentation that clustered around the wheel for ease of vision and manual access. These were the earliest and most concrete gestures Stevens made in the direction of making safety "visually palatable"—an effort that he redoubled in later years after consumer advocate Ralph Nader published his attack on the automobile industry, *Unsafe at Any Speed*.[6]

After the merger of Kaiser-Frazer and Willys-Overland in 1953, Stevens continued to work for the reconstituted company. In 1956 the Willys division launched a new line of four-wheel-drive "Forward Control" trucks and vans, based (like his old Jeep Station Wagon and Jeepster) on the chassis of a standard-model Jeep. A wide variety of these cab-over-engine vehicles were produced for general and specialized use until 1965, peaking in 1957 with almost ten thousand vehicles built. As was invariably the case with his automotive commissions, Stevens and his staff created many more vehicle types and styles for the line than ever saw production, including the interesting 1956 Commuter, a groundbreaking early minivan with six doors that was prototyped by the Reutter Company in Stuttgart but went no further. Not until the emergence of the Ford Econoline in 1964 would a similar minivan become commercially available.

1. Of the treatments, Stevens said, "It wasn't easy. They rough you around plenty" (quoted in Edward P. Halline, "Long Crippled by Polio, Fights Back to Recovery," *Milwaukee Sentinel*, 3 August 1947).

2. Brooks Stevens, "The de Sakhnoffsky L-29," *Automobile Quarterly* 6 (spring 1968): 453–57.

3. Brooks Stevens to Michael Lamm, 29 October 1969; Stevens to R. Perry Zavitz, 9 February 1970; Stevens to Michael Lamm, 22 April 1970, Brooks Stevens Archive, Milwaukee Art Museum.

4. Richard Langworth, *Kaiser-Frazer: The Last Onslaught on Detroit* (Kutztown, Pa.: Automobile Quarterly Publications, 1975).

5. Brooks Stevens to R. M. Langworth, 3 June 1975; Langworth to Stevens, 9 June 1975, Brooks Stevens Archive. See also Richard Langworth, "The Glorious Madness of Kaiser Frazer," *Automobile Quarterly* 9 (spring 1971): 266–81; Alex Tremulis, "Kaiser Frazer's Stylists," *Automobile Quarterly* 9 (spring 1971): 282–83.

6. Stevens routinely criticized Nader for his idealistic crusade against auto manufacturers, arguing (with some justice) that the consumer advocate knew little about the real world of car design. While working with AMC in the late 1960s, Stevens countered Nader's book with his own aesthetically sound safety measures, such as reflective tires and license plates, pop-out flush-mounted windows, and front ends that were pointed like boat prows that would glance off each other in a head-on collision. See Ralph Nader, *Unsafe at Any Speed: The Designed-in Dangers of the American Automobile* (New York: Grossman, 1965); Mervyn Kaufman, "Ralph Nader, Crusader for Safety," *Automobile Quarterly* 5 (summer 1966): 4–7; Brooks Stevens, "The Alleged Safety Car Need Not Be Ugly," 6 March 1968, and "Safety Car Features," 11 March 1968, Brooks Stevens Archive.

Excalibur J race car 1952

By 1951 Brooks Stevens was in a racing frame of mind. Three years earlier he and his design associate James Floria had helped to charter the first midwestern auto-racing club. He was steadily building his collection of antique and contemporary cars and had begun to travel to races across the country in the company of fellow enthusiasts at his design studio, including Floria and Anthony Reed. The previous year, a Racine newspaper had photographed Stevens in replica turn-of-the-century driving gear. In the article the designer proclaimed his desire to "combine our knowledge to blend with the fine Italian car—more grace, more flow of line— with the practicalities of the American car. If we can combine the two with American body dimensions, we'll really have something."[1] True to his word, Stevens approached the car manufacturer Kaiser-Frazer in late 1951 with the intention of designing and building the first authentic American-built racing car. "As a member of the Sports Car Club of America," he wrote, "and one who owns and operates several interesting European sports cars, it has always been desired to contribute something to the sport in an American-built vehicle within the reach of the medium-priced buyer enthusiast."[2]

Stevens's plan was to build his cars on the chassis of Kaiser-Frazer's recently introduced small model, the Henry J.[3] His choice was a natural one, as he and his staff were intimately familiar with the company's cars. Stevens was doubtless aware of the Henry J's poor reception on the market too and may have zeroed in on its chassis because he knew that there was readily available unsold stock. Of course his race car, dubbed the Excalibur J, looked nothing like the automobile whose inner frame it shared; it was instead an emulation of the Mercedes-Benz race cars of the 1940s. Designed by Stevens in conjunction with his staff designer Charles Cowdin Jr., the car was roughly tubular in shape and construction and was skinned in aluminum. The chassis itself was also considerably modified for racing, with steering, suspension, and even engine location all customized. It had virtually no compound curves, which would have entailed costly tooling. To reduce weight, the outer skin was made of aluminum, and street-driving necessities— including the windshield, bumpers, and headlights—were all removable for track racing.

Excalibur J race car 1952

Though Stevens had hoped to market the Excalibur J as a street car to a nationwide niche market, in the end only three of the cars were built. Costing less than three thousand dollars apiece—much less than the European cars in the same racing class—the cars were on the track by early 1952. Two were equipped with Willys-manufactured F-head engines, and the other with a Kaiser-Frazer F-head. Stevens had wanted to use an Alfa Romeo engine for the third car but decided at the last minute to "placate" his business partner. His initial impulse was borne out when two of the new cars were put through their paces at Sebring in Florida that spring. The Kaiser-Frazer engine burned out quickly, although the Willys survived well into the race and was running second when, according to Stevens, "a ten-cent oil seal let go and tore up the ring and pinion gear."[4] Later efforts at the track proved more successful, however. With the Kaiser-Frazer engine replaced by a Jaguar, Excalibur Js raced about twenty-five times and finished in first place on nine occasions, consistently beating out name-brand European sports cars. The car's greatest moment of glory was a victory at the U.S. Grand Prix in Watkins Glen, New York, in September 1953, with driver Hal Ullrich at the wheel.

The last of the Excalibur J cars was retired in 1958. The comparative success of this first American racer, however, was only the beginning of a long series of similar efforts on the part of Brooks Stevens and his eldest son, David. The Excalibur J, in the grand European tradition, was intended to be usable either on city streets or on the track. The race cars that Brooks and David Stevens built together, by contrast, were designed only for racing. David, a brilliant self-taught

Excalibur Hawk race car 1962

Brooks Stevens with a model for the Excalibur Hawk 1962

The Excalibur racing team ca. 1975
Left to right: mechanic Joe Zarconni, driver Ray Besasie Jr., and mechanic Alice Preston.

mechanic, outfitted a shop at his father's auto museum in Mequon, Wisconsin. The two collaborated on the design of a series of cars in the early 1960s, of which the most interesting was arguably the Excalibur Hawk of 1962. This car, which got its name from the extensive use of Studebaker Hawk parts in its chassis, anticipated certain styling touches used in the Corvette Stingray the following year. Like the J cars, the Excalibur Hawk was made of aluminum and featured a deeply scooped side that recalled the custom cars that Brooks Stevens had designed in the mid-1950s.

After the mid-1960s Stevens took a hiatus from racing, but he returned with renewed fervor in 1974. This time the Excalibur team was larger, with a more demanding schedule, and its operation was not integrated with the activities of the design office or auto museum. The cars were not custom products, but rather factory-built formula racers with minor cosmetic modifications. Though Stevens justified his new incursion into racing as a way of achieving name recognition both for himself and his sons' Excalibur business, in fact it was essentially an extremely expensive hobby. By the decade's end, Stevens's failing health and the mounting costs of maintaining his team put an end to his glory days on the track.

1. Patricia Reed, "Yes, You Really Did See It!" *Racine Journal*, 28 June 1950, 14.

2. Quoted in Richard M. Langworth, *Kaiser-Frazer: The Last Onslaught on Detroit* (Kutztown, Pa.: Automobile Quarterly Publications, 1975), 154.

3. On the Henry J, see Karla A. Rosenbusch, "1951–54 Kaiser-Frazer Henry J," *Automobile Quarterly* 39 (December 1999): 36–45.

4. Langworth, *Kaiser-Frazer*, 157.

Miller Brewing Soft Cross corporate logo 1953

The phrase "corporate identity" is commonly used to refer to a logo—a highly recognizable graphic image that identifies a company. Of course, this is a kind of shorthand. Corporate identity is actually a much broader thing, comprising elements as various as packaging, advertising, architecture, employee relations, and products themselves. The science of combining these factors into a public persona began in earnest in the 1920s. By the postwar period it was a nearly pervasive concern of American business. Industrial designers, although they often designed logos, were rarely given the responsibility for managing a corporation's whole public profile. Henry Dreyfuss performed this role to some extent for Honeywell, as did Norman Bel Geddes for the Toledo Scale Company and Raymond Loewy for Coca-Cola and Nabisco.[1] None of these efforts, though, equaled the scope of Brooks Stevens's work for the Miller Brewing Company.

Miller Brewing Soft Cross corporate logo 1953

Stevens's first design for the Milwaukee corporation was a 1939 streamlined delivery truck, identical in shape to the other streamlined vehicles that his firm executed at the time. Thanks to his close friendship with company president Frederick Miller, this commission led to a veritable flood of design work after World War II. In 1947 Stevens's firm designed another fleet of delivery trucks for Miller and followed it with a "courtesy car" with broadcasting equipment, as well as a custom station wagon in steel and wood for Frederick Miller and his family. The culmination of the promotional vehicles was the 1955 Miller High Life Cruiser. This was a bus that sported not only an interior display on the company's history and production methods but also a ten-foot fiberglass beer bottle on top that slid down into the vehicle body when the Cruiser was on the road.[2]

Miller High Life Cruiser 1955

Miller Brewing delivery vehicle 1954

Miller High Life beer bottle 1953

Miller delivery uniform 1959

Miller display 1961

Miller also turned to Stevens for a package redesign program that began in the late 1940s and lasted more than fifteen years. Stevens's head of graphic design during this period, Ray Anderson, was primarily responsible for these changes, which were planned from the start to be incremental—in Stevens's words, "evolutionary, rather than revolutionary."[3] The firm's most significant contribution during this period was the Miller "Soft Cross" of 1953. This masterpiece of corporate identity was devised by abstracting the intersecting ribbons that had previously been wrapped around the necks of the company's beer bottles. The new logo managed to

be both novel and traditional through its combination of Surrealist-inspired biomorphism with rigid symmetry and a somewhat antiquated typescript. It was so successful that it almost immediately displaced the company's older Girl in the Moon symbol and is still in use fifty years later in applications ranging from packaging to television commercials to an enormous rotating sign that was placed atop Miller's Milwaukee brewery in 1967.

Stevens and Anderson also designed bottles, cans, and box packaging for Miller. Because consumer research indicated that the company's name was much more recognizable than its brand name, High Life, these designs moved gradually toward an emphasis on the word Miller and its visual equivalent, the Soft Cross.[4] In a move to attract female customers to the brand, they introduced a wine bottle shape for the familiar clear bottle used by the company. They capitalized on the company slogan ("the champagne of bottle beers") with a golden can, whose color was carefully calculated to "look cold."[5] They also invented novel uses for the Soft Cross, such as a delivery man's uniform that turned its wearer into a walking version of the logo and a package that could be stacked in the store to compose an arresting display pattern.[6]

The combination of old and new used in the Soft Cross was also a feature of Stevens's other major project for Miller, a renovation of the company's physical plant in Milwaukee. The rebuilding effort began in March of 1950 and lasted five years, coming in at an eventual cost of $25 million. Stevens's part of the effort included the interiors of the Miller Inn and Caves, where visitors were received for tours; consultation on factory and office spaces; and most importantly, the new Miller Administration Building. In each of these areas Stevens and his staff were at pains to blend the new structures with the existing fabric of the brewery.[7] For this reason, the use of cream-colored Milwaukee brick predominated, and the character of many of the interior appointments was decidedly Germanic.

Miller Administration Building facade 1951
Miller Administration Building interior 1951

The only aggressively styled portion of the project was the Administration Building, an exemplary demonstration of Stevens's precept that "today's industrialist uses the 'front' of his plant (provided it is attractive) as he does the labels, packaging techniques and product design of his wares—to advertise and merchandise his products."[8] The Administration Building's facade was similar to a billboard; even its brass and stainless steel trim was meant to evoke the colors of beer and foam. The interior was an essay in sophisticated modernism, with a sweeping circular staircase, furnishings custom-designed by Stevens's office, an amber carpet woven to order in Puerto Rico, and a pseudo-abstract mural by Stevens's friend Edmund Lewandowski, head of the Layton School of Art.[9]

1. Russell Flinchum, *Henry Dreyfuss, Industrial Designer: The Man in the Brown Suit* (New York: Cooper Hewitt, National Design Museum, Smithsonian Institution, and Rizzoli, 1997), 140–46; Jeffrey T. Meikle, *Twentieth Century Limited* (Philadelphia: Temple University Press, 1979), 53; Raymond Loewy, *Industrial Design* (Woodstock, N.Y.: Overlook Press, 1979), 146. Most industrial designers' forays into corporate identity development were tied to logo graphics or to onetime display events such as those at the World's Fairs of the 1930s. See Roland Marchand, *Creating the Corporate Soul: The Rise of Public Relations and Corporate Imagery in the United States* (Berkeley: University of California Press, 1998).

2. "Courtesy Car with a Capital C," *Milwaukee Sentinel*, 17 April 1955; "'Brewery on Wheels' to Tour Nation," *Milwaukee Sentinel*, 17 April 1955.

3. Margaret Fish, "Blend Old and New," *Milwaukee Sentinel*, 17 April 1955.

4. "Miller's New Design Features a Display Plan," *Miller High-Lites* 15 (April–May 1961): 6–9.

5. David G. Meissner, "Label Change Involves Massive Problem Solving," *Milwaukee Journal*, 2 November 1967.

6. "Can Acquires Quality Image," *Food Engineering* 40 (January 1968): 44–45; A. C. Vosburg, "Driver-Salesmen Will Be Tailored for Volume Selling," *Miller High Life Impressions* 1 (July 1959); "New Miller Six-Pack Serves as Own Display," *Food Field Reporter* 29 (27 March 1961): 31. See also "Industrial Designer: Brooks Stevens," *Miller High-Lites*, March 1992, 8–9.

7. Margaret Fish, "Blend Old and New," *Milwaukee Sentinel*, 17 April 1955, 69; "Handsome New Guest Center Nearing Completion at Miller," *Milwaukee Journal*, 31 January 1951; "Miller Brewer Readies Quaint New 'Gast Haus,'" *Milwaukee Sentinel*, 29 April 1951.

8. Brooks Stevens, "Factories Also Have Faces," *Industrial Design* 8 (April 1961): 12.

9. "Five Year Expansion Trail Near End, Miller to Celebrate," *Milwaukee Sentinel*, 2 September 1951; "Lewandowski to Do Brewery Mural," *Milwaukee Sentinel*, 4 July 1951.

Die Valkyrie 1954
Gaylord Grand Prix 1955
Olin Mathiesson Scimitar 1959

Of the many routes that Brooks Stevens pursued to satisfy his automotive design ambitions, the one with which he had the most consistent success was the custom-built car. He had first acquired his taste for luxury autos through his collecting habit, and in fact his earliest custom design was his own rebuilt L29 Cord. In 1945 Stevens had designed his first unique auto from scratch for the actress Diana Lewis Powell (wife of William Powell, better known to moviegoers as the Thin Man). This was also Stevens's first chance to try out some of his wartime ideas, many of them borrowed from airplane design: windows and windshield that retracted with the push of a button, fluted stainless steel side panels, and a deep air intake in the front that suggested the front opening of a jet engine. One Milwaukee writer claimed that "Diana will look as though she's taking off any minute when she steps on the throttle, as the exhaust section is so fashioned that with oil mixed in with the gasoline the exhaust fumes will spew out in a fantail effect

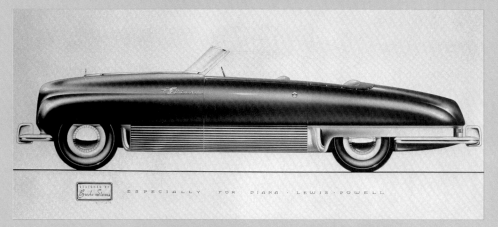

Custom car for Diana Lewis Powell 1945

like that of a jet propelled plane."[1] The "pontoon fenders" of the car were joined in a unified volume with the body, in the manner of a prophetic car that Stevens had designed in 1942 [see page 68]. The upholstery was executed in ivory leather with pillowed red leather accents— all in all, a car that the Milwaukee designer knew would make a sensation, even in Hollywood.[2]

After the Powell commission, it was some time before Stevens had another try at designing a truly opulent automobile. This may be attributable to his successes in the more pragmatic realm of mass manufacturing with Willys-Overland and Kaiser-Frazer. The time, difficulty, and investment involved in producing a one-off, or even a limited-run car, were disincentives under the best of circumstances. It was not until Stevens hired French public relations man Guy Storr that he found a means to overcome the inevitable logistical difficulties. Stevens had been intent on becoming a recognized name in European car design since being called in as a consultant for Alfa Romeo's 1800 Sprint Series in 1951.

Storr apparently decided that the fastest route to raising his client's profile overseas would be to create a centerpiece car for the Paris Auto Show of 1954.[3] Stevens came through with a stylish sports car built on a Cadillac chassis by Hermann Spohn of Ravensburg, Germany, an esteemed coachbuilder that had worked for Rolls-Royce and Mercedes-Benz. Financial backing came from a Cleveland city councilman and car enthusiast named Irwyn Metzenbaum. Stevens first called the new car the Excalibur (a name that he used repeatedly through his career) and also seems to have considered an alternate sword title, the Rapier.[4] Eventually he settled on the German name Die Valkyrie, possibly because the car's most dramatic touch was a deep central V shape in the center of the front bumper, meant to symbolize the car's powerful engine, a Cadillac V-8. The black and white graphic design of the car's sides was equally modish. As Stevens must have hoped, the Valkyrie looked right at home when photographed against the Paris skyline. With Storr's promotional help it was well received in France, and an unknown but presumably small number of Valkyries were sold at a comparatively staggering cost of $10,000 apiece, each customized to the specifications of the buyer.[5] Stevens purchased one of the cars for his wife, Alice, and she drove it until it entered the collection of the Brooks Stevens Auto Museum.

Die Valkyrie coupe rendering

Stevens's next act, the Gaylord, was even more dramatic and probably the apex of his career in custom car design. He was commissioned to create an automobile that, in the words of a writer for the journal Motor Trend, "had every advantage that money can provide."[6] The car's wealthy patrons, two self-described "auto-holics" from Chicago named Jim and Edward Gaylord, gave Stevens such latitude that the entire vehicle was planned before price was even discussed. He later described the nature of the assignment: "It was to have the spirit and functionality of the then relatively young Ferrari yet the silence and the sort of ride of a Rolls of that period. It was to be the most elegant two-place, short wheel-base, minimal mass, sporty boulevard car in the world."[7] Stevens's staff designer Gordon Kelly did much of the body design, while Jim Gaylord designed the chassis; at Stevens's recommendation, Spohn was again chosen as a coachbuilder. The Gaylords shared Stevens's conviction, premised on the example of early twentieth-century autos, that the car's front identity was of primary importance. Accordingly the car was festooned with dinner plate–size headlights, a vertical radiator grille with a classic flavor, and front fenders that Stevens compared with the "wings of the 1930s."[8] The car also featured a wraparound windshield (customized from glass plates from a Ford Thunderbird) and a hard top that retracted under the rear deck at the push of a button. To reduce noise, Stevens

Die Valkyrie coupe 1954

Gaylord Grand Prix automobile 1955

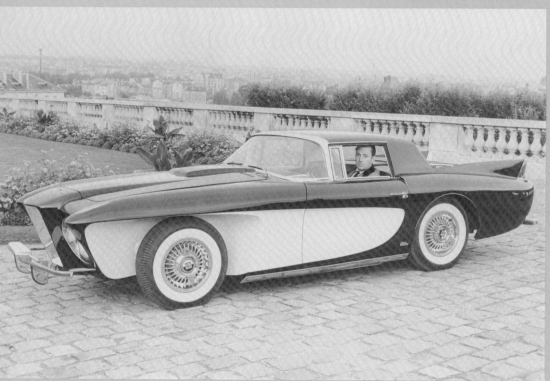

came up with the marvelous and expensive contrivance of padding each joint between the body and the steel frame with rubber cushions. The car proved to be another hit at the Paris Salon, but Stevens and the brothers Gaylord were never able to put their wondrous luxury car into production—only six were ever made. Some of their ideas did live on, however, in the Ford Skyliner and Thunderbird of the late 1950s, which borrowed the mechanism and lines of the Gaylord's roof.[9]

Though the Gaylord may have been, as one wag put it, "the latest word in super snob appeal," its innovations were far beyond the reach of any practical car manufacturer.[10] The same cannot be said for Stevens's Scimitar, made at the behest of aluminum manufacturer Olin Mathiesson. From beginning to end the Scimitar was intended to demonstrate the efficiency of constructing cars from the lightweight, rustproof metal. Stevens himself had a fair amount of experience with the material, having an aluminum kitchenware manufacturer among his clients. He had also encountered the advantages and disadvantages of aluminum in designing the Steam-O-Matic clothes iron in 1940. As a keen student of car design, Stevens was also no doubt aware of previous attempts to use the metal in autos, including several cars from the prewar period that were in his own collection. More recently General Motors had produced a version of the LeSabre entirely out of magnesium and aluminum, and Henry Kaiser (who was also in the aluminum production business) had tried to explore the material through Kaiser-Frazer, though he never got the opportunity.[11] Stevens himself had used aluminum in his race car, the Excalibur J, in 1952.

So the idea of an aluminum car was hardly new when Stevens's team set to work on the Scimitar in 1956. What was unusual was the attempt to prove that the metal could be used in a cost-effective manner in an industry dominated by modern steel construction. The Scimitar was, according to Stevens, "not to be a car of the future or even a drastic styling treatment, but to be a concept of today applicable to current manufacturing procedures."[12] This was a tall order. Although aluminum had undeniable functional advantages in the finished car, the raw metal cost about four times as much per pound as steel. More importantly, it was significantly more expensive to tool than sheet steel, because it could not be bent or molded over forms. Every shape in an aluminum body car had to be formed in individually built die presses. This meant not only a high initial capital investment but also an equivalent outlay whenever the body styling changed.

Rendering for the Scimitar showing **aluminum distribution** 1959

For a fierce proponent of annual model change, then, aluminum was not a promising material. Nonetheless Stevens was able to come up with a sleight of hand that justified his new project. His solution was to design three cars that were based on a single set of die stamps. Each of the trio was outfitted with a different roof structure, in such a way as to appeal to different sectors of the market. Stevens was sufficiently pleased with this strategy that he revived it later in his career when building his own Excalibur line of automobiles, and it was indeed an ingeniously polymorphic plan. The simplest of the three body types was a two-door hardtop convertible town car or coupe, in which the top retracted into the rear deck, as in the Gaylord. By extending the roofline backward and adding a sliding rear door, the coupe could be made into a more utilitarian "station sedan" family car with a fixed roof. Alternatively and most outlandishly, the

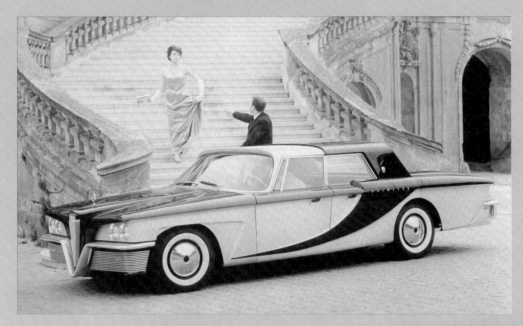

Olin Mathiesson Scimitar town car 1959
(left and lower left)

Rendering for the Scimitar phaeton car 1959

Rendering for the Scimitar station sedan 1959

Scimitar could be built as a sports car with a three-way roof. With the top fully closed, the car was a closed formal sedan; with the top fully open, it was a touring car; and with the roof half-closed, it was a phaeton—an aristocratic auto type that Stevens had explored previously in his design for the Willys Jeepster. Stevens conceded that this third body type was something of a luxury within the overall parameters of the project. It would doubtless have had a limited market when compared with the hardtop coupe and the fixed-top family vehicle, but as a promotional vehicle for Olin Mathiesson, the car was a perfect fit.

The varying renditions of the Scimitar were unified by identical color treatments in black and gray, distinguishing the steel and aluminum parts of the chassis. The notable motif was a curved form suggestive of the auto's name. All three types were realized in prototype form using chassis provided by Stevens's colleague at Chrysler Virgil Exner. The bodywork was performed by the Reutter Company of Stuttgart, Germany—a firm known mainly for its work with Porsche. As with the Valkyrie and Gaylord, the entire body of each car was built from scratch. Aluminum was used for the front and rear quarter-panels, bumpers, wheel disks, and front grille. The trim was also of polished anodized aluminum instead of chromed steel. Wherever possible, Stevens avoided placing pieces of metal atop one another to reduce tooling costs.[13]

The Scimitars premiered at the 1959 Geneva Auto Show. This final effort to gain acceptance in the European auto design world was not unsuccessful—the Scimitars drew a great deal of press, particularly in France—but it was nonetheless the last such attempt. By the early 1960s Stevens had become consumed with a project much closer to home: the formidable task of changing the fortunes of the Studebaker Corporation of South Bend, Indiana.

1. Untitled article, *Milwaukee Journal*, 14 July 1946; see also "Special Car Body Is Designed on Jet Plane Motif," *Automotive News*, 1 October 1945, 31.

2. "Looking Ahead," *Motor*, 26 June 1946, 439.

3. Guy S. Storr, "The Platform Does It," *Public Relations Journal* 11 (June 1955): 15.

4. "V-Eight Dominant," *Autocar*, 30 April 1954, 605.

5. Sanford Markey, untitled article, *Motor Trend*, February 1955, 39; see also "Die Valkyrie," *Car Life*, March 1955, 35; "U.S. Firm to Sell One-of-a-Kind Foreign-Built Cars," *Automotive News*, 4 February 1955.

6. Don MacDonald, "One for the Money," *Motor Trend*, December 1955, 36–37, 59.

7. Quoted in Alex Tremulis, "One Auto-holic's Views on Another's Ultimate Car: Gaylord," *Automobile Quarterly* 12, no. 4 (1974): 401–7.

8. Brooks Stevens, designer's notes for Gaylord Grand Prix, undated, Brooks Stevens Archive, Milwaukee Art Museum.

9. For more on the Gaylord, see Richard M. Langworth, "Gaylord from the Driver's Seat," *Automobile Quarterly* 12, no. 4 (1974): 408–11.

10. "Sports Car Salon," *Speed Age*, March 1956, 72.

11. "Light Metals in Automobiles," *Modern Metals* 7 (September 1951): 23–36. For a general account of the use of aluminum in postwar design, see "Promoting Aluminum: Designers and the American Aluminum Industry," *Design Issues* 9 (spring 1993): 44–50.

12. Untitled Olin Mathiesson advertisement brochure, ca. 1959, Brooks Stevens Archive.

13. Günther Molter, "New Theme…Old Variations," *Motor Trend*, June 1959.

Fig. 1 Brooks Stevens, 1961

The Enfant Terrible of Industrial Design
Planned Obsolescence and Other Crimes Against Modernism, 1956–78

When I redesign a 1961 model car I am not styling it for the man who bought one in 1960,
I'm styling it for the man next door who didn't buy it when his neighbor did.

Brooks Stevens (1966)[1]

Stevens discovered, quite by accident, that the easiest way to become famous was to become infamous. One night in 1954 he was scheduled to deliver a talk to the local advertising club in Minneapolis. Stevens arrived in the city the night before (having traveled on the Olympian Hiawatha train, which his firm had designed) and, as was his custom, sat down to organize projector slides and write out a few notes from which to speak extemporaneously. Mindful of the fact that he would be addressing a group of advertising agency executives, he impulsively hit upon the catchphrase "planned obsolescence" as a description of the industrial designer's mission. Probably without giving its meaning much thought, he used the phrase as the title of his speech the following day—a speech that was otherwise mostly interchangeable with the hundreds of other presentations of his firm's work he had done since the 1930s. The title raised questions, however, and Stevens felt increasingly obligated to define and defend it. Over the next years he gave those two words a good deal of thought indeed; despite the casualness of its conception, the phrase "planned obsolescence" would become his major lasting contribution to design theory.

By 1956 Stevens was presenting his philosophy of planned obsolescence at nearly every opportunity, having codified its

definition as "instilling in the buyer the desire to own something a little newer, a little better, a little sooner than is necessary." This was a formula that he repeated for the rest of his life, but it was not one that found widespread acceptance. Invariably his bolder declarations on the topic were the ones that were promulgated, such as "I believe in status symbols" and "our whole economy is based on planned obsolescence, and anyone who can read without moving his lips should know it by now."[2] If such comments were intended to raise hackles, then Stevens got exactly what he wanted. A particularly vituperative response was delivered by pop culture critic Vance Packard, whose 1960 book *The Waste Makers* quoted Stevens and then accused him of a sinister strategy of exploitation. Packard identified two types of planned obsolescence: that of quality (or "functional obsolescence"), in which objects were intentionally designed to wear out, and that of desire ("psychological obsolescence"), in which the approach was to make the product "old-fashioned, conspicuously non-modern." Both were equally suspect from Packard's perspective, because they amounted to a callow manipulation of the consumer.[3]

Though Stevens dismissed *The Waste Makers* as "a scare headline book," it seems clear that he lost the war of words with his critics.[4] Already by 1959 Volkswagen was proudly claiming in its advertising: "We do not believe in planned obsolescence. We don't change a car for the sake of change." And today planned obsolescence is certainly not a concept that finds many vocal supporters. Being a believer in the notion that all publicity was good publicity, however, Stevens enjoyed his notoriety. He was particularly delighted by an attack in the communist newspaper the *Weekly People* in 1958, which excoriated him for being "completely oblivious to the gross immorality of his venal posture" and accused him of turning art from an educating force into "a harlot that seduces the uneducated."[5] For years thereafter in his speeches, Stevens was able to number the communist press among his enemies, with implications that would have been obvious to Cold War–era audiences.[6]

Stevens's primary strategy, however, was simply to dismiss his detractors as cowardly or dishonest. In 1958, for example, he was the subject of an extensive profile in a men's magazine. He used the opportunity to lash out at designers who criticized his ideas: "I get some waving of the hands and disparagement from some of my colleagues who feel that I am too realistic, that I tell too much. I disagree with them. I believe in being totally frank. I can affect the public only a little bit anyway. I can't hurt the system even if I expose it." Stevens courted controversy by pronouncing industrial designers to be "ninety percent merchandiser and ten percent artist" and, to a certain degree, "charlatans" whose business was to pander to the bad taste of the consumer. "I could not go on a crusade for good design, I mean, really good, aesthetically good, artistically good design in a manufactured product because it wouldn't pay off," he continued. "We sometimes make things merely *striking*, and not actually good-looking, and therefore they have no aesthetic use for being."[7]

These sentiments were flagrantly contrary to the anti-elitist stance of the mainstream industrial design establishment of the day. Yet behind the inflammatory rhetoric there were subtleties to Stevens's thinking—nuances that Packard and his ilk, in their haste to demonize the idea of planned obsolescence, failed to engage.[8] The central observation behind the theory may have been Machiavellian, but it was also persuasive: "If companies did not bring out a new and better product each fall, volume would fall off, unit costs would increase, and employment would be reduced."[9] This dimension of Stevens's argument was simply an extension of the tacit assumption made by those who praised industrial design in the Depression era—that styling led people to buy things against their better judgment, to the overall benefit of the economy. Stevens also made a telling point concerning the resale value of obsolete designs. "The item you trade in is never junked, destroyed, or thrown away," he said. "It is moved into the used merchandise market and is bought by someone who might not have had the product in any other way. Think how many have been helped that way."[10]

The apex of Stevens's discourse on the subject was probably his 1960 response to a critique by industrial designer Walter Dorwin Teague. In his attack on planned obsolescence, Teague equated the concept with "just plain 'gypping,'" insisting that progress in the market would happen quickly enough through "honest, legitimate obsolescence, … [in which] we advance by making things more serviceable, less costly." He pointed to Detroit's ill-fated 1958 models, including the infamous Ford Edsel. These cars performed extremely poorly in the market—so much so that they created a minor recession—despite the fact that they were loaded with what Teague called "extraordinary elaborations." Stevens took up this challenge and tried to defend Detroit's sales strategies. Calling the styling splurge "an eye arrestor, a brand identifier, a come-on to the uneducated mind," he chalked up the 1958 market catastrophe to a slight error in judgment. Car designers, he wrote, had simply "outdimensioned and outchromed the most susceptible buyer."[11] In other words, Detroit's design failure had been one of degree, not one of kind.

Teague drew the opposite conclusion, presenting the 1958 debacle as a cautionary tale about all attempts to use design as pure sales technique. He advanced the well-worn chestnuts of American modernism, writing: "The function of design, simply put, is to realize the true character of the thing designed, and to reveal the values that have been put into it. If it is used for camouflage, it is being prostituted." It was this very dichotomy between "true character" and "camouflage," however, that

Fig. 2 (left) Exterior of Brooks Stevens Associates' new Wilson Drive Office, 1959

Fig. 3 (below) The drafting room of the new office. In the foreground are Ray Anderson (left) and Gordon Robertson (right)

Stevens was trying to escape. The true character of a product, he argued, necessarily includes its own marketability. The organic model of progress that Teague advanced was fine in theory, but in practice it could not work because it had no motivating device. It was, to Stevens, an idealism that the manufacturer could not afford. "Planned obsolescence versus 'natural' or 'genuine' obsolescence is not the point at all," he wrote in a stinging conclusion. "There can be no obsolescence *without* a plan."[12]

The centerpiece of planned obsolescence was the annual model change—a rapid overturn of product line that originated in the auto industry but became widespread among many large companies during the late 1950s. The demands of directing this amount of design work for several clients necessitated a larger office and staff, and in 1956 Stevens and his associates began planning a new building to house their expanding business.[13] In contrast to the stunning streamlining of the previous Water Street office, the new workplace was to be stylistically neutral— a subdued composition of light gray stone and glass. Its bland exterior and open, brightly lit workrooms suggested little of the style that Stevens's firm would bring to its commissions, and this was appropriate, because style was increasingly beside the point (figs. 2, 3).

In 1958 Stevens and his staff moved into the new three-story building at the intersection of Capitol and Wilson Drives in Shorewood, a northern suburb of Milwaukee. A rare surviving personnel roster from the previous year shows that on the verge of its transition the office included fourteen designers and two secretaries. Stevens and his three associates (Reed, Floria, and Hughes) each occupied their own rooms. Immediately below the four executives were Gordon Kelly, the head of transportation and product design, and Ray Anderson, who directed packaging, trademark, and presentation design. Kelly had five staff designers under his direct supervision: Myron Stevens, Bill Davidson, Robert Schouten, Joe Besasie, and David Nutting; his department also included specialist model maker Dick Frank. The smaller graphics department had only two staffers: Gordon Robertson and the airbrush artist Dick Rechlicz. Betty Meyer was personal secretary to Stevens, and Frances Lutz to the other three partners.

Once in the new space, Stevens immediately set about increasing this roster. Many of the figures who would come to play a leading role in the later stages of the firm were introduced shortly before or after the move to Shorewood; among them were Adrian Bonini, John Bradley, Bill Davidson, Stan Johnson, Peter Stacy, and Wayne Wagner. Many of these young men were handpicked from the Layton School of Art in Milwaukee, where Stevens lectured frequently and served as a member of the board of directors. Others came from further afield, including Davidson and Stacy, who had been trained at the Art Center School in Los Angeles. Despite their youth, the new staff members were extremely professional in their outlook and highly skilled. The overall production of the design office was heavily influenced by their personal styles and abilities; from this period onward, it becomes increasingly difficult to speak of Stevens's designs as the product of a unified vision. The sense of a generational shift was increased when several of the established figures in the office moved on to other activities. Most disruptive was the exit of James Floria, who left on extremely poor terms with Stevens personally, but the departures of Davidson in 1962 and Kelly in 1964 were probably more of a loss to the firm in design terms. Both proved their abilities in later years, Kelly at his own design office in Milwaukee and Davidson as the vice president in charge of styling at his family business, Harley-Davidson, where he became famous to millions of bikers as "Willie G." The most deeply felt loss of the period, however, was the death in 1965 of Stevens's longtime friend and confidant Anthony Reed, the firm's senior partner and most experienced engineer.

These changes set the stage for a gradual but pronounced evolution in the way that Stevens's staff did its business. Tom Green, a product designer who joined the office in 1967, describes this shift as typical for an industrial design firm of the day.[14] The basis of a designer's legitimacy, in Green's analysis, went through a three-stage development in the postwar period from authority to theory to demonstration. Early industrial designers had simply asserted their right to reshape the products of major companies, and they retained that right primarily through force of character. The academically trained designers and business school graduates who grew to maturity in the 1960s, however, were suspicious of this cult of personality. They ushered in a new approach in which theories about demographics, ergonomics, recognition factor, and other variables were put forward for study. As these hypotheses were tested and refined, the field of design entered its current orientation toward scientifically demonstrable results. Today it is not enough to grandly state, as Stevens often did, that a redesign campaign had multiplied sales figures; such claims must be proven through exhaustive verification and assessment.

This trend toward objectivity was, of course, antithetical to Stevens's personality and approach to design. He had always staked his career on intuition and charisma—qualities that were not easily quantified—and he had little patience with research. Asked about market research in 1990, he testily responded, "we didn't have any, we didn't do it, I didn't believe in it," even though he had in fact used such research several times in the 1940s, when it was relatively new. "The worst thing we'd be confronted with," he continued, "was if some client [asked], how can you be sure that what you've done for us with that refrigerator or this washing machine or this or this flat iron or whatever it is, is the right way to go? Don't you think we ought to ask some of the people around here? How do you know? Are you a prophet? How can you be sure? Well it is hard to explain, but somehow in those days I was able to convince them that whatever way I led them was the way to go in the market."[15]

It is easy to imagine that Stevens may have been frustrated as his natural authority became less and less effective. It is easy, too, to understand why he became gradually involved with side projects during these years. From his museum of antique cars to his racing teams to his quixotic decade-long attempt to build the Satellite Towers hotel in downtown Milwaukee, Stevens spent much of the 1960s and 1970s on extracurricular schemes. Many of the firm's commissions of the period, such as the development of 3M's corporate identity, were great marketplace successes but lacked the idiosyncratic character that Stevens had previously brought to his work. The exciting prophetic designs that the office did undertake during these years, such as the

Fig. 4 Rendering for the Brooks Stevens Design office in Mequon, 1970

promotional "showboats" designed for Evinrude between 1956 and 1962, were increasingly distant from the workmanlike products to which most of the staff devoted their time. Most disheartening of all, the client that Stevens and many of his staffers cared about most deeply, Studebaker, closed its South Bend automobile plant in December of 1963.

These developments eventually took their toll on Stevens both personally and professionally. Though his warm relationships with corporate leaders remained intact, his firm entered its first fallow period in and around the year 1970. With the Vietnam War on, the economy heading into recession, and the use of in-house design departments on the rise, business was hard to come by. This condition worsened immeasurably during another office move to Mequon, near the grounds of Stevens's auto museum. The planning of the new building was badly managed, and the staff was forced to work in a temporary trailer for several months (fig. 4). By the time the new facility was finally ready, Stevens had become clinically depressed. Only with the help of his sons and design staffers, and treatment with early chemical antidepressants, was he able to recover. Sadly, it looked as though Stevens's design career would end with a whimper rather than a bang.

1. Stevens, quoted in Gay Pauley, "Keeping Up with Joneses Called 'Healthy' Trait," *Pittsburgh Press*, 25 January 1966.

2. "Frank-Talking Designer Argues His Philosophy," *Milwaukee Engineering* 40 (April 1961): 12–13. See also "Designer Applauds Status-Seekers Who Keep U.S. Economy Booming," *Trenton Evening Times*, 19 January 1966; Jo Sandin, "Go Ahead—Keep Up with the Joneses," *Milwaukee Journal*, 12 January 1965.

3. Vance Packard, *The Waste Makers* (New York: David McKay, 1960), 54, 68. On Packard, see Daniel Horowitz, *Vance Packard and American Social Criticism* (Chapel Hill: University of North Carolina Press, 1994).

4. "Frank-Talking Designer," 12–13. For later attacks on planned obsolescence from a variety of perspectives, see Victor Papanek, *Design for the Real World: Human Ecology and Social Change* (New York: Pantheon Books, 1972); Nigel Whiteley, *Design for Society* (London: Reaktion Books, 1993). For a uniquely thoughtful and sympathetic response from one of Stevens's fellow designers, see George Nelson, "Obsolescence," in *Problems of Design* (New York: Whitney Publications, 1957).

5. "The Crime of 'Planned Obsolescence,'" *Weekly People*, 18 October 1958.

6. "Forty-five Apprentice Diplomas Given at Manitowoc," *Manitowoc (Wis.) Herald-Times and Two Rivers Reporter*, 17 May 1960.

7. Karl Prentiss, "Brooks Stevens: He Has Designs on Your Dough," *True Magazine*, April 1958.

8. Though no supporter of planned obsolescence, the Marxist theorist Stuart Ewen has pointed out this weakness in Stevens's most ardent critic: "Packard's analysis itself [was] neutralized by its fixation on questions of corruption and abuse." See "The Social Crisis of Mass Culture," in *The Captains of Consciousness* (New York: McGraw-Hill, 1976), 187–220.

9. "Designer Brooks Stevens Introduces OMISA's New Lines," *Outboard Marine International News and Notes* 3 (November 1960).

10. Sylvia Bernstein, "Have You Heard?" *Milwaukee Sentinel*, 15 November 1967. See also "'Planned Obsolescence' Goal on Products Told by Designer," *Milwaukee Journal*, 15 May 1956, in which Stevens argued that "the lifeblood of the traded-in automobile, refrigerator, or TV passes on to the good American consumer in a lesser income bracket who could not otherwise afford this luxury at its original retail price."

11. Prentiss, "Brooks Stevens."

12. Brooks Stevens and Walter Dorwin Teague, "Planned Obsolescence," *Rotarian Magazine*, February 1960, 1–5.

13. "New Offices at Shorewood," *Milwaukee Sentinel*, 5 May 1956.

14. Tom Green, conversation with the author, 2002.

15. Stevens, interview with Chip Duncan, 1990–91.

AMF Jet Trike 1956

"Around Christmastime, the windows of our favorite toy stores start to bristle with rocketry," the satirist Peter Blake wrote in 1964. "It is a heartwarming sight: There are not only small-scale models of brightly colored 'Ultimate Weapons,' but plenty of full-sized ICBMs as well, complete with atomic warheads designed to enable the Lovable Ones to zero in on the adult enemy."[1]

AMF Jet Trike 1956

As was often the case, Stevens was in on the beginnings of this particular trend. In 1956 he had secured a contract with the American Motor Foundry Company (AMF) of New York. AMF had recently absorbed the Junior Toy Corporation and the Binghamton Manufacturing Company (BMC), and Stevens was assigned responsibility for these subsidiaries in addition to the main brand. It was an opportunity for his designers to let their imaginations run wild; the products that were eventually produced, as lively as they were, only hinted at the science fiction–influenced renderings that inspired them.

In a 1959 essay written for a trade publication, Stevens remarked that "the boy who wishes his father were a jet ace or rocket pilot, and the girl who watches her mother operate a gadget-bristling stove, are not going to be satisfied with toys that are dull, cold, and inanimate." The rigid gender separation suggested by this observation was borne out by the firm's work. For girls, Brooks Stevens Associates had designed a full set of kitchen appliances for the Structo Company; for boys, they had done the 1957 Jet Trike. "At that time," Stevens explained, "rockets were playing an important part in the news, flying saucers were reported skimming the skies in several parts of the country, and new Nike bases were being built at several points. All three of these matters influenced the design of a new tricycle, which we believed would receive the plaudits of the young consumer. We were right, for it was an immediate sales success."[2] Stevens was right to say that rockets were in the news. *Sputnik* was launched in the same year as the Jet Trike, and at the height of the Cold War it is likely that the tricycle was intended to touch a nerve—a good example of another of Stevens's precepts, that a toy should appeal simultaneously to parent and child, though not necessarily for the same reasons.

Stevens also won AMF commissions for the design of a series of toy trucks, pedal cars, toy tractors, and bicycles. These assignments placed him in head-to-head competition with Cleveland's Viktor Schreckengost. Though best known for his painted ceramic vessels and sculpture, Schreckengost was also an accomplished industrial designer with particular experience in the bicycle and pedal-car industries. His main client in this area, Murray Ohio, was undoubtedly AMF's target when it hired Stevens. Both men had designed toy vehicles in the past; Stevens had done a line of "juvenile autos" and fire trucks in 1940 for the American National Company in Toledo, while Schreckengost's "Champion" pedal car for Murray was the top seller in the market. From 1957 on, the two designers competed in a back-and-forth of product-styling ideas, first in the pedal-car market and later in bicycles. As late as 1969 both men produced virtually identical "dragster"-style bikes for separate clients—Schreckengost for Murray, and Stevens for Sears, Roebuck & Co. Both the Murray Mark II Eliminator and the Sears Screamer sported wraparound handles, banana seats, and undersize front wheels (which Schreckengost purportedly borrowed from the Californian hobbyist's practice of mounting a tricycle wheel on the front of a bicycle, in emulation of a "chopper" motorcycle). The overall look of Stevens's bike for Sears was probably lifted directly from Schreckengost's, or possibly from the similar "Krate" bicycles that Schwinn began producing in 1968. Stevens did, however, add an optional flat-spoked "mag wheel," which, like its counterparts on drag-racing cars, produced an exciting roaring sound at high speeds.[3]

1. Peter Blake and Robert Osborn, *The Everlasting Cocktail Party: A Layman's Guide to Culture Climbing* (New York: Dial Press, 1964), 70.

2. Brooks Stevens, "Why an Industrial Designer in the Toy Industry," *Toys and Novelties*, March 1959, 378–79, 471.

3. For Schreckengost's designs, see Henry Adams, *Viktor Schreckengost and Twentieth-Century Design* (Cleveland: Cleveland Museum of Art, 1999); the Murray Eliminator is pictured on 137. See also Jane Dwyre Garton, *Pedal Cars: Chasing the Kidallac* (Atglen, Pa.: Schiffer Publishing, 1999), for more on both designers' pedal cars.

AMF Rocket tricycle 1958
BMC toy tractor 1954
Sears Screamer bicycle 1969

The Evinrude "shrieker" prototypes 1956–62

Since the inception of industrial design in the 1920s, the line between it and its more anonymous and less respected cousin, advertising, has been a blurry one. Brooks Stevens consistently tried to take advantage of this fact. He used design as a sales gimmick throughout his career, and never more effectively than in a series of nautical designs created for the Evinrude division of Outboard Marine Company between 1956 and 1962. In these confections of design, futurism, engineering, and silliness, Stevens reached the high-water mark of styling as a form of promotion, not only in his own career but also in the history of industrial design as a whole.

In all there were seven of these "shriekers," as Stevens called them. All were unique prototypes built exclusively for exhibit at the National Boat Show, which premiered annually in New York City and then traveled to Chicago and San Francisco. In each case, the mandate was the same: to design a radical-looking watercraft that would challenge conventional thinking in boat design. There was also a more important, if mostly tacit, mandate to create a glamorous showcase for the latest Evinrude outboard motor. Stevens later recalled: "I felt that the display of outboard motors behind long velvet ropes and flanked by batteries of salesmen was doomed. I was convinced that the only way to dramatize our motors was to dramatize our boats."[1] Since the design firm was also responsible for the motors themselves, it was possible to coordinate this visual pairing carefully. The strategy ensured that each year the Evinrude display at the boat show, which might ordinarily be overshadowed by companies with full-size vessels on view, would instead be a showstopper. More surprisingly, Stevens's inventions were convincing enough that they actually affected the real world of boat construction and marketing.

Evinrude Lark 1956

Of the seven boat show prototypes that were eventually built, the first was the one that would have the most direct influence on nautical manufacturers. It seems probable that when the prototype program was launched in 1956, no one involved expected it to be anything more than a onetime occurrence. Perhaps for this reason, Stevens fell back on his old standby of automobile styling. He produced the Lark, a sixteen-foot runabout in red, gray, and white that stood in vivid contrast to the boat designs then on the market, including the ones Stevens himself had produced in the past for Globe and Chris-Craft. The Lark was patterned after a sports car. It had full-length stainless steel trim, bucket seats upholstered in a harlequin pattern, and most dramatically, a rear end that sported a pair of fins. These contained lights and also acted as moorings for water-skiing cables, but their real purpose was to frame the new Evinrude thirty-horsepower motor that shared the Lark name. Stevens was justifiably confident in the impact that his creation would have. "Traditionalists may wail," he said, "but this new craft will cause a furor. We are reluctant to use the term 'dreamboat,' but it is nearly that, and certainly a prophetic design which we feel will influence other designers and builders."[2] As it turned out, the reaction was more dramatic than the designer could have anticipated. Most coverage of the boat shows in both New York

Evinrude Fisherman 1957

and Chicago featured photography of the Lark, and as Stevens had predicted, the boat industry took notice. One year after the Lark's unveiling, the Cadillac division of the boat-building firm Wagemaker launched a version of Stevens's design under the name "Sea Lark," which made the cover of *Newsweek*.[3] By 1960 most boat builders had sport models that were fitted with fins, metal trim, car-like flush door panels, and bucket seats—all features introduced by Stevens.[4]

Model for the Evinrude Starflite 1958

Given the general acclaim that the Lark had garnered, it was natural for Evinrude to repeat the performance. This time, all involved must have anticipated the press coverage they would receive, and they accordingly came up with the most "far-out" design of Stevens's career: the flying saucer–shaped Fisherman. The initial idea for a fishing boat was provided by Howard Larson, Evinrude's director of sales, who had noticed that these utilitarian craft had received virtually no attention from the design establishment. Stevens's firm took the idea and ran with it, inventing a boat that looked as if it had come from a sci-fi pulp novel. Fourteen feet in diameter and constructed of reinforced plastic, the Fisherman fairly bristled with conveniences: an eleven-foot mast that doubled as a folding umbrella and radio aerial; a ring of outward-facing angler's chairs upholstered in blue Naugahyde; and most outlandishly, a "Subsea Control" featuring sonar, a depth sounding device, navigation equipment, and a monitor that was hooked up to an underwater color television camera. (The Subsea Control was fictional but was rendered in the prototype as an impressive-looking set of dials and knobs.) Evinrude's outboards were again highlighted, this time through the ingenious contrivance of bubble-shaped glass "nacelles." All steering was accomplished by varying the speed of the two eighteen-horsepower motors, so there was no rudder. All in all, Evinrude explained, the craft "[relied] a bit on the inference of space travel, flying saucers, and other atomic-flavored thinking."[5]

Though it was less pertinent to the real world of boat manufacture, the Fisherman far outstripped the Lark in terms of press coverage. Journalists delighted in inventing descriptors for the space-age boat: "a mixing bowl with egg beaters," "a giant circular ashtray," "a seagoing yo-yo," "a modernistic cuspidor."[6] One Milwaukee writer summed up the general reaction: "Goggle eyed previewers agreed that it combined the elegance and beauty of a soup tureen, but there was some argument about whether it would float."[7] This question was settled in August. After being shown at several boat shows—spinning on a turntable while the umbrella went up and down—the craft was finally proven seaworthy. The test run was conducted on the Milwaukee River, where the Fisherman paraded past curious crowds at speeds between six and ten miles per hour, twirled on its axis, turned right angles, and finally was brought back ashore. Sadly, the boat was destroyed after being shown at the Brussels World's Fair in 1958.

For his next performance, Stevens sounded a more practical note and again drew upon his experience with auto design, this time approximating the function and styling of a contemporary station wagon. The boat was dubbed the Starflite, again in conjunction with the release of a motor (a new fifty-horsepower model) bearing the same name. The design, though stylish, was much more pragmatic than that of the other Evinrude showboats. Stevens wrote that "the proper utilization of space is more important in a boat than in any means of transportation with the possible exception of aircraft," and the flexibility of the Starflite reflected this principle.[8] The craft was fitted with an electrically powered telescoping cabin top and four seats that converted automatically to form sleeping bunks. It also had amenities such as cabinetry, a built-in refrigerator, and a two-burner stove—reminiscent of the streamlined land yacht Stevens had designed in the 1930s.[9] The one note of real showmanship was a Plexiglas shield placed over the motor, ostensibly to reduce running noise. The Starflite was shown at the New York boat show surrounded by a circular metal ramp, which permitted visitors a privileged view of the boat's interior.

Stevens and Evinrude continued to emphasize the theme of flexibility with their 1959 effort, the Housefloat. This ungainly creation was a modular waterborne living center that rode atop catamaran-like pontoons. Each of the six sections of the Housefloat was seven by eleven feet and was connected to its neighbor by extruded aluminum sliding joints. Customers were meant to begin by purchasing two modules and gradually expand to the full six as their family grew in size. (Stevens had created a waterborne metaphor for the rapidly expanding suburban population of the 1950s.) When fully assembled, the craft would have open deck area, cabins, a bridge, three pontoons, and two thirty-five-horsepower Lark motors. All of this, Stevens claimed, could be accomplished for a retail price of five thousand dollars—less than half the price of the previous shriekers. The pragmatism of the plan paid off. Plans were distributed to home hobbyists who wished to build their own versions of the Housefloat, and the Kayot Company in Mankato, Minnesota, soon put a line of similar pontoon-riding houseboats into production.

After the relatively sedate Starflite and Housefloat, Stevens returned to gonzo showmanship in 1960 with the Jetstream, a sixteen-foot sport runabout with thirteen-foot powered pontoons. When the boat reached three-fourths of its maximum speed, the pontoons lowered into the water and lifted the main hull off the surface, reducing drag and increasing overall speed. This dramatic creation earned Stevens the title of "the enfant terrible of industrial design" and attracted more press attention than all the previous showboats, including the Fisherman.[10] But if the design of the Jetstream was more exciting than that of the other Evinrude prototypes, it was also more exacting. To achieve the correct underwater hull shape, Stevens revived his collaboration with Douglas Van Patten, the naval architect who had assisted in the design of the Globe runabouts in 1946, to ensure that the engineering of the hull and pontoons would be accurate. The styling of the boat reflected these narrow tolerances by referring specifically to aircraft design, with a bubble-enclosed cockpit and a steering wheel that swung on a short boom from helmsman to copilot.[11] (Stevens would again use this idea, taken from military fighter planes, in a prophetic fuel cell–powered car called the Utopia the following year.) The boat ran on a new Starflite II seventy-five-horsepower motor—the most powerful in the Evinrude line—which was itself streamlined to tight tolerances. Stevens claimed that the graceful curves of the motor eliminated "talking surfaces," so that there was an overall noise reduction of 22 percent.

EVINRUDE
House float
...inexpensive elegance in living afloat

An original design by Evinrude and Brooks Stevens

Brooks Stevens with the model for the Evinrude Housefloat 1959

Advertisement for the Evinrude Housefloat 1959

The penultimate shrieker was a natural follow-up to the airplane styling of the Jetstream. As Stevens explained it, when he overheard spectators at the 1960 boat show exclaim, "I don't know how Evinrude will be able to top this—I guess they'll have to make the next one fly," he decided that the next one would do just that.[12] The solution was the Heli-bout, a speedboat that could be converted into a helicopter. Again, Stevens managed to feature the outboard motor, another seventy-five-horsepower Starflite, by having it power the rotors through the application of flexible driveshafts and reduction gears. Because the motor would be lifted out of the water while the craft was aloft, a special coolant system was planned for the stern. None of this engineering was ever put to the test; the prototype that was built for the boat shows was not light enough to achieve liftoff, and its rotors were only for display purposes. But the basic idea, Stevens insisted, was both aerodynamically sound and eminently practical: "You can take off from your swimming pool, patio or front lawn. In a matter of an hour or two you can set down

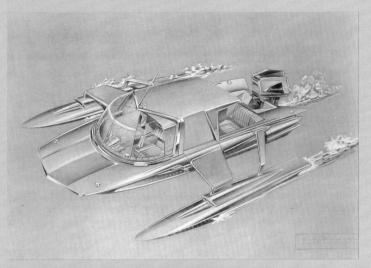

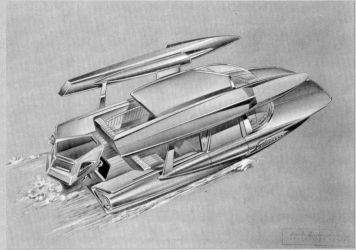

HELI-BOUT

Renderings for the Evinrude Jetstream 1960 (above, left and right)

Rendering for the Evinrude Heli-bout 1961 (lower)

on your favorite lake or stream and enjoy a pleasant weekend. . . . No more long hours of fighting traffic or looking for a place to put your boat in the water. How can you beat that?"[13] In terms
of styling, the Heli-bout echoed the most exciting prophetics of the past. Like the Lark, it had
two tail fins (this time tipped with stabilizing rotors), and like the Jetstream, it boasted a glass-
enclosed cockpit equipped with a swinging steering column.

Stevens's finale at the boat shows was, as the designer conceded, "a complete reversal of general
theme," in that it was dedicated to what had already been rather than what was to come.[14]
The 1962 Showboat, built by the Kayot Company, was a miniature version of a Mississippi River
steam-powered packet. Ingeniously, Stevens placed a grille in the foredeck,
which was vented through two otherwise fake smokestacks, creating
the illusion of actual steam power. In actuality the craft was powered by
a forty-horsepower Evinrude Lark engine, which could be controlled
remotely from a wheelhouse. The Showboat inspired a full-scale replica
called the Lady of the Lake, which Stevens designed in collaboration
with his old associate from the Globe Corporation, Russell Gage.[15]

The nostalgic Showboat was the last of the Evinrude shriekers. OMC made
the decision to enter the boat business for real and, perhaps feeling that
it did not want to compete with Stevens's imagination, had him concen-
trate on styling the company's expensive new tri-hull fiberglass boats.
During their seven-year run, however, the Evinrude prototypes achieved
a degree of notoriety that was unequaled in Stevens's career. Prior to each
boat show, newspapers in New York, Chicago, and San Francisco would
speculate on Evinrude's next outlandish proposal. Stevens's team kept
each new idea top secret, occasionally leaking an intriguing detail. When
the boats actually hit the display stand, they were wrapped in pedestrian ramps, signs, and lights,
making them seem even more extraordinary than they actually were. But through all of the
stagecraft, clever means were devised to draw attention to the motors themselves, which were
of course the real product on offer. Sadly, the very novelty of the prototypes meant that once
they had made their splash, they were not of great value to the company. The Heli-bout is the
only one of the prototypes known to have survived.

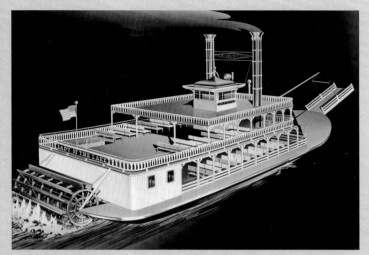

Evinrude Showboat 1962

1. "Runabout Aided by Two Pontoons," *New York Times*, 19 January 1960.

2. "Evinrude's New Lark Heralds New Morn in Boating," *New York Times*, 12 January 1956.

3. *Newsweek*, 15 April 1957.

4. Rick O'Shea, "Jet Stream Catches On," *Evansville (Ind.) Courier and Press*, 17 July 1960.

5. Advertisement for the Evinrude Fisherman, 1957, Brooks Stevens Archive, Milwaukee Art Museum.

6. "Disc Shaped Fishing Boat Unveiled," *Milwaukee Sentinel*, 25 May 1957; "Evinrude's Whirling Saucer Has Trial Spins,"
Motor Boating, August 1957, 114; Hank Bowman, "Water Line," syndicated press release, 1960, Brooks Stevens Archive,
Milwaukee Art Museum; "Evinrude 'Floating Saucer' Flouts Boating Traditions," *Milwaukee Journal*, 11 January 1957.
See also "Resemblances," *New Yorker*, 2 February 1957, 26; "Craft Built to Inspire Adventure in Design," *Chicago Daily
Tribune*, 8 February 1957, sec. 2; Til Ferdenzi, "Round Trip," *New York Journal-American*, 18 January 1957.

7. "Many Badger Exhibits in N.Y. Motorboat Show," *Milwaukee Journal*, 20 January 1957.

8. "He Has Designs on Your Boat," *Outboard Progress*, May 1960, 32–33.

9. "Sea 'Station Wagon' Rides High at Show," *Milwaukee Journal*, 16 January 1958.

10. Karl Prentiss, "Brooks Stevens: He Has Designs on Your Dough," *True: The Man's Magazine*, April 1958.

11. Rick O'Shea, "Jet Stream Catches On," *Evansville (Ind.) Courier and Press*, 17 July 1960.

12. Roger Williams, "Heli-Bout Proves Boat Show-Stopper," *San Francisco News-Call Bulletin*, 6 February 1961.

13. Ibid.

14. Brooks Stevens Associates press release, ca. 1962, Brooks Stevens Archive.

15. Dorothy Kinkaid, "New Boat on the Lake," *Milwaukee Sentinel*, 28 May 1963.

Allen-Bradley corporate logo 1958

One of the major sources of income for Stevens's design firm was the machine tool industry. While less exciting and romantic than his automotive and nautical projects, machine tools were the backbone of Milwaukee's economy in the years when Stevens's career flourished. Although his first allegiance was to Cutler-Hammer, thanks to his father's position in the engineering department there, his primary postwar client in the field was Allen-Bradley. The fit was a natural one. Even today Allen-Bradley retains a dominant presence on the Milwaukee landscape, with an enormous plant topped by an octagon-faced clock tower. The company was the city's best example of the benevolent paternalism that was common in corporate America in the early twentieth century; it even fielded its own basketball team and touring orchestra. In short, Allen-Bradley was a company that was highly conscious of both internal morale and external relations—two areas where industrial design might be of great assistance. In addition, the two brothers who ran the firm, Harry and Lynde Bradley, were both inveterate tinkerers who had a strong interest in art. They were perfect candidates for Stevens's particular charms, and it is unsurprising that they should have welcomed his input so enthusiastically.

Rendering for a Bradley washfountain 1938
Allen-Bradley motor control enclosures 1958
*Before and after redesign; Stevens's redesigned logo
appears on the enclosure to the right.*

Stevens's first Bradley-related commission came early in his career. Harry Bradley had invented a large semicircular stainless-steel washfountain for use by several people simultaneously, reportedly to eliminate long lines at the factory sink at the end of the workday. This simple but useful notion was quite distant from Allen-Bradley's usual product line, so the patents were sold to an independent concern in Menominee Falls, Wisconsin, which went on to manufacture the washfountains. When Stevens was hired to style the product, his firm provided a fairly typical design scheme based on horizontal speed lines. The washfountains proved a commercial success in a variety of locales, from factory floors to the restrooms at Wrigley Field. A version close to Stevens's original 1940 design is still produced by the Bradley Corporation in Menominee Falls.

It was not until 1958 that Stevens again heard from the Bradleys, but this time the relationship would be much more meaningful for both parties. Summoned at Harry Bradley's request by his assistant, Fred Loock, Stevens was asked to redesign the company's logo. Working under the leadership of Ray Anderson, Stevens's graphics staff retained the classic octagon shape but cleaned up the overall image and replaced the antique typeface with a tighter, more modern font. Subsequently the commission broadened into the project of redesigning all of Allen-Bradley's machine control enclosures, beginning with the 1961 "709" Series. In contrast to the "before and after" images that populated Stevens's early presentation books, in which the impact of the designer was quite dramatic, the difference between the new enclosures and their outmoded cousins is a subtle one. The new Allen-Bradley enclosures were no more rational or clear than their antecedents. They simply projected more authority or, as the company itself put it in advertisements, "aristocratic appearance." Like the octagonal logo itself, the redesigned box is devoid of its prior softness. It is crisply rectilinear and has little unnecessary shaping beyond the beveled "picture frame" of the front face, which emphasizes the simplified logo and push-buttons held within. Visual interest is provided by a contrast of finishes, rather than by color or shape. This overall starkness of form speaks to the narrowing scope of industrial design in the early 1960s; as is clear from comparison with the enclosure that Stevens did for Cutler Hammer in his early career, scrupulousness was now to be preferred to sculptural vigor.[1]

---

1. For more on Stevens and Allen-Bradley, see Gary Drinan, "Brooks Stevens: Bringing a New Look to A-B Products for More than Fifty Years," *Allen-Bradley Network*, March 1994, 1. The author thanks Jim Jerschefske for this reference.

Oscar Mayer Wienermobile 1958

"There's nothing more aerodynamic than a wiener," Stevens once remarked when asked about his most endearing design. While he did not originate the promotional vehicle—the Oscar Mayer Company of Madison, Wisconsin, came up with the idea in 1936—Stevens did create the classic shape of the famous frank when commissioned to redesign it in 1958. His main contribution, as he put it, "was to put the wiener in the bun."[1]

The original vehicle had been a low, inelegant truck with a giant hot dog riding atop it. Taking advantage of the possibilities of molded fiberglass construction, Stevens transformed the lower section into a sculptural form that was cast in sections from a hand-built full-scale model. He also claimed to have coined the term "Wienermobile," to replace the previous moniker, "Wiener Wagon," which he found to be antiquated. Finally, Stevens added a dramatic bubble cockpit to the front, creating a sense of space-age design that contrasted pleasantly with the fundamentally hokey nature of the project. Unfortunately this feature proved to be less than practical, as it leaked in rainy weather and created unbearable heat for the driver on sunny days. (Ironically Stevens himself had predicted these problems in his wartime dismissals of the bubble-topped plastic cars of the future.) He had a chance to correct his error a decade later, however, and replaced the open glass front with a "goggle-shaped" windshield that lacked science fiction connotations but had a great deal of personality nonetheless.

Oscar Mayer Wienermobile 1958

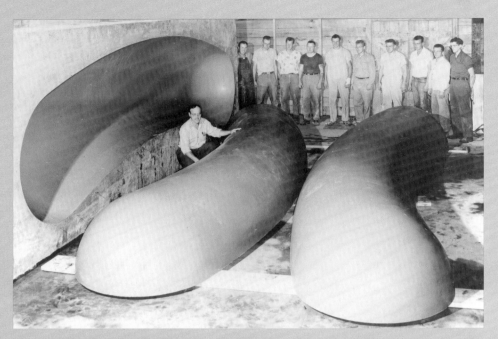

Oscar Mayer Wiener Wagon 1936
Casting the fiberglass wiener in two halves 1958
Oscar Mayer Wienermobile 1987

Many years after Stevens's redesign of the Wienermobile, his family once again became involved with the itinerant sausage. Oscar Mayer approached Brooks's sons Steve and David to build a new fleet of Wienermobiles in 1987, using the existing design as a mold. Within two years the brothers and longtime Stevens associate Alice Preston had built nine of the vehicles, using a Chevrolet van for a chassis base. Both Steve and David Stevens continue to work with the program as builders and troubleshooters—an end to the story that their father surely would have relished.

1. Brooks Stevens, interview with Chip Duncan, 1990–91, transcript, Brooks Stevens Archive, Milwaukee Art Museum.

Brooks Stevens Auto Museum 1959

It is hard to say just when Stevens first conceived the idea of building a permanent display space for his vintage automobile collection. The opening of the Brooks Stevens Auto Museum took place on September 2, 1959—the proud proprietor attended the event in a black and orange blazer and a leather motoring cap with dust goggles—but it was a long time in coming. Stevens had been building his collection since his acquisition of an L29 Cord in 1937. By 1949 he was in possession of sixteen cars, some of them antique and some of his own design.

Only six years later, that number had climbed to thirty-five, and he had started referring to the collection by the rather pretentious name of "Brookington Limited." For tax reasons and to solve the logistical difficulties of showing his cars only on an ad hoc basis, Stevens eventually resolved to build a permanent public museum facility for his collection. By 1957 the articles of incorporation for a new venue for the display of the autos had been drafted, and a site was soon chosen in Mequon, a suburb northwest of Milwaukee.

Taking his cue from the cars themselves (and perhaps from the new Disneyland theme park in California as well), Stevens had the museum grounds landscaped to suggest the early twentieth century. One approached the main building via a dirt road with a covered bridge, passing a lake with a 1911 steam-powered yacht. Behind the museum was a farmhouse that would be remodeled for office space and a "research and development" building. This small auto shop would soon prove invaluable as a space to construct automobile models under the watchful eyes of Frank Newschwager and Ray Besasie Sr., who had been Stevens's personal mechanics since the 1940s. In later years, Brooks's son David would take charge of the shop, to be followed by Ron Paetow. Among the cars that were built there were the prototypes of the Studebaker Gran Turismo Hawk and the Excalibur SSK roadster.

The museum itself had 12,500 square feet of exhibition space and, when it opened, displayed thirty-four autos, most of them from Stevens's personal collection, though a few had been borrowed from his friends in the world of car collecting. Among the star vehicles were a 1905 one-cylinder Cadillac roadster, a 1914 Marmon Wasp, a 1927 Hispano-Suiza town car, a 1930 L-29 Cord coupe custom-designed by Alexis de Sakhnoffsky, a 1939 Talbot Lago, and a 1928 Mercedes phaeton that had belonged to Al Jolson and would later serve as the inspiration for the Excalibur.[1] The museum also exhibited postwar vehicles that Stevens respected, including a 1954 Rolls Royce Silver Wraith town car. The collection would grow steadily over time, peaking at about seventy-five cars in the 1970s. Though the museum drew Stevens's attention (and resources) away from the design business, it did play an important role in inspiring his auto designs. It also served as a repository for the preservation

Brooks Stevens Auto Museum 1959
Stevens with a newly acquired 1950 Jaguar XK-120.
The two tone paint scheme was Stevens's own design.

of vehicles created by the firm, from a 1948 Jeepster and 1951 Kaiser to the 1961 Heli-bout and the Studebaker prototypes of the mid-1960s.

The museum took on new life in 1987, when its shop served as the construction site for the new fleet of Wienermobiles. Alice Preston, a longtime mechanic at the shop, took over as curator of the museum at that point and opened a restoration shop to defray the museum's expenses. Toward the end of his life, Stevens took some of the museum's antique cars to road rallies around the country—a final hurrah for his racing days. After he passed away, the museum stayed open for some time but finally closed in 1999. The cars were sold, with a good part of the proceeds from the sale going to the Milwaukee Institute of Art and Design.

1. For images and discussion of some of these cars, see Tom Burnside, "Selections from the Brooks Stevens Collection," *Automobile Quarterly* 2 (winter 1963): 400–405.

Willys do Brasil Aero 2600 automobile 1960

Thanks to the 1953 merger of Kaiser-Frazer and Willys-Overland, Stevens had the rare opportunity to redesign several of his previous efforts with a decade of hindsight. Although he had not done any work for Willys for several years, he had been actively involved in styling Kaiser-Frazer's passenger cars in the early 1950s and was also developing a new series of "Forward

Model for the Willys do Brasil Aero 2600 automobile 1959

Control" trucks for the 1957 model year. He was therefore a logical choice of consultant when, in 1955, the newly reconstituted firm Kaiser-Willys launched two South American spin-off companies called Willys do Brasil and Industrias Kaiser Argentina, centered in São Paulo and Buenos Aires, respectively. Under the leadership of Edgar Kaiser, these new firms quickly became (in Stevens's words) "an automotive onslaught" on a new marketplace, assembling and retailing cars not only from Kaiser-Willys but also from the French manufacturer Renault.[1]

Even though neither Brazil nor Argentina had a history of auto manufacturing, the venture was attractive on several counts. On a practical level, tooling dies and surplus parts that had already outlived their usefulness in the United States could be reused in a new market. In addition, the overall geopolitical circumstances in Latin America meant that the American government was eager to support venture capitalism in that part of the world. Stevens was acutely aware of this fact and described Brazil's "rocketing automotive industry" as a "bulwark against communism and Castroism in South America." Brazilian leaders and influential citizens, he claimed, "consider Castro an insane zealot—an idiot and a pawn—and feel that it will not be long before he is liquidated."[2] By the time Stevens was hired as a consultant for Willys do Brasil in 1958, the company was already one of the country's largest employers.

A slightly modified version of the 1946 Jeep Station Wagon had been produced in São Paulo beginning in 1954, and the 1951 Kaiser to which Stevens had contributed was introduced in Argentina two years later. This pattern of refurbishing old designs would continue under Stevens's watch. He first produced a new version of the Willys car that was closest to his heart, the Jeepster. The phaeton was given a new front end and a new name, the Saci, in honor of a gremlin in regional mythology. A handmade scale mock-up for the car is one of the rare survivals from Stevens's design shop; it shows the care and precision that craftsmen such as Dick Frank brought to the firm's models. The overall structure is made of painted fiberglass, with accents in metal, glass, paint, and reflective tape. Over the ensuing years Stevens executed several other updated versions of old Willys designs for the South American market, including a revised treatment of the station wagon called the Rural and a new pickup truck. Both featured bracketlike fenders over the back wheels, just like the original Jeepster and its new Brazilian variant, as well as special mudguards and stone deflectors to handle the rough roads of South America.

Another Willys do Brasil car for which Stevens acted as design consultant was the Aero Willys 2600. This short and comparatively luxurious passenger car was the first automobile to be manufactured in São Paulo entirely of Brazilian parts. It was an updated version of the 1955 Willys Aero, which had been successful in the United States and had been sold in Brazil previously. As was the case with Stevens's original work for Willys-Overland, the reuse of tooling

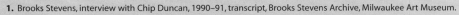

was a high priority. The only major metal stampings that were modified were the quarter panels and the new "slab-sided" roof (which was similar to that Stevens had used on his 1955 Gaylord), but the car also featured distinctive new hooded headlights and a radically simplified profile with a single medial strip of chrome. The car's grille was lifted from the Willys Rural in order to promote brand identity.[3] The quarter-scale model of the new Aero was produced in Stevens's design office shop and photographed in front of the new Eero Saarinen War Memorial Center in Milwaukee—the building that now houses the Milwaukee Art Museum.

Model for the Willys do Brasil "Jeepster," known as the Saci 1958

Willys do Brasil pickup truck ca. 1960

1. Brooks Stevens, interview with Chip Duncan, 1990–91, transcript, Brooks Stevens Archive, Milwaukee Art Museum.

2. Quoted in unidentified article, ca. January 1963, Brooks Stevens Archive.

3. Brooks Stevens, designer's notes on the Aero-Willys redesign, 25 January 1961, Brooks Stevens Archive.

Hotpoint Custom Trend appliances 1960

"The American consumer simply can't tell you what he wants until he sees it," Brooks Stevens said in 1960. "Oh, the homemaker might say, 'I want a thing that will wash, dry, iron and fold my clothes,' but can't be more specific."[1] Fortunately for American consumers, Stevens stood ready not only to give them what they needed but also to tell them that they needed it. He was a designer not only of products but also of lifestyle, and his ambition was to both conform to and reshape the patterns of the home. Stevens often spoke of "Mr. and Mrs. America" when describing the market for his designs, and he had in mind a relatively homogeneous public: white, middle-class, suburban, conventional families. These were the fictional people who appeared in advertisements for his lawn mowers, outboard motors, and station wagons, and they were the people whose lives he tried to understand and improve.

Custom Trend Gourmet Center 1960

Of Stevens's attempts to articulate a vision of domestic lifestyle, the most adventurous were a pair of prophetic designs executed for the appliance company Hotpoint in 1960. Made for the appliance show at the Chicago Merchandise Mart, these were something like the Evinrude "shriekers" or prophetic cars that Stevens had done—ideas that pointed the way to a possible future while creating publicity in the present. They were the last in a series of prototype appliances that Hotpoint had shown in Chicago annually since 1954 under the direction of Raymond Sandin, a Swedish-born architect who headed the company's design department.[2]

The series—fittingly entitled "Custom Trend"—managed to be both tantalizingly cutting-edge and profoundly conventional. Stevens's ideas did not depart from this pattern. One, the "Gourmet Center," was an amalgamation of most of the appliances in the average kitchen: a refrigerated storage area, a freezer, an oven and range, and a sink with running water. When not in use, this multitasking center folded into a wood-faced cabinet. By fusing together multiple appliances, Stevens perfectly captured the period ideal of entertaining with a minimum of fuss. The second design, a "Rotisserie-Barbecue," took this idea of flexibility and made it portable. The device was centered on a heating element that rotated from a vertical to a horizontal position, so that the user could cook either on the grill or on rotating spits. Stevens gave its copper-lined filtration hood, reminiscent of that on a French cooking stove, a "rather subtle provincial shape to soften the overall atmosphere of the appliance."[3] The whole affair was mounted on wheels so that it could be taken from kitchen to patio, in the spirit of the open plans of the era's houses. Like all of Sandin's efforts at Hotpoint, the focus was on "casualness" with an air of luxury—the ideal of a prosperous postwar America.

1. "Visionary Appliances Serve Practical Purpose for Firms," *Milwaukee Journal*, 10 January 1960. See also "Chicago Promises Leisurely Living," *Philadelphia Bulletin*, 6 January 1960.

2. Arthur J. Pulos, *The American Design Adventure, 1940–1975* (Cambridge: MIT Press, 1988), 130–35.

3. Brooks Stevens, designer's notes, undated, Brooks Stevens Archive, Milwaukee Art Museum.

Studebaker Gran Turismo Hawk automobile 1961

Studebaker—the largest auto manufacturer in America after the "Big Three" of Ford, Chrysler, and General Motors during the postwar economic boom—was until the 1960s firmly the design territory of Raymond Loewy. The aristocratic Frenchman first had input into the company's autos when he designed the 1939 Champion. The commercial success of that car meant that after World War II Loewy was able to displace Studebaker's own staff entirely. He set up a remote office in South Bend and began a campaign of independent design consultations that is unequaled in automotive history. Over the next decade he created a long list of classics, including the Commander, the Starliner, and the Speedster. These cars, with their stunning low hoods and muscular chrome articulation, had the distinct flavor of European sports cars and tended to be more successful aesthetically than commercially. In 1956 Studebaker finally canceled Loewy's contract; having merged with Packard, the company once again had an in-house design staff and felt that it could no longer afford Loewy's extravagant design fees.[1]

Brooks Stevens had always felt keenly competitive with the older and more famous Loewy, and in 1961 he had his chance to move in on his New York rival's territory. Having fallen on financial hard times, the South Bend auto manufacturer brought in Sherwood H. Egbert from the McCulloch Corporation, a company with which Stevens had a long-established business relationship. Egbert was also friendly with Stevens on a personal level and naturally was inclined to go to him for styling consultation. Furthermore, the two agreed that the company's present lineup was, as Stevens later put it, "a mish-mash multiple panic facelift of 1952."[2] Auto historian Richard Langworth, who interviewed Stevens extensively about his relationship with Studebaker, reported that Egbert had been impressed by the designer's recent low-cost alteration of the Willys Aero and thought he might be able to do the same with Studebaker's mainstays, the Lark

Studebaker Gran Turismo Hawk automobile 1961

and Hawk. "On the face of it," Stevens told Langworth, "the job was impossible. We had $7 million for tooling both cars—normally about enough to tool a Plymouth door handle! We also had only six months before 1962 introduction time. But Sherwood wasn't an automobile man. He didn't know it was impossible."[3]

Egbert may not have been an automobile man, but he must have been acutely aware that replacing Loewy with Stevens would cause a furor. The two designers had never been especially friendly, and after the Studebaker incident they became outright rivals. Stevens's 1962 Lark was only a slight modification of the existing Loewy design, focusing on those parts of the car that could be cheaply restyled. It was longer overall than previous Larks had been and was outfitted with a new instrument panel, grille, and hood ornament. Stevens's other car for the 1962 model year, the Gran Turismo Hawk, was another story. It could not have been more antithetical to

Loewy's style. The 1956 Hawk had been the last major remodeling that Loewy's office had executed for Studebaker, and it had many of the features that were common to his work for the company: relatively short overall length, pronounced fins, and luxurious curvature. Stevens's long, sharp, and finless Gran Turismo Hawk was a dramatic change of pace. The squared-off lines of the car stood in dramatic opposition to the muscular streamlining that Loewy had brought to all his work at Studebaker. While Loewy's Hawk had chrome detailing to spare, Stevens's had only a stainless steel base edge that ran continuously from front to rear bumper. The dashboard (designed in part by Gordon Robertson, a graphics specialist at Stevens's firm) was also wholly transformed through an aircraft cockpit–like treatment. It was composed of three separately angled sections made of walnut, so that each of the instruments faced directly toward the driver— an innovation that would later be implemented by Chrysler and General Motors. The rounded front grille recalled that on a Mercedes, in honor of the fact that Studebaker served as the German car manufacturer's importer. The car garnered an enthusiastic reception with the automotive press and the public alike, with sales three times those of the previous year's Hawk.[4]

Unfortunately, like Stevens's Jeepster, the Gran Turismo Hawk enjoyed commercial success for only one year. The company's fiscal struggles of the late 1950s were exacerbated by a labor strike in 1962, and by 1963 it had already begun a slide toward insolvency that proved irreversible. Stevens was not about to let his chance slip away, however, and embarked on an ambitious design program that projected the Studebaker line all the way through 1966. For the 1963 Lark and Hawk he modified his earlier designs only slightly, adding to the former a "vanity" with cup holders and makeup mirror that looks eerily like the appointments in a minivan of today. He also contributed a heavy-duty station wagon based on the Lark called the Wagonaire, which featured a sliding rear door that opened not only the back of the car but also the rear portion of the roof. Stevens had experimented with this idea previously in his prophetic Scimitar "station sedan" and knew that it dramatically increased cargo capacity—the Wagonaire could carry a refrigerator upright if need be.[5]

Lark Sedan Model 1962 (above)

Raymond Loewy, Studebaker Avanti 1963 (lower)

Such superficial alterations could do little to save the company, and Sherwood Egbert knew it. In a last-ditch attempt to regain momentum, he rehired Loewy to create a sensational new sports car. Loewy's avant-garde creation, the Avanti, is still considered to be one of the most iconic American automobiles. Streamlined into a gorgeous hourglass shape, with saucerlike headlights and nary a straight line, the Avanti was years ahead of its time—a fact that the market swiftly proved. Thanks partly to problems in production, the car was a famous commercial flop, the worst financial failure the company had ever suffered on a single automobile.[6]

Studebaker Sceptre prototype 1963
Interior of the Studebaker Sceptre prototype 1963

In December of 1963 the Studebaker plant in South Bend closed for good. Stevens was distraught; the best chance he had ever had to put his designs onto automotive assembly lines was ending. Perhaps unfairly, he blamed his adversary's Avanti for Studebaker's demise. "The public didn't understand that car," he remarked. "I wish now we had had that five million dollars for our 'family' cars. We might still be in business."[7] The "family" cars to which Stevens referred were the ones he himself had devised for the company, and even after the South Bend factory shut down, he continued to try to sell them to the higher-ups at Studebaker. A subsidiary plant in Hamilton, Ontario, did continue to manufacture the cars that had been planned for the 1964 model year, including Stevens's new versions of both the Lark and Hawk lines. Almost a decade and a half later, Stevens somewhat petulantly published a series of overlay design comparisons between this little-known 1964 Lark and the newly downsized 1977 Mercedes Benz 450 SEL, Cadillac Seville, and Chevrolet Caprice. His point, that he too had been ahead of his time, did not change the fact that in 1963 Studebaker was a closed book.

Incredibly Stevens continued to pour his resources into designing automobiles for the dying company. The situation was both desperate and quixotic and hence played perfectly to his strengths. Always drawn to extreme solutions, the designer planned a frankly futuristic car called the Sceptre. Intended as a replacement for the Hawk, the car was stylistically similar to the Gran Turismo from the side. The headlights, however, were unlike anything ever conceived: continuous bars of light that ran the full width of the vehicle. A small red safety bulb was mounted in front of each wheel well to improve nighttime visibility of the car from the side. (These lighting treatments, so familiar today, did not become standard in the auto industry until the 1980s.) The Sceptre also had a strikingly low slope on its front hood for a 1960s car, a powerfully shaped front bumper, and entirely flush sides. The interior was equally advanced, with space-age bubble covers over the radio and clock instruments and a beautifully sculpted "polo mallet" steering wheel. The Sceptre was never put into production, but its prototype survives at the Studebaker Museum in South Bend as a testament to Stevens's premonitory ideas about auto design.

In late 1963 Stevens and his staff came up with one more idea for Studebaker: a subcompact car with fully interchangeable fiberglass panels, ideal for a manufacturer with no remaining capital. But by then the end had come. Studebaker gasped along, turning out old model years with little or no alteration, and the Hamilton plant finally closed in 1966. Stevens did continue to work on non-automotive products manufactured by Studebaker, such as food industry equipment and home appliances, but he would never again have such a close connection with a legitimate auto manufacturer. It might be said that the only thing wrong with Stevens's work for Studebaker was its timing. Had Sherwood Egbert come to the company somewhat earlier, his attempts to revitalize its image might have had the chance to take root. But by the 1960s the intrinsic difficulty of competing with the "Big Three" would have eventually overcome any redesign campaign. For Stevens to pursue his vision of auto manufacture, he would have to take matters into his own hands. Appropriately enough, it was through Studebaker's demise that he had an opportunity to do just that.

1. Bruno Sacco, "The Studebaker Connection," in *Raymond Loewy: Pioneer of Industrial Design*, ed. Angela Schönberger (Munich: Prestel, 1990), 123–33.

2. Brooks Stevens to Robert B. Evans, 2 July 1969, Brooks Stevens Archive, Milwaukee Art Museum.

3. Richard M. Langworth, *Studebaker: The Postwar Years* (Osceola, Wis.: Motorbooks International, 1979).

4. On Loewy's and Stevens's Hawks, see Asa E. Hall, "1956–61 Studebaker Hawk: South Bend's Winged Warriors," *Collectible Automobile* 1 (November 1984): 58–70; R. M. Clarke, *Studebaker Hawks and Larks, 1956–63* (Cobham, England: Brooklands Books, 1989); Michael Richards, "The Way We Were: The Life and Times of the Studebaker Hawk," *Automobile Quarterly* 12, no. 3 (1974): 318–31.

5. "Studebaker Wagonaire," *Canada Track and Traffic*, February 1963; Kit Foster, "1964 Studebaker Wagonaire: The Last Wagon from South Bend," *Auto Week*, 2 July 2001.

6. On the Avanti, see Patrick R. Foster, "Going Out in Style," *Automobile Quarterly* 37 (October 1997): 6–19.

7. Unidentified press clipping, ca. 1964, Brooks Stevens Archive, Milwaukee Art Museum.

Series I Excalibur SSK Roadster 1964

The end of Studebaker meant that Brooks Stevens Associates no longer had an American venue for its automotive designs—a tragic outcome for many on the staff, none more so than Stevens himself. There was, however, a silver lining to the story. Through a bizarre turn of events, the passing of Studebaker led directly to the birth of the Stevens family's own business manufacturing cars in the style of a late 1920s Mercedes—an idea that Stevens called a "contemporary classic" but that soon earned the less grand title of "replicar."

Series I Excalibur SSK Roadster 1964

What Stevens originally had in mind for Studebaker was not a production car at all, but an automotive equivalent of the prophetic boats he had done for Evinrude between 1956 and 1962. Just as the outboard motor company had been overshadowed by displays of full-size boats, Studebaker was at a disadvantage at the national auto shows, where it had to compete with the splashy exhibits of the larger auto manufacturers. Stevens managed to convince the executives in South Bend to show a one-off "Mercebaker" as a conversation piece for the show. The car would have a body based on an antique Mercedes SSK of the 1927–29 period, but its chassis and engine would be taken from Studebaker's current stock. This idea was justified to some extent by the fact that Studebaker was Mercedes-Benz's American importer at the time, but at first the executives at the auto company were totally uninterested. As Stevens recalled, when he told Byers Burlingame (who had replaced the ill Sherwood Egbert as president) about the car he had built for the auto show, "there was a still moment on the phone," followed shortly by a dial tone.[1] Studebaker had recently promoted a new slogan—"the common sense car"—and this plan was as far away from common sense as could be imagined. Furthermore, the company feared that a positive reception for the show car might swiftly backfire when it became clear that no such car would be forthcoming. Having been involved with the Studebaker auto show display the previous year, however, Stevens was convinced that a note of excitement was sorely needed. The company's past exhibits had been no more interesting than the average parking lot—which, he observed sarcastically, would have at least one or two Studebakers in the stalls.

Determined to build his "Mercebaker," Stevens approached his son Steve to complete the construction. Though he was only twenty years old at the time, Steve Stevens was already an experienced car man, having been taught by his older brother, David. Over a period of six weeks in 1964, Steve and two friends—Ray Besasie Jr. and Jules Mayeur—built a prototype at the auto museum using a Lark Daytona chassis and engine from Studebaker, working from Brooks Stevens's concept and detailed drawings by staff designer Joe Besasie. Joe's brother Ray was responsible for the body, which was fabricated in aluminum, like the Excalibur race cars that Stevens and his sons had designed since 1952. The crew was fortunate in having an example close at hand in the form of the auto museum's 1928 Mercedes, which had previously been owned by Al Jolson and the great German race-car driver Rudi Caracciola. Though the replica was smaller and lighter than the original car and boasted a very modern top speed of 150 miles per hour, the Mercebaker had a full complement of antique touches: a belt to hold the bonnet closed, louvers in the hood, wire wheels, three-pipe external exhausts (supplied by the same German manufacturer that had made the pipes on the original Mercedes of the 1920s), motorcycle fenders in the rear, and most importantly, a classic high cowl and wedge-shaped radiator.[2]

Immediately upon completion of the prototype, Steve Stevens test-ran it briefly at the nearby track at Elkhart Lake and then towed it to New York for the auto show. While he was en route, however, Studebaker's executives informed Brooks Stevens that they would not be showing his "contemporary classic." Studebaker was backing out of the car business, and there would be no booth at the New York show that year, or ever again. When the Mercebaker arrived, its youthful custodian was stunned to hear the bad news. Fortunately Brooks Stevens was friendly with Gerald Martin, the director of the auto show. Through Martin's intercession the prototype made it to the floor as a product of Brooks Stevens Associates, rather than Studebaker. (Amusingly, it displaced the Ford Econoline van, which would go on to be one of the most successful new vehicles of that model year.) The crowd at the auto show was a perfect audience—many were collectors or admirers of classic autos—

1928 Mercedes-Benz in Stevens's collection

Steve Stevens, Jules Mayeur, Ray Besasie Jr. and David Stevens with the Excalibur Jr. Go Kart.

and the reception for the curious "old-new" car was enthusiastic. Steve Stevens, manning the booth at the fair, was repeatedly approached by prospective buyers and became convinced of the vehicle's marketability. He returned to Milwaukee and persuaded his father to put in the seed money necessary to put the car—rechristened the Excalibur—into production.

The car company that emerged was really the enterprise of Steve and David Stevens rather than their father. The pairing of the sons was a good one, as Steve was a natural salesman and David a skilled engineer. In 1964 the two were twenty-one and twenty-five years old, respectively, but unlike their father, who had never owned a pair of coveralls in his life, both were already accomplished auto mechanics and builders. David in particular had taken a direct hand in the repair and restoration of examples in the auto museum collection and had helped his

Rendering for the Spyder Excalibur 35X 1970
Designed by Brooks Stevens and Guy Storr.
Built by Michelotti Coach Works, Turin, Italy.

father design a pair of race cars based on the 1952 Excalibur J, as well as a go-cart called the Excalibur Jr.

By early 1965 there were already ten or more Excaliburs on the road. The first and most successful car of this kind to enter the marketplace, the Excalibur differed significantly from the less exalted "kit car," an outgrowth of America's thriving postwar hot rod culture that was built from preexisting parts. Kit cars simulated the look of older autos but were generally impromptu affairs without strict fidelity to historical precedent. The "contemporary classic," by contrast, would be a car that rivaled the original in both style and quality. It would once again make the golden era of autos available to a select but interested audience. Of course, the project was directly at odds with Stevens's usual advocacy of progressive design, an irony that was not lost on him. "It's a very odd situation for me," he wrote, "because I'm the man who coined the phrase 'planned obsolescence' in 1954. Suddenly I find myself in a venture that has no obsolescence—contemporary classics. Now I'm wearing my hat the other way."[3]

Though several other "replicars" based on Cords, Auburns, and other makes swiftly followed in the footsteps of the Excalibur, none had its staying power and notoriety.[4] Because of Stevens's capital and high profile, as well as the high quality of the cars, celebrities lined up to purchase them. One of the first buyers was Tony Curtis, whose Excalibur was delivered by Steve Stevens personally on the set of the film *The Great Race*. Other celebrity owners would eventually include June Allison, Sonny and Cher Bono, Dick Van Dyke, George Foreman, Jackie Gleason, Liberace, Dean Martin, Steve McQueen, Rod Serling, Rod Stewart, Adam West (television's "Batman"), and Phyllis Diller, who owned four.

Ownership of the Excalibur business stayed in the Stevens family until 1986. After the first few cars had been completed, the operation moved from the auto museum shop, first to an independent location with greater production capacity and then, in 1966, to a permanent facility in nearby West Allis, Wisconsin. By 1970 construction had gone over to a chassis built from scratch, fiberglass body construction, and a Chevrolet V-8 engine. An additional body type was also available, as the original roadster had been joined by a phaeton in 1966. Though different engines and other mechanical improvements came and went over the next decade, the design of the body did not change significantly until the introduction of the Series IV in 1980. These Excaliburs, designed mainly by David Stevens, were heavier, longer, and more luxurious than their predecessors—closer to the deluxe model 500/540K Mercedes of the 1930s than the SSK of the late 1920s. Brooks himself did not get deeply involved with the design of subsequent Excaliburs, but he did put considerable support—financial and otherwise—behind the project. In 1967 he and his longtime French public relations manager Guy Storr initiated a similar offshoot program called the Spyder Excalibur 35X, a replica of a 1930s Bugatti racer. Twenty-seven of these separate "replicars" were finally built in 1978 in Turin, Italy, using an Opal chassis. The idea was revived again in partnership with John DeLorean, only to be cut short by Guy Storr's death in a car accident in 1980.

There was very little original "design" in the Excaliburs, particularly in the first version that Stevens had done, and he himself had little to do with the company after it got off the ground. Nonetheless he gloried in his identification with the high-profile status symbol autos, speaking on the topic at the Society of Automotive Engineers conference and elsewhere. The cars came to define his aesthetic to the public more than any other product of his long career. Eventually the Excaliburs became a victim of their own success; the new models were so expensive that they could not compete with the number of earlier cars on the resale market (more than three thousand vehicles were made by the company between 1965 and 1986). Today none of the cars is in production, though former Excalibur mechanic Alice Preston continues to operate a business called Camelot Classics devoted to their repair and upkeep. Steve and David Stevens both live in Milwaukee, where they continue to be involved in automotive projects.[5]

1. Quoted in Richard M. Langworth, *Kaiser-Frazer: The Last Onslaught on Detroit* (Kutztown, Pa.: Automobile Quarterly Publications, 1975), 154.

2. Roger Hill, "Excalibur Rides Again at a Howling 150 MPH," *London Sunday Express*, 7 November 1965.

3. Unidentified article, ca. 1965, scrapbook, Brooks Stevens Archive, Milwaukee Art Museum.

4. For other examples, see "Reincarnated Classics," *Look*, 9 August 1966, 43–45; Mary Blume, "Instant Automotive Nostalgia," *International Herald Tribune*, 17 January 1968, 12.

5. The best accounts of the Excalibur story are Chris Poole, "Excalibur: An Invincible Tradition," *Collectible Automobile* 1 (November 1984): 8–27, and Jonathan A. Stein with Daniel Simkin, "Excalibur: Subtle Like a Broad Sword," *Automobile Quarterly* 38 (December 1998): 6–17. See also Sam Martino, "The Excalibur: Contemporary Classic," *New York Times*, 12 October 1975, 398; Mervyn Kaufman, "The SS Revived," *Automobile Quarterly* 3 (summer 1964): 196–201. The author thanks Steve Stevens, David Stevens, James Lee, and Alice Preston for their recollections and insights into the history of the Excaliburs.

An Adjunct to Sport (1964)

Private individuals in America and all over the world have for the last several decades performed in a hobby-like manner a service to the history of the automobile. Something which the automobile industry has not had the time to do or has not seen fit to do. The discovery and restoration of antique or classic automobiles has now become a most colorful and fabulous historical record of one of the world's largest industries.

Many an enthusiast has longed to find, acquire, and restore certain species of famous sports cars of the classic period. Perhaps the most famous European car of the period 1927–30 was the fabulous Mercedes SSK, a close coupled competition-type sports car built in Stuttgart with Teutonic elegance and functional superiority.

The supercharged SSK not only delivered startling performance, but its wailing blower was virtually a harbinger in sound of today's jet aircraft's ear-splitting wail. It is said that it was a fantastic experience to place one's foot down hard on the accelerator both from the standpoint of acceleration and a *sound* warning described as the "wail of the banshee."

Brooks Stevens, internationally-known industrial designer and for 30 years an avid collector and restorer of princely classic sports cars, has created in "retrospect" a contemporary classic: the Studebaker SS. This car, designed by Brooks Stevens especially for the New York International Automobile Show, consists of a standard Studebaker Daytona Chassis powered by a supercharged R-2 engine, disc brakes, four-speed gearbox, and modified close-ratio steering. The only change from the normal Studebaker chassis was to re-locate the engine 28 inches toward the rear. This car was built to be a replica in modern, low-dimensional proportion of the SSK.

Brooks Stevens, designer of the 1964 Studebaker regular passenger lines, hopes that enthusiasts unable to afford a $20 or $30 thousand restoration of an authentic classic Mercedes SSK, would consider the Contemporary Classic as a modern-day operational vehicle with the flavor of an elegant era in the sport. It is possible that if multiples of this car were built, a class racing group could be established for very colorful events on road circuits such as Watkins Glen, Road America at Elkhart Lake, and even in endurance runs at Sebring.

This car is not a pseudo-sports car or purely an exhibition piece. Its performance abilities would be highly respectable. It weighs less than 1800 pounds and its horsepower to weight ratio, its low center of gravity, and disc brakes would provide excitement in truly competitive performance. Imagine a dozen of these cars with the "wailing" of their Paxton blowers shrieking through the natural countryside beauty of Road America. This could be the glamorous re-birth of the hairy sports car driving era with all of its color and grandeur. The winner to be toasted in a trophy full of the best vintage champagne.

An important factor in this proposed "adjunct to a sport" would be the reliable and modern components that would insure the Contemporary Classic owner a safe, spirited ride on any highway without fear of expensive restored parts failures as sometimes experienced in operational restored cars. Many an aspiring car buff might get permission from his "Secretary of War" to buy one of these cars instead of a mink stole.

Viva the wail of the banshee!

Text by Brooks Stevens, excerpted from a promotional flyer for the Studebaker SS Roadster, distributed by SS Automobiles Incorporated, 1964.

Kearney and Trecker Milwaukeematic machining center 1964

Among Stevens's least known but most imposing designs were those for equipment used in the construction and machining industries. Milwaukee was a center for this business until recently, home to such heavyweight firms as Allis-Chalmers, Chain Belt, and Bucyrus Erie. Stevens worked with all of these firms, but he had an especially close tie to another company, Kearney and Trecker. Through his college friend Francis J. Trecker, Stevens secured work on projects as various as mining cranes, a corporate jet (the Trecker 166 of 1959), and a 1965 redesign of the company logo. The highlights of his work for the firm, however, were the 1964 Milwaukeematic Series Ea machining center and its subsequent redesign, the Series Eb. Although it looks to the uninitiated like something out of an early science fiction movie, the Milwaukeematic was in fact an extremely practical device. Its rotating head held a variety of tools for machining metal parts; through the use of a programming tape, the Milwaukeematic could be made to perform operations which each of these tools in sequence. Kearney and Trecker had manufactured a similar but much larger machining center called the Series II since 1958, and the Series E was a logical successor. It brought the same capacity and flexibility to much smaller outfits than could afford the previous model—shops that might produce batches ranging between five and one hundred pieces. The central problem in designing the sheath for the Milwaukeematic was keeping all mechanical parts shielded from chips and coolant while still visually lightening the ponderous device (which weighed in at more than ten thousand pounds). Stevens and his staff evidently succeeded, as their design won a prestigious Master Design Award from Product Engineering magazine.[1]

1. "Machining Center Brings Small Shops Automation," *New York Times*, 14 August 1966.

Kearney and Trecker Milwaukeematic machining center 1964

Kearney and Trecker Milwaukeematic machining center 1964 *(side view)*

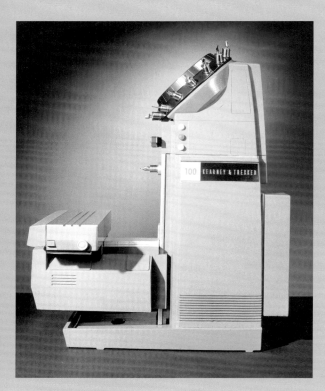

Satellite Towers Hotel Complex 1964

Stevens called his attempt to build the Satellite Towers Hotel "the most frustrating experience in my total professional and business life."[1] The ill-fated project had its first stirrings in 1960, when Milwaukee's mayor, Henry W. Maier, asked Stevens to offer an opinion on the construction of a new convention center and hotel for the downtown area. At the time there was an explosion of similar developments in small cities across America. Conventions had traditionally been a cash cow for larger metropolises such as Chicago, New York, and Los Angeles, but they seemed an easy way for less prominent places to become travel destinations and earn valuable tourist dollars.[2] As luck would have it, Stevens met shortly thereafter with an entrepreneur named Charles F. Mullen, who lived in Milwaukee and had also considered the possibility for a new convention center in the city. Using four dimes encircling a quarter to illustrate his idea, Mullen made a pitch to the designer: instead of an enormous facility under one roof, why not build a single meeting space with amenities, ringed by "satellite" hotel towers?

The plan had numerous logistical advantages, at least in theory. Each of the satellite towers would be identical in construction, allowing for the extensive use of prefabricated and precast elements. Separate investors could be lined up for each satellite, so that investors could retain control of their own building. During slow times of the year one or more of the towers could be shut down, saving heating and cleaning expenses. The quality and capacity of the amenities in the site's central tower could be much higher than those of a smaller hotel. Most importantly, at least from Stevens's perspective, the design would be novel and eye-catching. Skywalks connecting the towers in midair would make the complex an icon for the city and would in turn afford hotel residents a commanding view of Lake Michigan. The Satellite Towers would be a grand architectural gesture that, in Stevens's mind, would do for Milwaukee what the Eiffel Tower had done for Paris.

The plan that Stevens and Mullen originally developed in 1964, relying heavily on the talents of Stevens's staff designer Wayne Wagner, called for a low central building surrounded by six satellite hotels of 150 rooms apiece. A first floor of enclosed galleria sales space would interconnect all seven buildings, and curved concrete arms suggesting an abstract fountain would visually tie together the towers' upper stories. Over the ensuing year this plan was modified to reduce costs. In the new version there were only four hotels, but each would contain 250 rooms and be topped by a rotating restaurant, with each one featuring a different type of cuisine: French, American, Chinese, and in a nod to Milwaukee's ethnic heritage, German. The central tower grew in height in the new plan and was thought out in more detail. It would now have underground parking and a roof garden with a pool that could be frozen over in wintertime for skating. The fountain motif was jettisoned for a cleaner look that placed more emphasis on the transparent skyways between the towers.[3]

Satellite Towers Hotel Complex 1964

Unfortunately Stevens knew little about the difficulties of constructing a major urban land-mark. As he put it, "my zeal matched only my naivety [*sic*] in understanding the processes of city government."[4] Immediately after the Satellite Towers project was unveiled, it ran afoul of entrenched interests in Milwaukee. These included the proprietors of existing hotels in the city, who did not welcome the idea of new competition, and an influential local economics professor named Manuel Gottlieb, who preferred to see Milwaukee retain its small-town character rather than become a hub for conventions.[5] The site that Stevens and Mullen had chosen—a downtown block bounded by Fourth, Fifth, and Wells Streets and Kilbourn Avenue—was adjacent to an antiquated auditorium built in 1909 and a sports arena dating to the 1950s. Though the Satellite Towers backers hoped to see their facility connected to these older buildings via an underground tunnel, other constituencies wanted to raze the whole site and start afresh, perhaps building a mall of green space extending from courthouse to river. At the same time, many Milwaukee leaders hoped to attract the lucrative American Legion Convention in 1968, an event that would require many more hotel rooms than existed in the city. This concrete goal gave the Satellite Towers proposal a sense of urgency and practicality that it might have otherwise lacked.

Thus a great diversity of opinionated parties converged on the Milwaukee Common Council, the governmental body that would determine the fate of the project. Although Stevens and his allies had the strong backing of Mayor Maier, several of the aldermen on the council were hostile to the plan. Things came to a head shortly after the proposal, in its revised one-plus-four-tower configuration, was officially submitted to the council in September of 1965. In order to move ahead with construction, it was necessary to gain not only a lease for the land from the city but also a fifteen-year tax freeze on the property. These measures would help to offset initial capital outlays and attract investors to the project. After a struggle the freeze passed the Common Council by a single vote, only to be struck down in the state Supreme Court as a result of a lawsuit initiated by Professor Gottlieb. The plan was dealt a fatal blow in August of 1967, however, when the American Legion, lacking confidence that the new hotel would be completed in time, withdrew its plan to hold its convention in Milwaukee. This lost the city upward of $15 million in revenue and was the occasion for acrimony on all sides; for all practical purposes, the Satellite Towers idea was dead.

Model for the Satellite Towers Hotel Complex 1965
Hyatt Regency O'Hare Hotel completed 1970

Stevens soldiered on nonetheless, trying in vain to rally enthusiasm for his idea. In despair of succeeding in Milwaukee, he and Mullen formed a group called the Satellite City Design Corporation and proposed the same basic plan to other midwestern cities, such as Detroit, Kansas City, and Saint Louis. Mullen also approached a Milwaukee hospital in the hope of having the same design put to an alternate purpose.[6] Ironically the Hyatt Corporation did build a hotel strongly resembling the Satellite Towers in Chicago near O'Hare Airport, but it did so without involving anyone in Milwaukee with the design or construction of the facility. This, of course, infuriated Stevens, who tried unsuccessfully to sue Hyatt for patent infringement.[7]

Insult was added to injury in 1970. The Common Council, under the leadership of Alderman Robert J. Jendusa Sr. and at the recommendation of a blue-ribbon panel headed by Robert E.

Dineen, determined that the proposed Satellite Towers site would instead be used to build an exposition center with no hotel facilities. A new structure was designed by Chicago architectural firm Welton Becket & Associates and was completed in 1974 at a cost of $13 million, as opposed to the admittedly conservative $18 million that had been projected for the Satellite Towers. The official government mandate for the building was that "strong emphasis was to be placed on functionalism, before considering aesthetics" and that "it was to be remembered that the city would be selling basically only one commodity: space." These objectives were certainly carried out in the final design, which Stevens excoriated as an "enclosed parking stockade."[8] Clearly he was hardly objective on the matter, but it would be difficult to characterize the new exposition center as anything other than a disaster of urban planning. Connected via an "Astro-Walk" to the adjoining buildings, the new center was grouped with the existing auditorium and arena under the name MECCA (Milwaukee Exposition, Convention Center, and Arena). Despite the intent of its builders, the complex was not as profitable as had been hoped, with each of its three parts going empty for over half of the year.[9]

Welton Becket & Associates (Arthur Love, design manager), MECCA (Milwaukee Exposition, Convention Center, and Arena) completed 1974

Even in his last years, Stevens still believed in his old idea. In 1993 he initiated a letter-writing campaign to drum up interest in the Satellite Towers anew, to little effect. In an epilogue that would have given him grim satisfaction, however, the 1974 conference center, along with the old arena, was demolished in 1998 and replaced by new structures. Only the oldest of MECCA's three parts, the auditorium, was considered to be worth renovating.[10]

1. Letter to Barbara Dembski, 17 December 1976, Brooks Stevens Archive, Milwaukee Art Museum.

2. "When Conventioneers Hit Town," *Business Week*, 14 January 1967, 158–62. According to the article, other small municipalities that had built or were building convention centers included Duluth, Nashville, Charlotte, Fargo, and Anaheim, as well as somewhat larger cities such as Miami, Houston, and Cincinnati.

3. "The Satellite Plan . . . a Bold New Design," *Hotel Bulletin*, March 1967, 10–11, 26; Robert Dishon, "Satellite Towers Proposed by Stevens Here," *Milwaukee Sentinel*, 29 July 1965; Satellite Towers Development Corporation press release, 17 May 1967, Brooks Stevens Archive.

4. Brooks Stevens to Hal C. Kuehl, 14 May 1973, Brooks Stevens Archive.

5. Brooks Stevens to Robert E. Dineen, 1 June 1967, Brooks Stevens Archive.

6. Charles F. Mullen to Congressman Henry S. Reuss, 7 March 1967, Brooks Stevens Archive.

7. Charles F. Mullen to Curt Morsell Jr., 29 December 1969, Brooks Stevens Archive.

8. "Satellite Hotel of One Thousand Rooms Proposed for Auditorium-Arena," *Milwaukee Journal*, 2 October 1965.

9. Ello Brink, "Civic Center's MECCA Is a Design Disaster," *Milwaukee Journal*, 3 June 1973; Barbara Dembski, "Dark MECCA Stirs Worries," *Milwaukee Journal*, 12 December 1976.

10. The most complete and objective account of the failure of the Satellite Towers and the building of MECCA is "The Development of MECCA," in "Milwaukee Exposition and Convention Center," pt. 1, unpublished manuscript, Milwaukee Public Library. See also "Satellite Hotel Is Proposed for Milwaukee," *New York Times*, 2 October 1966. The proposed Satellite Towers site is now occupied by the Midwest Express Center.

3M corporate packaging 1965

Stevens's designs rarely betrayed much of an influence from the fine arts, except when that influence was in vogue. This was true of his firm's use of biomorphism in the 1950s in the Miller "Soft Cross" logo and Formica "Skylark" pattern, and it was again the case in 1965, when Stevens took a page from the sketchbook of painter Piet Mondrian in redesigning the packaging of Minneapolis office products company 3M. Earlier that year the fashion designer Yves Saint Laurent had initiated the craze for verticals, horizontals, and primary colors with his "Mondrian" collection of short dresses. More than just a fashion statement, the new style was a brilliant triangulation between Saint Laurent's designs, the severe paintings of the prewar Dutch abstractionist, and the emerging style of pop art. Although Stevens's use of the same geometric imagery lacked the iconic power of Saint Laurent's couture, it was nonetheless a masterstroke of corporate identity.

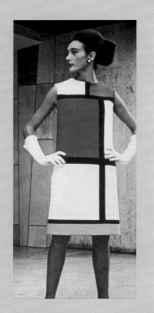

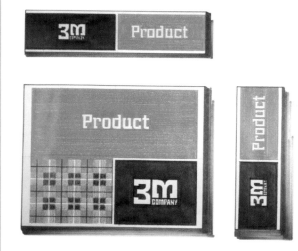

Yves Saint Laurent Mondrian dress 1965
3M packaging rendering 1965

3M had more than thirty-five thousand products, which lacked consistent graphic treatment prior to the 1965 redesign effort.[1] Needless to say, Stevens had never tackled any corporate identity commission of this magnitude, but he did have some experience with the problem of tying together disparate products. In 1945 he had been hired to provide similar brand identity for a Minneapolis-based department store company, Gamble-Skogmo. Working in cooperation with his client's design director, George Bohlig, Stevens and his graphics staff developed a seven-part division of products, each of which had its own stylistic identity and brand name: Hiawatha (sporting goods), Varcon (auto supplies), Homeguard (paints and building supplies), Artisan (tools), Coronado (radios and home appliances), Farmcrest (farm implements), and Crest (automobile tires and tubes). He also consulted on some product designs for the firm—such as radios, refrigerators, car batteries, and washing machines—and even assisted in the preparation of in-store displays. Gamble-Skogmo proudly reported the results to its satellite stores: "We now have expert color advice, engineering knowledge of processes and materials, vast research and survey files, architectural and decorative talent as well as top esthetic judgment, available at all times....When your new packages come through in the standardized colors, in unified proportions, with the same style type; when your products are better looking than any others on the market; when you store is expanded and becomes a lively beehive in a beautiful, colorful background with a modern front, take pride in the fact that much time and effort have been expended to achieve this."[2]

The experience with Gamble-Skogmo no doubt helped Stevens in tackling the vast job of redoing 3M's corporate identity. As in the case of the department stores' branding, the challenge was to create a graphic treatment that could fit a wide range of products. After experimenting with several geometric frameworks suggested by Mondrian's paintings, Stevens and his graphic designers Ray Andersen and Wayne Wagner settled on a simple tripartite division. The smallest of the three rectangles would invariably contain the new 3M logo, designed by New York firm Gerald Stahl and Associates in 1961. (This logo was an ingenious creation in itself, in which the 3 and the M were the same shape but rotated ninety degrees from each other.) A slightly larger rectangle would contain either the name of a 3M-owned subsidiary brand, such as Scotch or

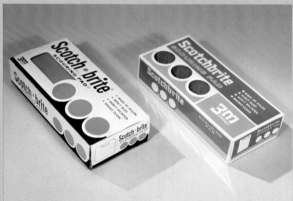

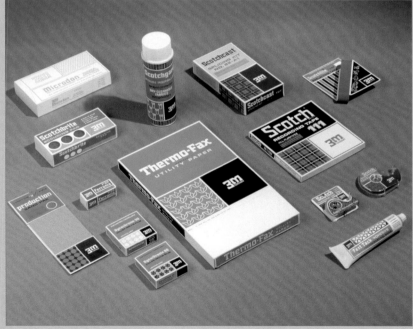

ABCDEFGHIJK
LMNOPQRSTU()
VXWYZE12345
6789!?"-';:
abcdefghijklmy
nopqrstuvwxz

Clockwise from top left:

**Gamble-Skogmo
packaging** 1948

**Variations in
packaging layout**

3M typeface

3M Brand Development

**3M corporate packaging:
Ferrania Film**
before and after redesign

**3M corporate packaging:
Scotchbrite scouring pad**
before and after redesign

Wollensak, or else a distinctive decorative pattern; sometimes these patterns were based on the previous packaging for the product in order to promote brand recognition. Finally, the largest rectangle held the name of the product, rendered in a typeface designed by Stevens's firm.

This system was applied universally to 3M's products. Because many of the product packages were to be designed by staff at 3M's subsidiaries, the company produced and distributed plans showing how to balance consistency and flexibility in using the new design in varying shapes and scales.[3] Stevens, who had once said that "art for art's sake is simply not salable in the market place of consumer goods," had successfully adapted the language of abstract art to the exigencies of the multinational corporation.[4]

1. "3M Adapts Mondrian for Its Packaging Program," *Women's Wear Daily*, 7 December 1965; "Mondrian Does a Job for 3M," *Modern Packaging* 38 (December 1965).

2. Untitled article, *Tempo*, May 1947.

3. "Photo Products Have New Look," *3M Sales Digest*, June 1966, 1; "It's the Design That Counts," *Minneapolis Star*, 21 December 1965; "Company's Packaging Given Unified Look to Support Corporate Identity," *3M Ambassador*, October–November 1965, 1, 3.

4. "Frank-Talking Designer Argues His Philosophy," *Milwaukee Engineering* (April 1961), 12–13. Stevens's package designs were used by 3M until 1977, when they were displaced by a new treatment by New York designers Siegel and Gale. 3M's corporate Web site features an excellent history of the company's graphic identity and packaging.

Evinrude Skeeter snowmobile 1965

For the Outboard Marine Corporation (OMC), snowmobiles were a natural. Virtually all of the commodities sold by the conglomerate—garden equipment, outboard motors, boats—were used only in the summertime. Yet the company was located in Wisconsin, which has a long, deep winter. Snowmobiles could be made using much the same approach, and even some of the same mechanical parts, as other products manufactured by the firm. Stevens's office was also a natural choice as a design consultant for the new project. John Bradley and Tom Green, both of whom had worked on the Evinrude account since their entry into the design firm in the late 1950s, had strong working relationships with the OMC engineering staff and were given the responsibility for styling the new snowmobiles. In its overall aesthetic the Evinrude Skeeter that emerged in 1966 was, unsurprisingly, closely related to the outboard motor shrouds done at the time by the same team of people.

Evinrude Skeeter snowmobile 1965

Unlike the motors, however, snowmobiles were an unknown quantity. Both Bradley and Green recall spending a great deal of time with OMC's engineers in developing the new product mechanically and ergonomically.[1] Even so, the early machines were plagued by unsatisfactory engines and poor maneuverability. An aggressive campaign of improvements ensued, and though the exterior rigging of the snowmobiles—paired skis in the front, caterpillar tracks to the rear—did not change much over the next decade, annual styling changes reflected the internal changes. Of particular note was the introduction of the Skimmer in 1968, which corrected the heaviness of the earlier models and was accordingly sleeker in its overall lines. Various prototypes were also developed, including a Skeeter Jr., for young riders; an Aquaskeeter, with removable flotation pontoons; and a fully enclosed model called the Skeeter GT. The program culminated with a 1976 prototype that featured a bicentennial color scheme and a rear spoiler like that on a racecar. Its extraordinarily low center of gravity was accomplished by literally inverting the standard chassis used by the company.[2]

Unfortunately, just as this machine was unveiled, OMC announced that it was getting out of the snowmobile business. Many of the company's competitors in the lawn and garden and marine products markets—such as Bolens, Wheel Horse, and Mercury—had seen the wisdom of competing for a piece of the wintertime market. By the 1970s supply began to outstrip demand, and along with several other companies, OMC withdrew from snowmobile manufacture. Today there are only three major snowmobile producers in America; one of them, Polaris, continues to work with Brooks Stevens Design.

1. John Bradley, interview with the author, 17 July 2002; Tom Green, interview with the author, 22 July 2002.

2. Brooks Stevens, designer's notes, 23 April 1975, Brooks Stevens Archive, Milwaukee Art Museum.

American Motors proposals 1967–69

Brooks Stevens's auto design career was a series of courageous jousts at America's "Big Three" automakers. Marketable eccentricity had been the leitmotif of his work for Willys-Overland, Kaiser-Frazer, Studebaker, and even his family's own car manufacturing concern, Excalibur—which he liked to call the "sixth largest car manufacturer in America," adding, "there is no seventh."

Stevens had no real disagreement with the way that Chrysler, Ford, and General Motors did business; he merely objected to the narrow range of designs that their dominance created. His last tilt at this state of affairs was staged between 1966 and 1969, when he was retained as a consultant by the American Motors Company (AMC) of Detroit.

AMC had been formed in 1954 as a result of the merger of two of the largest independents in the country, Nash and Hudson. After early success in the marginal compact car market, notably with the popular Rambler, AMC entered into direct competition with the Big Three's larger vehicles. Under the direction of in-house designers Richard (Dick) Teague and Fred Hudson, the company responded to cars like the sensational Ford Mustang with their own "pony cars" and sports cars with sloping "fastback" rear ends and blunt, shark-nosed fronts: the 1965 Marlin, the 1967 Ambassador, and the 1968 Javelin and AMX. The new direction played to Stevens's tastes and strengths, and once introduced to the fray by his friend Teague, he eagerly plunged in. Beginning in earnest in 1967, Stevens and his staff (particularly Peter Stacy, Tom Green, and Dave Coleman) produced a huge number of designs and redesigns. On two occasions, the Milwaukee team produced full-size models (for the projected 1972 American and Ambassador), only to have their ideas largely passed over for more conservative in-house designs.

Brooks Stevens and Peter Stacy (right) with full-size model for the 1972 AMC American 1967

If Stevens had one piece of advice for AMC, it was that the company should try to make cars that looked different from those of the Big Three. The closer the company hewed to the precedent established by its larger competitors, he argued, the more it would struggle financially. In-house designer Teague, who felt that the executives at AMC were too conservative, encouraged

Stevens and his staff to push the envelope of model change—probably not because he intended to use the proposed designs, but rather in the hopes that competition with the Milwaukee team would induce his own stylists to be more creative. This goal was not shared by several men within the company's leadership, however, who subscribed to what Stevens called the "me too pattern."[1] AMC vice presidents Gerald Meyers and Victor Raviolo were particularly risk-averse and hoped to ride the wake of their larger competitors rather than break off in a new direction. Under Raviolo's influence the company came close to severing its ties to Stevens in late 1967 and finally did end the contract in early 1969.[2]

Brooks Stevens and Jim Jeffords with the AMX-R Prototype ca. 1968

During his three-year association with AMC, however, Stevens and his designers did originate several ideas that proved to be valuable to the company. Of particular interest was a prototype version of the AMX with a rumble seat and slightly modified styling. Called the AMX-R, the car would have competed against the Ford Trans Am in the market. To help promote this effort, Stevens enlisted his friend the racecar driver Jim Jeffords, who accompanied the prototype to various events around the country. The strategy did succeed in generating a good deal of press for Stevens's new client.[3] Stevens may also have played a small part in encouraging AMC to return to its old focus on compact cars in 1970 with the Gremlin and Hornet. As early as January of 1967, he had singled out a "low end, high volume" subcompact as his primary design goal for the company, and he could legitimately claim that his proposals had pointed the way toward the new autos (even so, he complained that the Gremlin was too much like the Chevrolet Nova for his taste).[4] More important than any individual styling touch, however, was the general spirit of adventurousness that Stevens and his staff brought to their proposals. As late as 1975, when Teague's unique Pacer was released, Stevens's advocacy for a policy of distinctive design was still resonating within the company, and as Peter Stacy has pointed out, the strategy of maintaining an outside "satellite studio" to energize an in-house design staff is now a commonplace practice in the car industry.[5]

In later years the relationship between Stevens's firm and AMC revived, thanks in part to a stint by Brooks's son Kipp as a designer at the auto company beginning in 1974. After Kipp became the head of Brooks Stevens Design in 1978, he and his father were able to weigh in on a new version of the Jeep Wagoneer, which had descended from the Willys Jeep Station Wagon. Stevens had designed the original Wagoneer in 1962 for Kaiser-Frazer and had given the similar 1963 Studebaker Wagonaire an innovative sliding rear roof that enabled it to carry tall loads such as refrigerators. The new Wagoneer that father and son helped to style was substantially the same car, although in response to the energy crisis of the late 1970s, AMC vastly improved its fuel economy. Lee Iacocca finally purchased American Motors for Chrysler in 1987, putting an end to the era of the American independents, and the new owners retired the Wagoneer in 1991. It was the first time in forty-five years that a Brooks Stevens car design was not on the market.[6]

1. Brooks Stevens to Roy D. Chapin, 17 September 1967, Brooks Stevens Archive, Milwaukee Art Museum.

2. Fred Hudson to Brooks Stevens, 15 November 1967; Brooks Stevens to Roy D. Chapin, 19 March 1969, Brooks Stevens Archive.

3. The AMX-R was only one of several experimental sports cars based on the AMX. On Dick Teague's most impressive effort in this area, the AMX/3 of 1969, see Michael Lamm, "Mid-Engine Marvel," *Automobile Quarterly* 41, no. 3 (2001): 4–17; David W. Bird II, "Dick Teague, Automotive Renaissance Man," *Automobile Quarterly* 30, no. 2 (1992): 4–19.

4. Brooks Stevens, "Design Concept and Marketing Goals for an American Motors Corporation Product Program for 1970-X," designer's notes, 1 January 1967, Brooks Stevens Archive.

5. Peter Stacy, interview with the author, 16 September 2002.

6. For a general history of AMC, see Patrick R. Foster, *American Motors: The Last Independent* (Iola, Wis.: Krause Publications, 1993). On Stevens's Wagoneer and other designs for Jeep, see Patrick R. Foster, "Jeep," *Automobile Quarterly* 39, no. 3 (1999): 53–69.

AMC Hornet 1970

Concept rendering for the AMC Jeep Wagoneer 1980

Kaiser Jeep Wagoneer 1962

Mirro Manhattan cookware 1968

Never one to undersell his designs, Stevens credited his firm's work for the cookware company Mirro as the factor that made it "the Cartier of the aluminum business."[1] Under its old name, the Aluminum Goods Manufacturing Company, the Manitowoc, Wisconsin, concern had been one of Stevens's earliest clients. In 1962 the company rehired him to do a makeover of its pots and pans, and David Nutting and other product designers at the office began introducing crisper contours and increased color to the line. The kitchenware environment at the time was dominated by harvest gold and avocado tints, and Stevens regarded the prospect of adding color to Mirro's traditional black and chrome with some hesitation. Hue therefore crept in slowly, beginning in 1962 with a "prestige line" trimmed in charcoal blue. At the same time, Stevens and Mirro experimented with alternate methods of attaining a distinctive look, such as sharply faceted handles and oval and square cross-sections. In 1964 they introduced some of the earliest Teflon coatings to be used in cookware.

Stevens with Mirromatic percolator 1963

A fully colored line called Manhattan was finally launched in 1968. The shades nutmeg brown, antique white, and Wedgwood blue were chosen. These selections were motivated in part by a desire to convey aristocracy—the blue suggested chinaware, and all the colors were meant to coordinate well with crystal and silver—but more important, the three colors were innocuous enough to still seem "foody" yet neutral enough to allow for flexibility in decorating and entertaining.[2] After all, Stevens regarded the kitchen as "Mrs. Housewife's office" and was intent on making Mirro's aluminum not just attractive but also an accessory within a designed environment.[3] He advocated an individualized and highly decorative approach to the cooking space, in contrast to the clean, quasi-scientific "continuous kitchen" of earlier decades. In 1963, in fact, his office designed a "test kitchen" for Mirro's plant, where salespeople gave cooking demonstrations to visitors. Though the room was dominated by white appliances and birch and mahogany cabinets and trim, Stevens hoped someday to produce appliances whose colored front panels could be replaced, mixed and matched according to the whim of the household.[4] Perhaps a more accurate indication of where his sympathies lay was the kitchen in his own home, which he and his wife redecorated with pink walls, chairs, and appliances and a green and white check tile floor. "It's really pink," Alice Stevens exclaimed, "and looks just beautiful."[5] Unfortunately, Stevens's personal tastes did not always win out in his professional life. After Manhattan cookware's inaugural year in blue, white, and brown, Mirro decided to add two more colors to the line: harvest gold and avocado.[6]

1. Gay Pauley, "Keeping Up with Joneses Called 'Healthy' Trait," *Pittsburgh Press*, 25 January 1966; see also "Designer Applauds Status-Seekers Who Keep U.S. Economy Booming," *Trenton Evening Times*, 19 January 1966.

2. Anita Black, "Cookware Goes Elegant," *Milwaukee Sentinel*, 17 July 1968.

3. Brooks Stevens, "Future Appliance Design—Color Them Avocado?" (lecture presented at the American Home Appliances Manufacturers Conference, 1969).

4. "New Mirro Test Kitchen," *Mirro Mixing Bowl*, spring 1963, 4, 6–7; Donna Wirth, "Percolated Kitchen Plans," *Milwaukee Journal*, 18 June 1963; Jo Sandin, "Go Ahead—Keep Up with the Joneses," *Milwaukee Journal*, 12 January 1965. For a critical view of the "continuous kitchen," see Ellen Lupton and J. Abbott Miller, *The Bathroom, the Kitchen, and the Aesthetics of Waste: A Process of Elimination* (Cambridge: MIT List Visual Arts Center, 1992), 50–59; for early commentary on designer colors in the kitchen, see Christine Frederick, *Selling Mrs. Consumer* (New York: Business Bourse, 1929), 12–13.

5. Marilyn Gardner, "Soft Colors Used to Set Tone in Kitchen of Fox Point Home," *Milwaukee Journal*, 29 July 1962, p. 7.

6. "Rainbow in the Kitchen," *Milwaukee Sentinel*, 3 September 1969.

Mirro Manhattan cookware 1968

Mirro Test Kitchen 1963

Future Appliance Design—
Color Them Avocado? (1969)

This rare transcription of a talk delivered at the American Home Appliances Manufacturers' Conference records not only Stevens's sentiments on the use of color in the kitchen but also the colorful and intuitive character of his extemporaneous speeches.

Mirromatic Electric Skillet 1963

I think any industrial designer that dares to come before you wearing a Bonnie and Clyde suit, a pink shirt, and a polka dot tie must be an expert on color in the appliance field. But we really think this is one of the most important and most flexible aspects of design in the appliance field. Color is important to the area of manufacturing, and it's not as expensive as tools and dies. It's not a $150,000 check every time we try to change the illusion of a given product.

We've had color spasms, I'll have to call them, in the past. I can remember red ranges and other colors; bright chrome yellow as far back as the late '30s. Attempts were made to color refrigerators. There seemed to always be someone who wanted to move away from the clinical appearance of the all-white, bloodbank appearance of the refrigerator, range, washer, and dryer.

As I say, we have had these cycles on several occasions, and they would seem to be there for a while and be what is now termed "mod," I guess, and then they would disappear.... When you picked strong colors such as red and yellow, positive tones, the consumer became frightened; either did not like red or yellow therefore white was neutral and safer, or the kitchen didn't happen to be in a color scheme with which that seemed to blend. The consumer has very strange ideas sometimes that things have to match one another. I think we are moving away from that.

During these periods of color exploration, the manufacturer became nervous because it was an inventory problem. We saw it in outboard motors. Certain manufacturers attempted this, offering you the bonnet for the enclosure of an outboard motor in any color you wished, to allegedly match your boat or match your miniskirt, or swimming suit or whatever. Inventory problems were tragic in that area. The Mercury people tried it; McCulloch Outboard, or the then Scott Atwater, tried it. It was a very, very serious situation, because what dealer, what sales manager, what manufacturing executive wanted to go out on a limb and say, let's make x-hundred thousand or whatever in green, blue, yellow, and so on?

So trying to guess the marketplace is difficult. Well, now we've had a strange recurrence of the color desire. I think in the last four years a new tone which we will say followed the copper tone approach which is certainly a relative neutral. And we had suddenly the emergence of what we call "avocado." There are a million shades and tones of avocado, but it has apparently become a relatively safe neutral as against black or white. The consumer reacted rather well to this. It arrived in the other major appliances at the shows in Chicago and in other parts of the country, and I think the most plausible explanation might be that it was a pleasing, individualized departure from the clinical look, but more importantly than that, it gave the writers something to write about….

Suddenly, avocado moved from the washer-dryer, range and refrigerator onto almost everything we have. Now you can have a rubber fly swatter in avocado, I'm quite sure. The floor mats and the wastebaskets and the little ladder from which to reach the coffee off the top shelf are all in avocado. I've watched this with great amazement. I watch it still, because it's lasted quite a while. We kept saying, well, this too will pass, like many of the other fad-type color spasms; but it seems to stay and maybe we have some staying power in what is now called a "third neutral."

One of our assignments for one of our largest appliance people, the Mirro Company, became interesting and one that had to deal with this problem. [The company was] suddenly faced with the fact that color is an important aspect of this world today in the marketplace; and our aluminum, polished, chromed, or satined or whatever, is, God knows, a neutral. But how do we play the game? How can we stay in the race? Shall we just take the aluminum vessel—I have tried to get the people in Manitowoc to refer to our products as "vessels," not pots and pans—let's not just take our aluminum vessels and dip them, or literally immerse them in color or paint because our consumer then may never know they are aluminum. In other words, this little girl behind the counter who has been there for an hour and a half, or maybe a week if she's an old employee, certainly doesn't have the full sales story of the light weight and all the other things that we claim. And so our consumer may walk right by thinking this is [a] heavy steel vessel and not realize that it is aluminum. Therefore, I begged them to allow some of that flavor to remain. In other words, let's keep some of our character and image and the functional side of our way of making vessels still visible to the consumer.

And [Mirro] immediately said, well of course, we will make them avocado. And I thought, my God, I guess you just call up some places and order the frit or whatever they call it and it's automatic—that's the only color they've got. I said, gentlemen, let's watch this more carefully than that, because perhaps avocado might be on the wane and it would be tragic for us to arrive next January or July or whenever, and be on the end of the miniskirt or the maxiskirt, whichever fad was up or down for the moment. Well, what color would we dare use? This, of course, then became the program. Now, I'm going to start with a few slides, if I may, and just take you through prophetic situations wherein I think color will be involved. And remember, it is one of your most inexpensive tooling procedures.

Excerpted from Brooks Stevens, "Future Appliance Design—Color Them Avocado?"
(lecture presented at the American Home Appliances Manufacturers Conference, 1969).

Lakester combination dune buggy/speedboat 1969

In the late 1960s Brooks Stevens finally met his match: a San Francisco boat show promoter named Tom Rooney, who was perhaps the only one of Stevens's many collaborators who outstripped him in terms of enthusiastic stage management. Working with a custom cabinetmaker named Don Price, Rooney had previously produced boats in the shapes of a Pepsi bottle, a jukebox, and a guitar; clearly he was not a man who stood on design principles. His interest in Brooks Stevens arose as the result of a published prophetic vehicle called the Lakester, which had been conceived by the design office in 1960, most likely as a prospective Evinrude boat show prototype. This "boaterized" dune buggy was meant for general fun in a large beach area.

Lakester combination dune buggy/speedboat 1969
Wrigley's Gum boat 1973

Its fifty-horsepower outboard engine hooked up via a power takeoff shaft to the differential on the rear axle of the car, allowing the vehicle to be driven short distances over the sand. Its owner could then detach a fourteen-foot runabout boat out of the buggy shell, reconnect the outboard's motor to its propellers, and be cruising across the water in no time.

The buggy portion of the Lakester was custom-built, mostly out of Volkswagen parts, and had an infinitely variable gearbox like that on a garden tractor—another area of expertise for Stevens's staff. Rooney thought the Lakester would make a perfect conversation piece for the 1969 boat show, and Stevens was glad to comply.[1] The partnership led to several other cooperative ventures between the two natural-born hucksters. In 1971 the pair launched the Boataloon—a watercraft that dangled from a hot air balloon—which, according to Rooney, "[enabled] boatmen to change lakes without fighting traffic and [assisted] fisherman in sighting schools of fish from the air."[2] Two years later they conceived a waterborne equivalent to the Oscar Mayer Wienermobile: a catamaran with pontoons in the shape of sticks of Wrigley's gum for the 1973 shows in San Francisco and Chicago.[3] That was the last product of the partnership, but Rooney continued to work with the Stevens firm's former staff designer Stan Johnson throughout the 1970s.

1. Parton Keese, "Designer of Post-War Jeepster Turns Sports Car into Speedboat," *New York Times*, 9 January 1970; Brooks Stevens, designer's notes on the Lakester, 1969, Brooks Stevens Archive, Milwaukee Art Museum.

2. "Designer Produces an Outboard Motor Boat That Flies," *New York Times* 3 January 1971.

3. "A Cabinetmaker Builds Some Weird Creations," *San Francisco Sunday Examiner and Chronicle Datebook*, 14 January 1973; Rick Talley, "Chew-a-Boat This Year's Show Hit," *Chicago Today*, 31 January 1973.

Lawn-Boy mower 1970

Lawn-Boy mower 1970

A sweeping shift in the design profession occurred in the 1960s, when renderings executed in Magic Marker and models made of paperboard became widespread. Up to this point, drawings had always been done painstakingly with colored pencils or an airbrush, while models had been made of clay or plaster. The parallel inception of felt-tips and thin cardboard, usually seamed using an automotive bonding agent, made the two-stage process of planning a design much quicker. It also meant that the finished drawings and models were more informal, an indication that clients were sufficiently experienced with industrial design that they no longer required the highly polished presentation materials that consultant designers had provided in the past. Though not as profound as the later influence of computers, these developments in the styling process had a definite impact on the products of the day. Because of the tendency of markers and paperboard models to promote flat planes that intersected with sharp edges, products made using these techniques tended to be blockier than the industrial designs of previous decades—an aesthetic that one Stevens staff designer, Tom Green, describes as "chamfered."[1]

Within Stevens's oeuvre this trend is especially visible in the area of lawn equipment. His long-time client Outboard Marine Company (OMC) had made a few lawn products in the late 1930s but did not enter the market heavily until 1952, when president Ralph Evinrude made the decision to purchase the Lamar, Missouri, manufacturer RPM (Rotary Power Mower Company). This small company had produced the first rotary lawn mower—a relative rarity until OMC began producing the design in huge numbers under the brand name Lawn-Boy. Despite some concerns about their safety, rotary mowers accounted for more than over half of all mower sales by 1955.[2] Stevens's firm was tapped to style the new products and their many spin-offs, including riding mowers, edgers, trimmers, weeders, and tillers. Product design staffer David Nutting was first put in charge of the account, later to be replaced by Stan Johnson and Tom Green. The office's involvement in lawn equipment eventually led to large commissions with two other companies: Bolens of Port Washington, Wisconsin, and the German manufacturer Gutbrod. Just as he had done in the case of Evinrude's sea blue outboard motors, Stevens proposed an environmentally appropriate "grass green" for the Lawn-Boy mowers. Over the years other colors were introduced, along with innovations that reduced the noise and vibration of the equipment. From a design perspective, however, the signal advance in the lawn equipment produced by Stevens's designers over time was its increasingly angular, choppy look. Renderings of mowers and garden tractors from this period show the use of felt-tip pens to delineate the new style, which was the antithesis of the streamlining favored at the firm in earlier years.

1. As an example of a similar trend in designs produced outside of Stevens's office, Green pointed to the paradigmatic shift in auto design from the smooth contours of the Jaguar XKE to the Pontiac GTO. He also mentioned the use of monofilament-impregnated clay in General Motors' model shop as another innovation that engendered the increasing use of hard edges and defined planes.

2. Virginia Scott Jenkins, *The Lawn: A History of an American Obsession* (Washington, D.C.: Smithsonian Institution Press, 1994), 113–15; Jeffrey L. Rodengen, Evinrude, Johnson, and the Legend of OMC (Fort Lauderdale: Write Stuff Syndicate, 1993), 66.

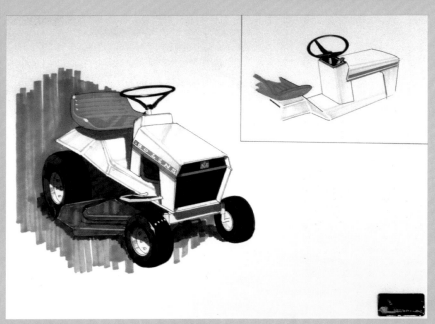

Rendering for a Bolens lawn tractor ca. 1970

Bolens lawn tractor ca. 1970

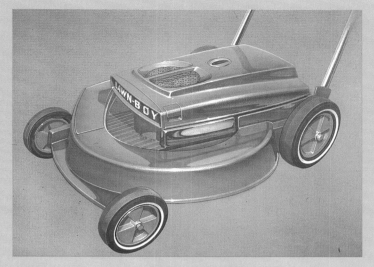

Renderings for a Lawn-Boy mower 1970

Fig. 1 Brooks Stevens, ca. 1975

The Seer That Made Milwaukee Famous
Reluctant Retirement, 1978–94

You cannot mention to me a product that we might not have touched somewhere.

I mean, if you said refrigerators, washing machines, lawn mowers, outboards, boats, airplanes.

…Why, suggest something. Think of something and ask if we've had anything to do with it.

Brooks Stevens (1990)[1]

In 1954 Stevens, asked to name his favorite design among all those his firm had handled, responded, "none, because every one would have to be restudied for the tastes of tomorrow."[2] At the end of his career, he had not changed his mind. "Would I change anything now that I did in the past?" he said. "Hell yes! Everything! Because it's all outmoded."[62] By the time he retired, he had designed approximately three thousand products for almost six hundred clients over the years, and he was by no means ready to quit. Unfortunately he was given little choice in the matter.

Following the difficult years of the early 1970s, Stevens lifted his spirits by getting involved once again in racing, this time with Formula Atlantic cars and a large team of drivers and mechanics. He also managed one final triumph. A hybrid electric car designed for the local manufacturer Briggs and Stratton landed him once again in the pages of the nation's newspapers and magazines. Stevens had weathered his difficulties of the previous decade with his spirit and ingenuity undimmed. His health, however, was seriously weakened. Sidelined in 1978 by serious heart problems, he handed the reins of his forty-three-year-old firm to his twenty-seven-year-old son Kipp (fig. 2).

Like his brothers, Kipp Stevens had taken to car design early in life. While his brothers stuck with the automobile business, however, he channeled his enthusiasm into his father's profession of industrial design. He attended Syracuse University's program in the field, studying under Arthur Pulos, and despite some expectation that he would return to Milwaukee upon graduation, he decided to go to Detroit and try his hand at auto styling. Thanks to his father's friendship with designer Dick Teague, Kipp got a job in the exterior styling department at American Motors. From there he went to New York City, where, ironically, he landed at Raymond Loewy's design office. (When Loewy discovered that his old archrival's son was working in the office, he tried to have the young man fired, but cooler heads in management preserved his position.) Thanks to the recession of the mid-1970s, however, the New York design firms were struggling. Kipp left for a brief stint in the Henry Dreyfuss office and then worked for ex-Loewy staff designer Chuck Mauro. Finally, in 1978, he did return to Milwaukee to work at his father's firm as vice president. Within two years he found himself the head of the office.

The transfer of leadership from father to son made for pronounced changes at the firm. The elder Stevens had always

Fig. 2 Kipp Stevens, 2002

Fig. 3 Brooks Stevens Design offices today. Designed by
Kahler-Slater Architects, Milwaukee, 1997

disliked design by committee and had as a consequence run his business as if it were a capitalist system in miniature. He liked to give individual designers their own projects and herd them (or have one of the senior designers herd them) through to conclusion. He did not like projects to be diluted by multiple voices. Each staffer was given a chance to prove himself, and each was rewarded accordingly. Some found their specialty to be model building, while others gravitated toward graphics or product design. Rarely did Stevens direct these movements within the staff; he simply created an atmosphere in which employees found their niche. Kipp Stevens, who had been schooled in the theoretical model of design popular in the early 1970s, had a very different approach. His focus was on teamwork, research, and the sharing of information—all goals that had been emphasized in the New York offices where he had honed his skills. Technological advances in the design process itself made for even greater changes in the daily rhythm of the staff. Under

Kipp's leadership the firm was an early practitioner of computer-aided design; the last time a clay model was constructed at the office was almost a decade ago. The culture of the office too altered dramatically. In Brooks's day it had been a "boys' club," where staffers routinely worked overtime in a partylike atmosphere. There were no women on staff but the secretaries. Today's design office is much more diverse, and though it still has camaraderie, one sees in the current staff a team of professionals rather than an unruly fellowship (fig. 3).

In many ways, then, the design office that still carries Brooks Stevens's name bears little resemblance to the firm that he operated for more than forty years. Yet toward the end of his life Stevens found a way to connect with the designers of the future. He continued to preside over his auto museum (hiring seasoned mechanic Alice Preston as director of the institution), made some efforts to put his papers and memorabilia in order—materials that now form the Brooks Stevens Archive at

Fig. 4 Brooks Stevens's retrospective exhibition at the Michael Lord Gallery, Milwaukee, 1987

the Milwaukee Art Museum—and submitted to numerous interviews. He also had the chance to teach for the first time in his life. This opportunity arose as the result of a rekindling of his long-standing relationship with the Milwaukee Institute of Art and Design (MIAD) and its predecessor institution, the Layton School of Art. During the 1980s MIAD heaped honors on the man whom it regarded as a father figure, making him a trustee, establishing a chair of industrial design in his name, and bestowing a doctorate upon him. In 1989 the gallerist Michael Lord took up Stevens's cause and staged the first retrospective for the designer since 1950, further raising local interest in his work. Between 1992 and 1994 curator Gary Wolfe and archivist Michael Bersch staged three exhibitions about the designer at MIAD's newly christened Brooks Stevens Gallery of Industrial Design (fig. 4). Two other shows were organized in 1991 in Madison: *Styled to Sell*, at the Wisconsin Historical Society, and *Designs in Motion*, at the Madison Art Center. Stevens continued

to teach at MIAD until his last days, even when confined to a wheelchair. Teaching gave him a chance not only to impart the wisdom of his decades in the field but also to voice his opinions about contemporary design. He railed against the car industry, which he accused of "a blandizement of form and lack of visual identity."[4] He spoke approvingly of the updating of some of his designs for the present day, such as the Harley-Davidson "Heritage Classic" motorcycle, based on the 1949 Hydra-Glide, and the Jeep Cherokee, styled by his firm and based on his Wagoneer for Kaiser-Frazer and American Motors. Most of all, he spoke with satisfaction of the fact that industrial design had become "an absolutely necessary profession that good manufacturing could not do without."[5]

Brooks Stevens died at the age of eighty-three on January 4, 1995 (fig. 5). He had been the last surviving founder of the Society of Industrial Designers, so his passing was literally the end of an era. It was an occasion to celebrate his achievements;

newspaper obituaries across the country listed his best-known designs and hailed him as "one of the founding fathers of industrial design."[6] For all the respect paid to him, however, Stevens did not live to see his place in design history rise to a level commensurate with his achievements. This apparently bothered him but little. "I have never designed something to be placed in an art museum," he once said. "Art for art's sake is simply not salable in the market place of consumer goods."[7] Accordingly, he had shaped his career to fit the path of profitability, rather than notoriety. He had decided to stay in Milwaukee, where the work was; and despite his many forays into the publicity game, he had spent the majority of his career promoting the names of companies, rather than his own. If he had paid a price for these choices in terms of personal fame, though, that was more than offset by the fact that the products he had shaped were as numerous, as widespread, and as successful in the market as those of any industrial designer who had ever lived. When Brooks Stevens was asked, in 1990, about the way he'd like to be remembered, he responded with a blend of pride and humility: "We only had to satisfy the client, and not to tell the world we did this refrigerator for ABC Manufacturing Company. So the things that went out on their own became successful and in many cases increased sales by thousands of percent—not hundreds, but huge volumes— and that stands on its own."[8]

1. Stevens, interview with Chip Duncan, 1990–91.

2. Luc Fellot, "Brooks Stevens," *L'Automobile*, February 1964.

3. Quoted in Perry Lamek, "Designing the American Dream," *Milwaukee Magazine*, August 1987, 46–52, 128.

4. Quoted in "Styled to Sell: The Industrial Designs of Brooks Stevens," *Industrial Design* 38 (November–December 1991): 12.

5. Stevens, interview with Chip Duncan, 1990–91.

6. "The Way Things Look," *Boston Globe*, 15 January 1995.

7. "Frank-Talking Designer," 12–13.

8. Stevens, interview with Chip Duncan, 1990–91.

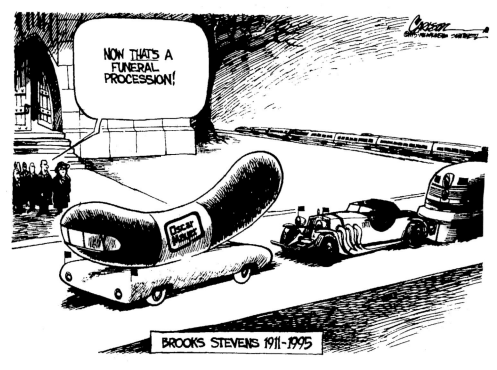

Fig. 5 Stuart Carlson, obituary cartoon for Brooks Stevens. Originally published in the *Milwaukee Journal Sentinel*, Jan. 6, 1995

Briggs and Stratton hybrid electric automobile 1979

The period in which Brooks Stevens and his son Kipp effectively shared the leadership of the family design firm was relatively brief, lasting only from 1978 to 1980. During these two years the elder Stevens was plagued by heart problems, which soon forced him to take a less active role in the firm. Brooks and Kipp did, however, collaborate on one important project: a hybrid electric car for the Milwaukee engine manufacturer Briggs and Stratton. Stevens had a long-standing relationship with this company and its leaders, particularly Fred Stratton, and had done design work on its motors on and off for decades. Stevens also had a long-standing interest in alternative fuels for cars. He had helped to design the steam-powered Paxton for the McCulloch Corporation in the 1950s and owned a Detroit Electric car dating to about 1915. He had also proposed two prophetic electric vehicles in the early 1960s: the Utopia passenger car, which was perfectly symmetrical front to back and featured a flat interior floor with swivel chairs, and the Gondola Terra motor home, an electric updating of the Zephyr land yacht, which he had designed for William Woods Plankinton Jr. at the beginning of his career.[1]

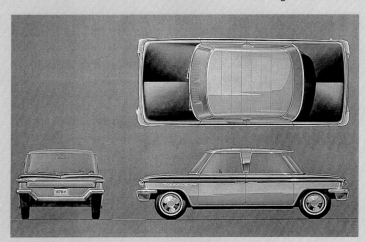

As for Briggs and Stratton's interest in the hybrid, the impetus was, as so often with Stevens's automotive projects, promotional in nature. The manufacturing company had just unveiled a new twin eighteen-horsepower engine, and combining it with an array of electric batteries to drive a car seemed like a perfect marketing ploy. After an initial surge of interest in electric vehicles following the Clean Air Act of 1967, they were again in the news as a result of gas shortages caused by the Arab oil embargo of the mid-1970s. Environmentalists, consumer activists, and automakers alike jumped at the opportunity to advocate the development of efficient electrics. Stevens regarded the auto industry's "Arab cheating solutions" with some asperity, commenting that "General Motors responded by dusting off fiberglass electric car prototypes from the late '60s, American Motors repainted a fiberglass 3-passenger electric car prototype built in the late '60s in conjunction with a well-known battery company, and many inventors, scientists, and ecologically minded citizens rushed to the drawing board and/or model shop and we began to read of the miracle of the electric car from the west coast to the east coast to the Texas border."[2] In addition to the mainstream car manufacturers, several other companies experimented with electrics at the time, including the McKee Engineering Company (the 1977 Sundancer), General Electric (the 1978 Centennial Electric), and Globe Union (the 1977

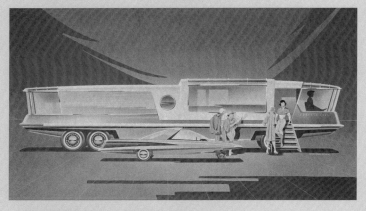

Utopia prophetic automobile 1960
Gondola Terra mobile home 1963

Endura, which Stevens's office also helped to design).[3] Briggs and Stratton was unusual, however, in building a hybrid instead of a full electric.

The hybrid that the Stevens office produced, with assistance from a Briggs and Stratton engineer named Doug Janisch, was novel in both concept and appearance. Its most distinctive innovation was the use of six wheels. Stevens admitted that this gave the car a desirable "unorthodox appearance" but pointed out that there was actually a tremendous practical advantage in the system. The front and back axles were not powered at all, while the center pair of wheels was attached to a drive train that could be powered either by battery power or by the Briggs and Stratton gas motor. This hybrid system helped to ameliorate the central problem of pure electric cars, the fact that range and performance are achieved at each other's expense. In comparison with an electric auto, the hybrid accelerated more quickly, had improved hill-climbing power, and remained mobile after its batteries had run out of power. The use of six wheels also permitted

Fiberglass model for a Briggs and Stratton motor 1982

Modeling the Briggs and Stratton hybrid electric automobile February 1979
Left to right: Jeff Shabowski, Kipp Stevens, Dick Frank.

Briggs and Stratton hybrid electric automobile 1979

the rear of the car to be constructed with a "captive trailer" that carried the eight hundred pounds of batteries necessary to power the vehicle electrically. This load was carried entirely on the rear pair of wheels, whose suspension was separate from the front four. The trunk of the car was located directly over the battery pack and gave access to the lower compartment so that the batteries could be easily replaced. The compartmentalization of the battery weight provided for an overall increase in maneuverability, smoothness, and acceleration. Because of its unusual internal construction, the car was cobbled together from a variety of bought and customized elements. Its armature was rebuilt from parts acquired from Marathon Electric, which had built a van along similar principles; the front end of the chassis also incorporated parts from a Ford Pinto. The body, by contrast, was entirely custom-built, apart from doors and a windshield taken from a Volkswagen Sirocco.

Briggs and Stratton's investment on the hybrid paid generous dividends. The car received an amount of national publicity that Stevens had not enjoyed since the days of his Evinrude proto-types of the late 1950s, including a placement on the cover of *Motor Trend* magazine. To maximize public impact, the design team styled the exterior of a carrier truck that conveyed the hybrid from place to place. Its rear end bore words that might have served as the motto for Stevens's entire career: "You may be following your future." Sadly, Stevens himself was able to take pleasure in his last major design achievement only vicariously. He was hospitalized for triple bypass heart surgery while the design of the hybrid was in its early stages; although he helped to develop the original concept for the car, the responsibility for developing the body styling to comple-tion fell to Kipp Stevens. Brooks soon recovered and returned to work at the design office, but he would not live to see his many prophetic electric cars realized in the marketplace. Only now, thanks to improvements in battery technology, are hybrid and fuel cell cars such as the Toyota Prius, Honda Insight, and General Motors Autonomy becoming commercially available.[4]

1. Brooks Stevens, "Tomorrow's Luxury Land Cruiser," *Automobile Quarterly* 1, no. 1 (1962): 78–84, 98.

2. Brooks Stevens, "The Electric Car—Miracle or Myth?" unpublished article, January 1979, Brooks Stevens Archive, Milwaukee Art Museum.

3. The spate of electrics was also spurred by Congress's adoption of the Electric and Hybrid Vehicle Research, Development, and Demonstration Act in 1976. On the period, see Ernest H. Wakefield, *History of the Electric Automobile: Battery-Only Powered Cars* (Warrendale, Pa.: Society of Automotive Engineers, 1994); Sheldon R. Shacket, *The Complete Book of Electric Vehicles* (Chicago: Domus Books, 1979). Kipp Stevens recalls that his father's office contributed mainly to the front end of the Endura.

4. For an overview of contemporary examples, see Jonathan Ringen, "Nonpolluting Cars," *Metropolis* 22 (August–September 2002): 106–9. On the general history of electric cars, see Ken Ruddock, "Recharging an Old Idea," *Automobile Quarterly* 31, no. 1 (1992): 30–47; Jim Motavelli, *Forward Drive* (San Francisco: Sierra Club Books, 2000); David A. Kirsch, *The Electric Vehicle and the Burden of History* (New Brunswick, N.J.: Rutgers University Press, 2000); and Michael Brian Schiffer, *Taking Charge: The Electric Automobile in America* (Washington, D.C.: Smithsonian Institution Press, 1994).

Back of Briggs and Stratton hybrid auto carrier 1979

Brooks Stevens ca. 1955

Brooks Stevens Associates, Staff and Other Colleagues

Brooks Stevens staff Christmas party, 1952.
Seated, clockwise from left: Dick Frank, Gordon Kelly, James Floria, Ralph Knudson, Charles Cowdin, Jr., John Hughes, Anthony (Tony) Reed, Betty Meyer, Brooks Stevens, Betty Dolan, Ray Anderson, Frank Shade, Hal Nickel, Tsugio Kubota, Richard Rechlicz.

Staff with Petipoint Iron 1941

Clockwise from top left:

Tony Reed, senior designer, ca. 1949

John Hughes, senior designer, with Stereo camera, 1956

Betty Meyer, personal secretary to Brooks Stevens, 1958

Jim Floria, senior designer, 1958

Clockwise from top left:

Gordon Kelly, head of product design, 1956

Dick Frank, model maker, 1958

Gordon Robertson, graphic designer, 1948

William G. Davidson, product designer, 1958

Guy Storr, public relations manager, 1958

Clockwise from top left:

John Bradley, product designer, 1967

Wayne Wagner, graphic and architecture designer, 1969

Peter Stacy, product designer, 1967

Dave Coleman, product designer, 1967

Clockwise from top left:

Stan Johnson, product designer, 1969

Adrian Bonini, graphic designer, 1969
Tom Green, product designer, 1969

David Nutting, product designer, 1967

Clockwise from top left:

Chuck Kiesow, staff designer, ca. 1975

Ray Anderson, head of graphic design, ca. 1975

Alice Preston, mechanic and Auto Museum director, 1994

Richard Rechlicz, airbrush renderer, 1974

Louis Netz, staff designer, 1974

The Industrial Designer is No Miracle Man

BROOKS STEVENS—1943
Industrial Marketing Magazine

To the editor: I should like very much to collaborate with you on a general article in connection with postwar product design for industry, as you suggest, in which we cover the fields quite completely. At the moment I am engaged in postwar product design programs for more than twenty manufacturing firms throughout the United States covering the fields of machine tool design, household appliances, refrigerators, outboard motors, passenger cars, truck, aviation, and others.

I have felt for the last year that most of the publicity articles, even institutional advertising, on the marvels of the postwar world have been terribly exaggerated, and in no way represent the practical manufacturing side of the picture. It is all very well for theorists and artist designers to project the fantastic all-plastic world which will be the fruits of victory after this horrible war, but, unfortunately, they do not consult those manufacturers and engineering departments who will somehow have to work these fantastic things out, or explain to the public why they have been misrepresented.

Unfortunately, these presentations have been primarily examples of art work with little basis for sound and practical manufacturing considerations. They have appeared glamorous and have attracted the eye, but they have led the public to believe that on Armistice Day one will rise from a plastic bed, bathe in a plastic shower, drive to work in a plastic car, and so on. These exaggerations, if not tempered, may cause a serious condition in the consumer's mind regarding the first postwar merchandise.[…]

If the glamour publicity has made a serious impression, Mrs. Housewife will say, "where is that round plastic refrigerator with the revolving shelves which I saw in all the magazines?" The dealer will fumble and try to explain. Mrs. America will then depart from the store saying, "Well, I know it's coming, so I'll wait till you have it in stock. Result—poor consumer acceptance to immediate postwar products.

If you ask the question—"then why not make the glamour products now?"—the answer is that it would be neither patriotic nor possible to do a twelve to fifteen month tool-up job before the war is ended.

Even this is based on the assumption that most of these things can be done, and I believe that I could go on for two thousand words explaining why most of them cannot be done. In addition, we must consider the fact that it is not written everywhere that the American consumer will accept these radical departures in everything from his toothbrush to his automobile even if they could be produced immediately. This country's progress has always been evolutionary and not revolutionary.

I should like to do a story for you with a title something like this: "The Industrial Designer is No Miracle Man." This might seem like a strange title for an article to be written by one in that profession. However, the point I should like to stress and illustrate by actual examples is that there is nothing miraculous or magnificent about the industrial designer's profession. He is terribly dependent upon the established engineering departments— in fact all the departments within his client's own company, and he merely collaborates with them, offering an outside point of view on certain phases of the product design which he has trained himself for and specialized in as a full-time job.

Many pseudo-stylists can turn out beautiful airbrush renderings of the way they would like things to be, but there always comes the horrible day of reckoning when these drawings must either be translated into tools, dies, and production, or thrown away as a needless expense. I have worked for over one hundred manufacturers, in as many fields of product design, and am pleased to say that the products have been built, reached the consumer, and have proved successful instead of remaining forever in a picture frame, demonstrating only wishful thinking insofar as the way that product might have been made.

If my approach and thinking along this line interest you, please advise me and I shall go to work on a rough draft. Please be advised that the story will be on the conservative side, but in so being it will be one that the average manufacturer will recognize as a possible link with the future instead of the theories of the long-haired artist who is satisfied to project his own whims on paper with the frame of mind that "everyone is out of step but my son John."

The Industrial Designer Is No Miracle Man
How the industrial designer functions and what this one thinks about some postwar designs being shown

The title of this article may seem to be a strange one in view of the fact the writer is engaged in industrial design. The reason for my choosing it is because I believe firmly that the industrial design profession has proven itself as a necessary and sound independent service available to all industry in times of peace or war.

In an effort to prove its soundness and its usefulness, I feel called upon to differentiate between the serious business of industrial design, in contrast to the tendency to prophesy and wave the magic wand of the airbrush gracefully over a paper surface depicting the wonders of the manufacturing world of the future.

Strangely enough, the wilder the predictions and the more fantastic the rendering, the more renowned the author of designer seems to be. This has resulted in a false and dangerous impression on the part of the manufacturer, and when I say manufacturer, I refer to perhaps the chief engineer, or someone within an organization who is responsible for actually carrying out the ideas of the new product and translating them into production. He will invariably ask, almost at his wits' end: "What makes this artist feel, first of all, that there is anything terribly remarkable

about his contribution to a total picture compared to certain of the engineers within the company who have worked long and tedious hours to prefect the product, make it work, and see that it's produced and delivered on time? Why must there be fanfare and full-page advertisements of this self-established miracle man who may have contributed to the appearance design alone?"

I have had the chief engineer of an automobile manufacturing company ask me why the stylist should receive glamorous publicity and great acclaim, when the engineers who developed its chassis, its engine, its very life, go unmentioned and are merely taken for granted. These are the reasons why I say that the industrial designer is no miracle man.

It is relatively easy for him to imagine and create fabulous products for the future world which, seemingly, erase the difficulties of the past. Button-pushing, remote control living, with hardly the necessity to think, flows smoothly from the orifice of his airbrush-flying automobiles, mechanical kitchens, refrigerators that literally hand you the food you want, and many other intriguing devices-yet, all these must be engineered: some way must be found to manufacture them, to make them work, and to produce them at a reasonable price. Considering some of the ideas that have been advanced in magazines, the job which lies ahead in the engineering department may well be the miraculous phase of a given development.

Industrial design can be justified as a profession because independent designers, operating alone or with a staff, are able to establish operations in their own location to serve a considerable number and types of industries. They are specializing in a phase of the work for which they are particularly talented. The question arises as to why an individual manufacturer should not maintain his own industrial designer of staff. My answer to that question is that the industrial designer can better serve a number of businesses through the lack of monotony and the regimentation brought about by continually working in one field. His exposure to trends, acceptances, and the progress of all fields of industrial design make him better suited in each individual case for the offering of a fresh viewpoint unhampered by constant proximity to one line of work.

Basically, the industrial designer in peacetime is a product appearance designer with some ability to simplify and suggest easier manufacture and lower cost of the product with which he may work. In some instances, there have been definite functional improvements and basic principles have been improved, but this probably was not promised or counted on when the designer was called in for consultation. Through discussion, collaboration, and cooperation, he may, by provoking enough questions or offering enough suggestions, arrive at something in the way of a functional improvement, which goes beyond product styling.

It is this very phase of the work—this collaboration, this cooperation—that is so necessary to the success of an association between the industrial designer and his client. The manufacturer needs the designer or he would not have called him in. But it must be realized how completely the designer needs the manufacturer and all his departments. If any industrial designer knew all there was to know about the past manufacturing histories of all the companies he might work for, and types of products he might work with, he would probably be a dangerous person to society. He depends completely upon the knowledge and experience of the men in the engineering department, sales department, and advertising department, and knowledge of the policies of the management. It is with these departments as tools that he does his best work. He becomes the hands and the coordinator of ideas pertaining to appearance design for the company whose departments and men have a full-time job in the particular phase of the work in which they are engaged.[…]

The industrial designer has been referred to as a "streamliner, a corner rounder, a hump smoother," and many other equally inaccurate terms. One does not streamline a one hundred ton sheet steel stamping press because it is stationary! One does not streamline a bathtub or a jukebox, for there is nothing in life which calls upon their being aerodynamically treated in form.

The term "streamlined" has become terribly hackneyed and trite for if has been applied to everything from airplanes to ladies' hose! It is not a new term by any means, for we have an interesting brochure in our files colorfully describing the 1911 Hupmobile car, and it makes a great point of the Hupmobile Runabout with

is "streamlined cowl." We have a copy of a design patent issued in 1897, or thereabouts, to an individual covering the design of a "streamlined" railroad train. It is remarkably close, in principle at least, to what has been done on the railroads today.

Product appearance design or product stylings are better-generalized terms for that all-important phase of the work engaged in by the industrial designer. Point of sale appeal and eye appeal can safely be considered in all products. A drill press can be styled so that when the machine tool buyer receives some direct mail advertising, and providing he knows the company who builds the machine, is convinced by its declaration of performance, and is agreeable to the price quoted, he may then actually be swayed by the final impression of a clean, good-looking, "proud to own" piece of equipment.

I have been asked the question, "Why style an electric control case of a starter housing when it may go in the basement or will be unseen, for the most part, in the shop?" The only answer is that some salesman originally must sell the device. If we are only successful in impressing him with his own product, we will have made great strides toward an increased sales volume. If he can remain with the buyer five minutes longer and as a final rebuttal speech allude to its clean lines and efficient styling, that, too, may be chalked up as an additional sale. If we are only successful in providing the advertising department or agency with better pictorial subject and more intriguing copy, these things alone may justify product styling.

We cannot always count on styling alone. No one is foolish enough to believe that a streamlined or styled tractor will make a farmer part with hard-earned money. But we can feel that if he is in the market for a tractor, and two manufacturers' products are being considered and they have equal performance and equal prices, the better-looking tractor may win out. It is a reasonable gamble, to say the least.

The question of how the industrial designer can successfully work on an automobile one day, a washing machine the next, and a lady's compact after that has often confused the average person. The answer, I believe again, is his complete freedom for appearance design thought: his cognizance of trends and acceptances; and his basic knowledge of the elements of good proportion and form, that can be applied in some was to any product that is designed for manufacture. The industrial designer must go beyond drawing pictures. He should carry each and every commission through at least three stages of development.

The first and most important stage of the work, after a thorough understanding of the problem at hand, is the preliminary design stage. This is often the longest and most difficult part of the work. Hundreds of rough sketches, which could hardly be called examples of artwork, may be the result. Many of these the client may never see. Many of them he will see, because they will provide the vocabulary of ideas, which are reasonable in the mind of the designer after having fully exploited the possibilities through this preliminary sketch method. It is now necessary to have the most important conference of the entire program, during which the engineers will weed through the preliminary ideas, criticizing and explaining the advantages of some and the disadvantages of others. This is where understanding, cooperation, and collaboration are most necessary, for it is from this vocabulary of ideas that a single course of action is chosen.

The second stage constitutes the final designing and the refinement of the most acceptable basic idea, and it is at this time that more finished, colored renderings or picturizations of the product, as it will finally appear, are required. It is during this stage that mock-ups, or scale models, may be necessary to completely show the design. In the automotive field, great care is taken and considerable expense incurred in the execution of finished work or plaster models which, when surveyed by the average person, will appear to be the real thing. They will be complete in every detail except for motive power.

After this stage, more conferences are held, final details ironed out, colors, finishes, nameplates, and the like, are refined and decided upon. The designer then proceeds with the third stage of his work, which is the execution of finished dimensioned working drawings for all parts of the product over which he has had jurisdiction, and he must then be available and on hand for consultation when the product has been completely tooled and is going into production. This shows how necessary all of the people involved in a complete product design development are to a successful solution.

To return again for the moment to prophecy, especially that of postwar prophecy, I feel it is dangerous and unwise to depict too wildly the mechanical marvels of the postwar period—especially when it involves the translation of airplanes, automobiles, and railroad trains, immediately into the field of plastics. We are apt to be jumping from ashtrays, calendar pads, and table-model radios, directly into products so large that the materials will not, with present experience and knowledge, do the jog. The element of danger involved in this type of prophecy is that we are going to have to look forward to a difficult tax situation, unknown markets, and not the least of our worries is the unknown time of this reconversion.

It is unfair and unwise to lead the public to believe that the day after our final day of victory they can be assured of plastic automobiles for $400 each, privately-owned helicopters within the automotive price range, and household appliances that will almost eliminate the necessity of domestic help. Industry cannot patriotically develop, tool up, and most important of all, put these dream products to test during the carrying on of the war. Therefore, the only logical and possible recommendation is to begin with the tools and dies, ideas and designs, equipment and methods, which were not doing badly before Dec. 7, 1941.

I do not mean to say the industrial designer is not trying, during this period, to improve those products through the medium of practical revisions in existing tools and new and fresh styling, at least to offer some reward for victory. But, if we must look forward to a consumer mind that has been propagandized into believing he will have a revolutionary and miraculous new product immediately, we may have a reluctance to purchase the immediate postwar products. If that occurs, and we have 130,000,000 people deciding to wait for the colorful magazine prophecies, we may look forward to twelve or eighteen difficult months which, believe me, will be difficult enough under any circumstances.

Future Body Styling in Retrospect

BROOKS STEVENS—1949

Will future motor cars look like an airplane with fanatical adherence to aerodynamics as a formula for the family passenger car body design? This question is interesting, and a most appropriate one to offer answers to in this particular stage of the American motor car development. It is particularly interesting and significant (because of the public's pent-up expectancies of postwar automobiles) that the realization that much of the extremely radical prophecy material, together with actual modified versions of these extreme predictions, have shown the public that advertisement and showroom flare should not be the dominating factor in the choosing of the motor car; that the ultimate living with the vehicle in a practical and economic manner is now provoking a screening operation on the buyer's part that demands sound body design— and this may produce the guiding light to the manufacturer in his true desire to give the public a product with merchandising appeal and functional integrity. The race for the streamlined zenith in form for the sheet metal mass which encloses the passengers who ride in today's automobile has produced a group of contenders who now may well heed a storm-warning.

In New York, a year ago, I had the pleasure of meeting with a prominent English magazine editor on a regular visit to America's motor kingdom, and I heard him state to a group of questioning writers and press people an interesting and rather concise description of the Englishman's opinion of the American automobile. In an engaging and clipped British accent he quoted as follows: "Gentleman, the Amarikan mota cah looks like an inflated am-lett with a chraome-plated mustash."

This analysis is a natural and humorous exaggeration, but not without foundation. The pontoon full-length fender and full-width body type now running through about half of the industry begins to take on the singular appearance shape of one large envelope with a superstructure or window group above, and depends quite thoroughly upon ornamental grill-work and applied chrome gimcracks, referred to as speed lines and/or buffer strips, for individuality and identity. This gradual arrival at the same set of conditions for five or six makes does present the true problem of how to distinguish one from the other without memorizing details or requiring close scrutiny of a nameplate.

Along with this development of a large single mass, with the maximum utility of the interior for the passengers, we have plunged headlong into the serious consumer attitude regarding maintenance and repair work. We are now undoubtedly at the crossroads, and in the existing laboratory of consumer approval and disapproval we have already seen two widely divergent policies on how to individualize and throw off the lethargy of identity oblivion. One prominent manufacturer, having waited the longest in the postwar retooling program, undoubtedly made the decision to heed the public's reaction to the early postwar full-blown streamlining attempts with voluminous sheet metal skin dimensions, low silhouettes and high, wide hood conditions, and concluded that the economic leveling process in business and trade would flavor the prospective purchaser's outlook with conservatism and minute evaluation of function for a relatively long ownership and investment period. In doing so, a completely retooled line of cars, with a full new stamping investment involved, was produced to answer the arguments against sheet metal width, difficult entry and exit conditions, head room, clearances, excessive overhang, and body element repair costs. The public's blunt statements about the impracticality of the immediate postwar automobiles purchased in the first rush-and-bloom of availability made its strong impression on this manufacturer who waited and then decided to appeal to the conservative transportation-minded more-cautious customer of the present day. It will be interesting to watch the longer-range exposure of this thinking in the immediate competitive picture.

Another manufacturer has just announced a new model which presents perhaps the most daring aerodynamic and aircraft styling allegiance to reach full production in the motor car field. The extreme contrast between these two approaches will provide the most interesting barometer for the future. It is interesting to note, however, in the more advanced and airplane type contender, that we have certain functional elements from a body design standpoint which are greatly improved functionally. I refer to the dropping of the bonnet mass in profile to provide improved vision, dispensing with the broad, high, relatively useless bonnet over which the average and shorter individual cannot adequately see from the low seat heights of the present cars.

FUTURE BODY STYLING IN RETROSPECT is the title of this paper, and in clarification I should like to point out that it is undoubtedly time for the body designer to look back with a certain amount of reverence for evaluation of the good points of the past motor car trends. This is the time to consider that similarity of form will lack identity, together with the consumer public becoming adamant with cars that do not fit in older garages, with fender dents involving a week's wages for repair and stream-lining (or pseudo-streamlining) being carried to the point of danger in the careful and safe handling of the car by the average driver. The crowded parking area problems are not to be ignored because it can conceivably affect the retail trade, shopping, and crowded business tempo.

Being involved in the overall profession of industrial design, and realizing that every product—from the cigarette lighter, household appliance, the automobile and the railroad train— all must appeal to the same consumer, we are more cognizant of the consumer's true use problems and demands than we are influenced in forcing him to accept illusions of speed and dash at the "impulse point of sale," later resulting in disappointment.

With the close relationship and interest in the automobile industry involved in professional life, I have fallen into the clutches of the fascinating hobby of antique automobile collecting and restoration. This offers a strong contrasting note to the incessant demand for fresh creative thinking in this particular field, and also provides an opportunity for true appreciation and study of good designs for their period in the past. [...]

For a few references to interesting retrospective details, I might point out that during the Minneapolis Aquatennial Tour this past July, one of my associates and I were hurtling through space in a recently restored 1914 Marmon Wasp Raceabout, and the weather was extremely hot. Directly ahead of me on the center line of a 9-ft. long low narrow bonnet was perched a nickel-plated Motometer, the trademark of a definite motoring era. Our concern, with a relatively tight engine, was heat, and I fixed my eyes comfortably upon the red mercury tube of the Motometer to watch its climb or level as we proceeded on the Tour. How amazingly simple and functional and logical this device now seems compared with forgetting completely to check the modern heat indicator aid, or trying to ferret it out from the cluttered instrument boar of the modern motor car before it has reached the boiling point and damage has been done to the mechanism. It was never necessary to drop one's eyes from the safe road position, and a careful check was never a difficult movement.

In this regard I still maintain that on the modern and future motor cars bonnet ornaments are superfluous as they are used today. Abstractions of the human form, birds, aircraft, and guided missiles seem to have taken over at the point where the radiator cap and Motometer was perched in functional dignity twenty years ago. I firmly believe in the smooth, unadorned hood, but if tradition will not let us discard this feature forever it may be possible to produce a dignified emblem in the form of a shield or coat-of-arms motif translated into the glamorous new art of combining transparent plastics with chrome-plated metals to include, on the back side, the heat indicator device as modern Motometer.

The hood and vision conditions of older models, wherein both fenders could be seen with ease, and a view down through the catwalks was possible, certainly was better from a safety angle than our broad motorboat bows over which we now attempt to see. The postwar Kaiser-Frazer car dared to shorten and drop a gracefully rounded bonnet toward the road for leading the way toward improving this prominent vision restriction in other makes. Its educational value and leadership has been followed and carried to a greater degree in the recently announced 1950 Studebaker.

Headroom conditions, ease of entry and exit for older or incapacitated persons, are points that should be reconsidered in the future body design. This does not mean that we shall go backwards, because it is entirely possible to style even the most practical set of functional conditions. The inception and design of the Willys Jeepster, in which I had the extreme pleasure of collaborating, proved several things in its daring and unorthodox presentation to postwar markets. It proved that the public was not wedded to an industry-accepted pattern and that a vehicle could have its own look and personality provided it was understandable to the average person as related to its intended function. It was felt that the sportsman and the youth of the nation had definite and strong memories of the true open car, or phaeton, last seen in the '30's, and that automatic, electronic, hydromatic, button-pushing convertibles of today were extremely expensive for this smaller market. The Jeepster has certainly been America's most recent sports car and undoubtedly paved the way for the Dodge Wayfairer Roadster and the Crosley Hot-Shot. The Jeep StationWagon, likewise, could never be looked upon as a streamlined vehicle, but captured its share of the utility market with a "stationwagon look" that the public immediately accepted as practical. It then went beyond this point to being accepted also as cute and smart, finding its way even into the carriage trade vehicles.

In the standard four-door sedan body of the future it would be well to look back and strive for functional improvement in the overall car. Excessive overhangs, both front and rear, have undoubtedly created illusions of length – in fact, not only illusions of length but actual length not completely controllable in many garages constructed as recently as a decade ago. The public has looked behind these false fronts by now, realizing that they enclosed very little more than space.

The hood conditions have been covered in previous remarks, which leads us to the windshield of the present day car. I am as well versed on the difficult problem of the "A" pillar post as the next man, but in looking back it must be pointed out that they have been narrower even in the mass produced sedan. The extreme slant, or rake, of the modern windshield has produced an accessory visor industry. In earlier days a visor function was built into the roof of the car. If we have made the public visor-conscious, we may have to provide it integrally with the car roof.

Door openings in some of the largest automobiles in current models are extremely difficult to maneuver through. Certainly these openings can be enlarged even though the silhouette is lower. Window sizes can increase with enlarged doors and should be kept adequate in height even with the lower roof line. It may be necessary to drop the belt line and thin the transverse curvature of the roof in order to provide these openings, but certainly there is no law in modern motor car design which places the lower window sill line at the passenger's shoulder level.

In looking back again it is most interesting to trace the history and derivation of the instrument panel and its cycle of existence. In the early 1900's instruments were at a minimum. The speedometer, however, was apt to be a free-standing unit in the front cockpit of the car, mounted low, even on the floor boards in some instances. A larger step was taken when a dashboard introduced on which a few instruments were mounted. Later, in the '20's, a tremendous stride was heralded when instrument groupings were brought together into one unit, reposing under a common glass. We have been through a recent decade or so of instrument panels extremes wherein every trick in design fabrication, raw materials, lighting, and position was exploited. Many of them became an outright game as to where the controls were actually hidden and which way you moved them if you found them. The "organ console" key arrangement, fairly adequate in the daytime, after an extensive training course required virtually the knowledge of the Braille system at night to find the hot air "IN" switch or the refreshed, revitalized air "ON" switch. We now find ourselves reverting back to instrument clusters divorced from a dash board, and some have found their way on to the steering column again, not unlike the memorable instrument box on the impressive Packard Twin Six of 1917 or thereabouts.

Interiors are a golden opportunity for a designer who chooses to look back and translate some of the earlier thinking into the period ahead. Early limousines and broughams for milady were beautifully turned out in everything from silks to needlepoint and grosgrain trim. The modern motor car is definitely purchased by Mrs. American and should be keyed to her feminine likes and tastes. As in those earlier cars, interior schemes borrowed on the home, and today we can borrow on modern upholstery and interior fabrics that are reminders of the warmth and livability of the davenport and easy chair. The average man driver today chauffers his sedan to work where it is parked all day and returns again in the evening. The woman driver spends a good part of her day handling her marketing travels as well as her social activities in an automobile which she wants to be attractive, feminine and admired, as well as a comfort to herself when she is alone with it.

Striking Kaiser-Frazer interiors, based on feminine appeal, individual and striking color combinations, with a new fabric and texture approach have led the way in this direction. When these designs were being originally prepared, fabric houses proudly showed what they referred to as their "automotive line" which was composed of a line of fabrics used in the immediate past by other manufacturers in the industry. As design consultants to the Kaiser-Frazer Corporation, we asked why we could not work from fabrics and colors borrowed from the living-room and the home, at which point the warning flag of conventionalism was raised to the masthead. Experimental combinations were pushed through, and I believe we are safe in saying that the general theme of this procedure will continue.

A final interesting parallel of a retrospective motor car style has been the introduction of the hardtop convertible or the sports sedan. Some of the most striking stylings of the late '20's were cloth covered hardtop sedans with open car window advantages. This offers the person who has objections to the true convertible automobile the sporty appearance of this individualized type of car.

In conclusion, I do not think that we must completely align ourselves in the design of future motor cars with the rocket and projectile design formula as pseudo-sales stimuli to the buying public. The American automobile, for many reasons, has reached a level of investment to the consumer which is extremely high, and the "whim" buyers are going to be few and far between, and *they* will think twice before turning over from two to three thousand dollars for something that looks like it's doing 100 miles at the curb but is so designed that you must crawl into as you would a fighter plane.

A careful homogenizing of good, safe body dimensions for the human beings who must live within, together with cautious over-all extremity dimensions, and the serious consideration of the not-too-careful driver who is bound to continually be involved in minor fender fractures and the like, can produce an automobile that adequate styling will enhance and sell. In short—everything in moderation.

Let us look doggedly forward for an improved product, but cautiously in retrospect, to make the best of the good things tried and true.

The Clarification of "Planned Obsolescence"

BROOKS STEVENS—1958
Industrial Designer, Fellow A.S.I.D.

The industrial designer in today's business world should be basically a business man, an engineer, and a stylist—and in that direct order.

Being a businessman is entirely important to the successful professional industrial designer in order that he may understand the problems underlying business conditions that exist with his client and within the industry in which he intends to serve that client. These business conditions may definitely alter his thinking with regard to the design approach. Product design, successfully handled by a specialist in the field, must comply with the conditions within the industry and definitely fit the marketing circumstances which may differ tremendously from a washing machine to a lawn mower or to an automobile. Even though we are dealing with the same consumer—Mr. and Mrs. America—for consumer goods, so to speak, the marketing problems and the business atmosphere of the different manufactures may vary even geographically, and certainly varies with the conditions of the money markets in the areas served.

The industrial designer must be enough of an engineer to understand manufacturing problems, plant techniques, equipment limitations, material uses, and costs. It would be useless for the professional stylist or industrial designer to foist a so-called absolute design, artistically speaking, upon his client, and in turn his client's market, without regard for its engineering flexibility, its conformation with plant equipment, and costs of production. Engineering must certainly guide the industrial designer in his product planning and no amount of design for design's sake should interfere with this formula.

The industrial designer, of course, creates his special niche in the economic and business life of his country by adding the stylist's touch to make manufactured products desirable to the consuming public and to give the products that last degree of "buy-appeal" necessary to make the sale. Styling, at the absolute expense of the best business approach, the best engineering approach, and the proper manufacturing approach and its costs, would be superfluous and unnecessary.

The industrial designer is not a fine artist producing works for exhibition purposes only. It is all well and good to talk about the relationship of art to industry, and art for art's sake, and to stress the point that the industrial designer must add the esthetic touch to big business and force business to recognize what is the very best in design and art, but art for art's sake is not saleable in the market place of consumer goods.

The industrial designer's first obligation is to his client primarily because he is retained by his client and derives his income for his services from that manufacturer. His next obligation is, of course, to the economy of the nation, and if his contributions to his client are properly handled and taken care of, this obligation to the economy is automatic. The consumer obviously benefits from this service and its subsequent carrying out by the manufacturer into the finished marketable goods in that he attains a distinctly higher standard of living, and we must remember that it is the consumer's own choice in the market place as to whether he buys a product or not..when and if he pleases.

The 1958 automobiles exemplified by certain makes were very good examples of styling errors, esthetic concepts that were not of the proper acceptable standard, and these examples were met by consumer refusal. A recessionary atmosphere followed in direct proportion to this motor car purchase refusal and these potential customers were referred to as "lookers" and not "buyers." A chain reaction was then begun when the 1958 automobile was distasteful to the public as a largest single purchase, no new TV, no new washer, no refrigerator, et cetera. Only then did the ivory-towered intellectuals and newspaper commentators and TV commentators come forth to condemn everything in business, including, of course, "planned obsolescence," and with this condemnation they decided to support and publicize the need for the European small car—why doesn't America have a Volkswagen, et cetera—and the crucifixion of Detroit and its chrome-plated befinned monsters continued to be the front page news. It even reached certain stages of the government and the presidential speeches were flavored with people buying things that were extreme or unnecessary.

Now, as negative as the 1958 automotive model acceptance seemed to be last year, I am quite sure that the recent introduction of the '59 models has already reversed the trend and that the smaller, unadorned European type car may be buried again because there is such great acceptance to the '59 models from Detroit. There is certainly one definite esthetic improvement in the 1959 cars and that is a much more restricted use of chrome trim and superfluous moldings. The trim is much more tastefully done, doing a much better job of accenting the basic sculptured forms.

I believe that ten points are necessary in clarifying "Planned Obsolescence" and I should like to begin with the definitions originally given over five or six years ago when this philosophy was first utilized in public addresses.

"Planned Obsolescence" was then defined as… "the desire to own something a little newer, a little, better, a little sooner than is necessary."

Point No. 1. in the clarification of this philosophy would be that this does NOT mean organized waste because used articles are not generally discarded or thrown away upon replacement by new ones. They move into the used product market to reach someone of lesser purchasing power in a much finer condition than the subsequent buyer could otherwise afford. This is certainly exemplary in the used car market. There are people who are able to buy fine automobiles today of one year's age with less than fifteen thousand miles for a very much reduced price. These people could otherwise not afford transportation perhaps of any reliable kind.

Point No. 2. It is erroneous to state that people are *duped* into buying things unnecessarily. They are NOT led into the market place by law enforcement officers; the products they buy are of their own choosing and they result in pleasure and satisfaction of ego. I am certainly not one who feels that keeping up with the Joneses is normal.

Point No. 3. This attitude and general philosophy keeps employment at the highest possible record, and purchasing power at a maximum, and in turn these combine to increase the standard of living for all.

Point No. 4. It is false to assume that annual models of products are not improved with new functions as well as style. These products are a much greater value at a comparable cost to previous models.

Point No. 5. New model announcements annually create an atmosphere charged with public interest and anticipation, and prosperity for sales and industry, which can only benefit the customer who is the very worker then provided with a job and subsequent purchasing power.

Point No. 6. The continual manufacture of any given-model-year automobile would soon produce a blandness of interest, and sales only to those who needed a vehicle due to car age and mechanical fatigue.

Point No. 7. The loudly publicized smaller unadorned automobile in America is a case in point. This car is not easy to build in the United States for appreciably less money and will not compare in pride of ownership with a one-year-old Oldsmobile Holiday Coupe in desirability or in cost.

Point No. 8. If this smaller less adorned automobile were the answer to the American economy why then did the very nicely styled 104" wheelbase Willys automobile pass out of the American market? It was a victim of more impressive used cars for less money.

The Rambler story, which is often utilized to point up the lack of need for "Planned Obsolescence," and the desire on the part of the public for a small European type car, brought back the 1951 Rambler tooling in 1958 and offered the Rambler America model. It was, however, outsold by its bigger sister, the 108" wheelbase Rambler by many, many thousands of vehicles.

It is also interesting to note that the medium sized sister, the 108" Rambler, was not adorned, and in 1957 was forced to sprout fins on its rear quarter panel, and in 1959 has expanded these fins to move forward into the rear doors, and has also increased its chrome side appliqué trim.

Point No. 9. The cry for rationality, the so-called chrome-less practical cars and products, is a step toward regimentation, lack of identification, and a blandness of acceptance, which can only be cataclysmic, economically.

Point No. 10. The tenth and final point must obviously be this. "Planned Obsolescence" is not an unsound philosophy and planned obsolescence versus "natural" or " genuine" obsolesce is not the question at all. In manufactured products today improved by research and development based on industry profits there can be no obsolesce without a plan. These products are not born, they do not grow in the ground, but are man-built and planned.

In closing, may I state that regimentation of any kind is dangerous and borders on socialism and a low standard of living.

Industrial Design—Economic Visual Aid

BROOKS STEVENS—CA.1960

Improved product design made *more* desirable to *more* people through greater *appearance* appeal will insure high levels of employment and economic stability. Thus industrial design becomes an Economic Visual Aid.

It is indeed a great honor to address the membership of the S.I.A. on this occasion. As a professional man, one engaged in industrial design, I would like to point out, of course, the relationship to industry and business. The professional industrial designer was brought about by the need for consulting services in connection with assisting business to continue its high level of sales and employment. The profession, in a sense, is not new except by advertisement and recognition. We have always had the industrial designer with us and among us. This man has quietly been the draftsman, the craftsman, the engineer, the builder, the factory worker, who unconsciously or consciously tried to make whatever product he was fabricating appear as pleasingly as possible as he built it. This is a definite addition to *pure function*. The relationship to business and economic life is of tremendous importance at this moment, and has always been, for we must remember that a form of business has been man's life from the earliest beginnings. If we go back to the historical times of the Neanderthal or cave man, we find the early beginnings of trade and barter and the ability to acquire possessions. There was also the problem of survival—the strength of groups of individuals or clans or bands of people- and trade an business took place among these people purely from the standpoint of acquiring sufficient food or firewood, or shelter to perpetuate their comfort and their lives. This early man was one of our earliest industrial designers in a sense because from a standpoint of pride and with the desire to impress his fellow clansmen or his competitors he

began to decorate himself either with skins or pain as in the case of many native tribes in foreign countries, our own Indian tribes in America. All of this was a part of presentation or doing business by impression. The problem of business and its necessity to human survival and a good way of life has always been a factor in ultimate war and strife. This human urge to acquire and to clothe oneself and to have possessions and ultimately, when the introduction of currency in some form, whether it was gold and later credit, emerged we had entire nations fighting one another for purely and basically business reasons.

The nationalistic urge was generally the advertising banner of the crusade but in most instances it certainly had to do with the acquisition of possessions or strengthening of position from which further business or barter or trade could be practiced. With the emergence of Christianity into this world a great deal of this terrorism and almost savage warfare and vandalism began to take on slightly different aspects. But as we became theoretically more civilized and educated, cultured and worldly-wise the gold problem, the land problem, the need for markets, for trading areas, etc., continued as the goal to the business men of those historic periods. As a result a good deal of our world war problems have come about through economic problems among nations. Business is one of the most important factors in the world today, and as a professional man serving business, I can only stress that good business, high levels of economy and good trading habits are completely necessary in a peaceful world if we are to ever have long periods of prosperity.

Man has always followed some form of sign in the heavens, celestial navigation, the Wise Men who followed the Star. Columbus who began his pursuit for a new trade route to India certainly had to do with business and gold for the Queen of Spain. He used the stars and their guidance for his navigation problems with a small fleet of ships. Through the definitely primitive degrees with which these ships could be navigated during that period errors in navigation were made, the ships slipped off into different courses than he contemplated, and Columbus is credited with discovering the New World, at least in that particular period of history. In discovering the New World he discovered new areas for pioneers, for trade, for business, and history moved along to the point of the actual industrial revolution, the Machine Age, and the emergence of industrial design in its most embryonic form.

Again, I must refer to the fact that there has always been some form of designer or stylist quietly at work. Certainly, with the creation of the railroad train, the "Iron Horse," man was confronted with the deep need to sell this new mode of transportation to a fearful public – a public who feared the billowing smoke and the noise and sparks and flames that the Iron Horse gave forth. Therefore, this engineer, this designer, this artist, and builder, this stylist, consciously went to work on the aesthetic style of the railroad locomotive and its coaches to improve the appearance and intrigue the public. These efforts resulted in locomotives festooned with brass, gold trim, striping, leaded glass, church type windows in the coaches, painted side panels with views of the countryside depicting the areas through which the train would travel. All of this was done to take away the fear, to intrigue the people to try out this new mode of transportation, this wonderful new horizon for travel. In 1902 the automotive industry, still in its infancy – less than 5 years – brought forth a man names Ransom E. Olds who had built originally the famous Oldsmobile curved dash car, but sold out to larger interest and re-entered the field with the Reo – taken from his initials. This particular automobile he advertised to the American public as his "farewell car". The utmost in what could be done in automotive transportation for that day, never to be exceeded, and yet look at the horizons that have been discovered in this particular industry in the years that have followed. In 1912 the Titanic, the unsinkable ocean liner, the finest design in the world, left Europe for its maiden voyage to the United States. On board were all the promi-

nent business men of that day clamoring for cabins, paying fantastic rates to have the prestige factor of riding on this wonderful new unsinkable ship. Through some simple quirk of fate, a mistake of man, a human frailty, the Titanic found itself among ice floes. She hit one in her most vulnerable spot. She was not unsinkable and many of our high caliber business men passengers dies in this tragedy. We have carried on, however, with shipping throughout the world hoping for better ships, safer ships. Even the Andrea Doria incident proves that this goal has not been entirely reached, not even in the modern day unsinkable ocean liner. However, the loss of life was absolutely minimum in this tragic disaster. In 1927 the aircraft industry, also embryonic, in its development came forth with a pioneer in the form of Lindbergh who flew the flimsy Spirit of St. Louis across the ocean to Paris and accomplished the reverse of Columbus' famous voyage in a flimsy craft also, and started the era of transoceanic travel. Today I fly to Paris in 6 hours on a luxurious airliner 40,000 feet above the water.

In 1929, shortly after the Lindbergh triumph, we could have looked upon American as Boomtown, U.S.A. Then the crash of the stock market. A Financial House of Cards. We had to learn this lesson of extending ourselves on margin, how to operate in the investment and securities and stock market without this type of inflated gambling. In 1929 the average worker's wage was $25 a week, considered rather good in these prosperity times of 1929. Thirty years later this same worker has $83 per week. The life insurance business in 1929 had $18 billions of dollars at work in industry and business. Billions of anything become numbers hard for the public to understand. Thirty years later in 1959 we had $101 billions in life insurance at work—savings—in business and industry. Actual monies in savings banks today as compared to 1929 are 20 billions today as against 4 billions thirty years ago. The automotive picture is a tremendous advance, from 1929 with 23 million automobiles to 1959 with 55 million automobiles.

I maintain that my philosophy of planned obsolescence, defined as the desire to own something a little newer, a little better, a little sooner than is necessary is a very sound approach to a high level economy for the world. Some of my colleagues have chosen to disagree with me even in public print, and have referred to the fact that this sounds like organized waste and they champion the cause of natural or genuine obsolescence. I am forced to remind them that there can be no obsolescence in product design, in business approaches without a plan. "Keeping up with the Joneses," is healthy American ego. There is nothing wrong with this and those who cy out strongly that this is a wrong attitude for the American, I am sure would be found upon observation to be driving a Cadillac car. I believe in planned obsolescence as having been the manner through which we have raised the standard of living for our people. We must think of the used product market – the second hand automobile with 12 thousand miles on it, which can be purchased by a low income worker who could not aspire to a brand new one. He finds this automobile to have many unused miles in it, and if properly cleaned up and simonized, he can be just as proud of the temporarily until he is able to trade upward to a bran new, larger, more expensive car. He was not concerned to have all the money in hand as was the Frenchman five years ago to buy this automobile in America, because by the down payment method and the monthly payment he literally rents the car, perhaps for the rest of his life, not ever really owning any one version of the automobile. Certainly years ago, when the procedure for owning your own home came about with the purchase of a piece of land, a mortgage and monthly payments simulating rent, allowed more to move from less desirable rented quarters, tenements, hotels, boarding houses and the like, to have their little parch of lawn, to have their rotary lawnmower, a TV set, to rent those as well on a down-payment basis. They have their TV, their washing machine, their dryer, their automobile, the outboard motor, all in the same year, not one every year and be deprived in the meantime.

The creation and stimulation of desire has put more people to work and in turn made more desires possible to fulfill than anything else we have ever know in the world today. Labor has had a difficult part of this picture in having been passed through a period of unfortunate education during the Roosevelt era of requesting more paid holidays, more time off, more leisure time, and by this I do not mean the fact that we have attained the goal of a Saturday and Sunday weekend to enjoy the family, to go boating, to cut the lawn, to drive our automobiles. I am speaking of this unfortunate mental concept of leisure time *today* on the part of the worker by the *hour*, meaning few minutes out of every hour earned, not really worked, disinterested, no pride in the product that they produce. I have heard this blamed on automation and mass production. This, I feel is unfortunate and wrong, for in Germany they are in a fine position today to absolutely show us that even though in the Volkswagen plant there is the highest degree of automation, the individual worker looks upon the Volkswagen as his product and is proud of it.

Now, I say, back to work. American must resume interest in the job she has to do internally and the job she has to externally if we are to ask "Why the Moon"? Man has always followed the star for some light in the heavens to lead him to some new discovery, perhaps to feel that he was getting closed to God, in Whom he believed. A goal in space, again new horizons, opportunities for exploitation, expansion of Science, travel, understanding, religion, again nearer to God, perhaps; but certainly not to be put in the last category the most marvelous possible diversion from internal world conflict. A focus on space and exploration for trade, business, betterment of man. What greater persuasion could there be from sending intercontinental missiles from somewhere in Russia to smash New York or Chicago or Detroit? Whom would this impress or what propaganda value could this possibly be when now the goal of the two largest powers in the world is to see what's on the other side of the moon?

We look forward to wondrous careers in business and in the professional life of tomorrow, avenues of advancement, in materials, and products not yet dreamed of by the public. We are involved in planning these products. Planned obsolescence will rule tomorrow's world and space exploitation with a long period of interest and satisfaction from the wonders of science and man made opportunity. Certainly, there is nothing to worry about from the standpoint of what to do in the future, business-wise.

The Brooks Stevens Archive at the Milwaukee Art Museum

CHAN HARRIES, ARCHIVIST

The story of the Brooks Stevens Archive began in 1935, when Stevens himself—acutely aware of his own place in history—first began documenting the activities of his design firm. The Milwaukee Art Museum acquired the Archive in 1997, as a gift from the designer's family and the Milwaukee Institute of Art and Design, which had cared for the materials since shortly before Stevens' death. The collection is composed primarily of audio/visual materials in numerous formats, including:

1. several thousand photographs and corresponding negatives in both black and white and color, in a wide variety of sizes;

2. black and white and color slides, primarily in 35mm and lantern sizes;

3. moving images on reel-to-reel and video cassette formats;

4. reel-to-reel audio tapes, some of which are speeches given by Stevens.

Also included in the Archive are paper documents, which span the length of Stevens' career. Perhaps the most important documents are a series of scrapbooks, arranged chronologically, which contain newspaper clippings documenting Stevens' career and civic life in Milwaukee. Other paper documents are divided into two series: professional and personal. Included in the professional series are an incomplete run of client files, which contain correspondence, design notes, and other miscellaneous items concerning the client. Among the personal items include materials concerning the failed attempt by Stevens to construct a hotel/convention center (the Satellite Towers) in downtown Milwaukee; correspondence concerning the Kaiser-Frazer company and other auto commissions; programs from exhibits of Stevens's work; and copies of articles and speeches for professional societies.

The archive is open to researchers by appointment only. For more information or to search the photographic contents of the archive, please visit the Milwaukee Art Museum website at **www.mam.org/brooksstevens.**

General Bibliography and Scholarly Design Monographs

GENERAL

Adams, Henry. *Viktor Schreckengost and 20th Century Design* (Cleveland: Cleveland Museum of Art/University of Washington Press, 1999).

Albrecht, Donald, and Robert Schonfeld. *Russel Wright: Creating American Lifestyle* (New York: Cooper Hewitt, National Design Museum, Smithsonian Institution/Harry N. Abrams, 2001).

Doordan, Dennis P., ed. *The Alliance of Art and Industry: Toledo Designs for America* (Toledo: Toledo Museum of Art/Hudson Hills Press, 2002).

Doordan, Dennis P., ed. *Design History: An Anthology* (Cambridge: MIT Press, 1995).

Eidelberg, Martin, ed. *Design 1935–1965: What Modern Was* (Montreal: Musée des Arts Décoratifs de Montreal, 1991).

Flinchum, Russell. *Henry Dreyfuss, Industrial Designer: The Man in the Brown Suit* (New York: Cooper Hewitt, National Design Museum, Smithsonian Institution and Rizzoli, 1997).

Forty, Adrian. *Objects of Desire: Design and Society Since 1750* (London: Thames and Hudson, 1986).

Harris, Neil. *Cultural Excursions: Marketing Appetites and Cultural Tastes in Modern America* (Chicago: Chicago University Press, 1990).

Hillier, Bevis. *The Decorative Arts of the Forties and Fifties: Austerity/Binge* (New York: Clarkson N. Potter, 1975).

Jackson, Kenneth T. *Crabgrass Frontier: The Suburbanization of the United States* (New York: Oxford University Press, 1985).

Kaplan, Wendy, ed. *Designing Modernity: The Arts of Reform and Persuasion 1885–1945* (Miami Beach: The Wolfsonian/Thames and Hudson, 1995).

Lambert, Susan. *Form Follows Function? Design in the 20th Century* (London: Victoria and Albert Museum, 1993).

Lhamon, W. T. *Deliberate Speed : The Origins of a Cultural Style in the American 1950s* (Washington : Smithsonian Institution Press, 1990).

Margolin, Victor, ed. *Design History/Theory/Criticism* (Chicago: University of Chicago, 1989).

Meikle, Jeffrey T. *American Plastic: A Cultural History* (New Brunswick, NJ: Rutgers University Press, 1995).

Meikle, Jeffrey T. *Twentieth-Century Limited: Industrial Design in America 1925-1939* (Philadelphia: Temple University Press, 1975).

de Noblet, Jocelyn, ed. *Industrial Design: Reflection of a Century* (Paris: Flammarion, 1993).

Plummer, Kathleen Church. "The Streamlined Moderne," *Art in America* 62 (Jan-Feb. 1974, p. 46–54).

Pulos, Arthur J. *The American Design Adventure 1940–1975* (Cambridge: MIT Press, 1988).

Pulos, Arthur J. *American Design Ethic: A History of Industrial Design* (Cambridge: MIT Press, 1983).

Schonberger, Angela. *Raymond Loewy: Pioneer of Industrial Design* (Munich: Prestel, 1990).

Sparke, Penny. *As Long As It's Pink: The Sexual Politics of Taste* (New York: Grosset and Dunlap, 1949).

Stayton, Kevin, and Brooke Rapaport, et al. *Vital Forms: American Art and Design in the Atomic Age, 1940-1960* (Brooklyn: Brooklyn Museum of Art/Abrams, 2001).

Votolato, Gregory. *American Design in the Twentieth Century: Personality and Performance* (Manchester: Manchester University Press, 1998).

Wilson, Richard Guy, Dianne H. Pilgrim, and Dickran Tashjian. *The Machine Age in America, 1918–1941* (New York : Brooklyn Museum/Abrams, 1986).

ABOUT BROOKS STEVENS

"The Crime of 'Planned Obsolescence,'" *Weekly People* (Oct. 18, 1958).

David, Tom. "Brooks Stevens: A Designer of Our Time," *Innovation* (Winter 1995), p 39–42.

Davis, Tom. "A Giant by Design," *Wisconsin Trails* 44/1 (Jan./Feb. 2003), p. 26–32.

"Brooks Stevens—Trend Maker," *The Boating Industry* (Jan. 1963).

Hayes, Paul G. "The Designer Who Roared," *The Milwaukee Journal Magazine* (Dec. 6, 1992), p. 5–17.

Grossman, Ron. "The Idea Man," *Chicago Tribune* (June 3, 1991), p. 1, 5.

Hertzberg, Mark. "Brooks Stevens: His Designs Still Too Advanced for the Market," *Beloit Daily News* (Jan. 20, 1977).

"Is This the Year of the American Revolution?," *Autocar* (Jan. 6, 1950).

Lamek, Perry. "Designing the American Dream," *Milwaukee Magazine* (Aug. 1987), p. 46–52, 128.

Lynch, Kevin. "Designs in Motion," *Capital Times* (Aug. 15, 1991), p. 1-D, 8-D.

"The Man Who Put a Whole New Spin on Design." *International Herald Tribune* (July 19, 1991), p. 8.

McDonnell, John. "A Life of Creating." *Autoweek* (July 29, 1991), p. 15.

Prentiss, Karl. "Brooks Stevens: He Has Designs On Your Dough," *True Magazine* (April, 1958).

"Prophet With A Purpose," *Let's See Milwaukee* (Jan. 23, 1959), p. 8–11.

Puelicher, Gertrude M. "Brookington Limited," *Exclusively Yours* (April, 1955), p. 12, 14, 26.

Rosenbusch, Karla A. "Brooks Stevens, 1911-1995," *Automobile Quarterly* 34/2 (July 1995), p. 110.

"Ten Men in Your Life," *House & Garden* 92 (September 1947).

Wilkerson, Isabel. "The Man Who Put Form on Your Harley, Color in Your Kitchen," *New York Times* (July 11, 1991).

Woodhouse, Anne. "Industrial Designer Brooks Stevens: Businessman, Engineer, and Stylist," *Wisconsin Academy Review* (Fall 1993), p. 10–14.

BY BROOKS STEVENS

"The de Sakhnoffsky L-29," *Automobile Quarterly* 6/4 (Spring 1968), p. 453–457.

"The Ego and the Image," letter to the editor, *Industrial Design* 7/8 (Aug. 1960), p. 10.

"Factories Also Have Faces," *Industrial Design* (April 1961).

"Planned Obsolescence: Is it Fair? Yes! Says Brooks Stevens; No! Says Walter Dorwin Teague," *The Rotarian* (February 1960), p. 2-5.

"Styling the Hiawatha," lecture, May 18, 1973. Reprinted in *The Milwaukee Railroader* (Third Quarter, 1997), p. 4-22

"Tomorrow's Luxury Land Cruiser," *Automobile Quarterly* 1/1 (Spring 1962), p. 78–84, 98.

"Why an Industrial Designer in the Toy Industry," *Toys and Novelties* (March 1959), p. 378–9, 471.

"Your Victory Car," *Popular Mechanics* (Dec. 1942), p. 82–85, 162.

WEB RESOURCES

The Brooks Stevens Archive at the Milwaukee Art Museum
www.mam.org/brooksstevens

Brooks Stevens Design
www.brooksstevens.com

Industrial Designers Society of America
www.idsa.org

Index

Photographic Acknowledgments

All images are from the Brooks Stevens Archive at the Milwaukee Art Museum, except for those noted below:

Auburn Cord Duesenberg Museum (p. 35, fig. 4; p. 41, upper); Brooks Stevens Design (p. 180, figs. 2, 3; p. 185, upper right); Chicago Landmarks (p. 58, top center); Formica Corporation (p. 112, upper); Hagley Museum and Library (p. 16, fig. 7); Henry Dreyfuss Collection, Cooper-Hewitt, National Design Museum, Smithsonian Institution (p. 16, fig. 6); Hyatt Hotels Corporation (p. 162, lower); Michael Lord Gallery (p. 181, fig. 4); Milwaukee Journal-Sentinel (p. 182, fig. 5); Milwaukee Public Library, Milwaukee Road Archive (p. 101; p. 102, lower left; p. 107); Milwaukee Public Library's Photo Archives (p. 163); Doug Mitchell (p. 40, all photos); Roger Morrison (p. 147, lower right); Norwest Collection, Minneapolis Institute of Arts (p. 60, lower right); Oscar Mayer Company (p. 146, all photos); Penn State University Libraries, Special Collections Library (p. 5, fig. 2); Alice Preston (p. 118, lower right; p. 194, lower right); SC Johnson (p. 90, upper); Studebaker National Museum, South Bend, Indiana (p. 152, lower); Norm Swinford (p. 54, upper right, lower right); University of Texas at Austin, Harry Ransom Humanities Research Center (p. 15, fig. 5 [photograph by Maurice Goldberg]; p. 60, middle right [photograph by Maurice Goldberg]; p. 63, lower right [photograph by A. B. Bogart]).